WAR
of the
WINDSORS

WAR
of the
WINDSORS

The Inside Story of Charles,
Andrew and the Rivalry That
Has Defined the Royal Family

Nigel Cawthorne

WELBECK

Published in 2023 by Welbeck
An imprint of Welbeck Non-Fiction Limited
Part of the Welbeck Publishing Group
Offices in: London – 20 Mortimer Street, London W1T 3JW &
Sydney – 205 Commonwealth Street, Surry Hills 2010
www.welbeckpublishing.com

A CIP catalogue record for this book is available from the British Library.

ISBN 978-1-80279-718-3

Typeset by seagulls.net
Printed and bound by CPI Group (UK) Ltd, Croydon, CR0 4YY

10 9 8 7 6 5 4 3 2 1

CONTENTS

"Charles has always been jealous of Andrew. He had a very successful military career for twenty years. So as soon as the Queen has gone, the daggers are out."

Lady Victoria Hervey

CHAPTER ONE
ANCESTRAL AMBITIONS

In July 2020, an astonishing photograph emerged. It showed disgraced socialite Ghislaine Maxwell, who had recently been arrested by the FBI for sex trafficking, sitting on the throne used by the Queen at her coronation in 1953, waving regally, in a flagrant breach of protocol. The photograph had been taken during a private tour of Buckingham Palace organised by her long-time friend Prince Andrew, who was (at the time the photograph emerged) embroiled in a sex scandal concerning his unsavoury friendship with Ghislaine's ex, the convicted paedophile Jeffrey Epstein.

Sitting next to Maxwell, on the throne once occupied by the Duke of Edinburgh, was Oscar-winning Hollywood actor Kevin Spacey, who had problems of his own with allegations of sexual misconduct.

Their visit to the throne room took place in September 2002, shortly before Spacey became artistic director of The Old Vic theatre on London's South Bank. There, at the culmination of his tenure in 2011, Oscar-winning director Sam Mendes directed Spacey in the title role of Shakespeare's *Richard III* – the bloodthirsty tale of a prince who seized the throne after murdering his older brother and, probably, the two princes in the Tower. If Andrew had done that himself, he would now be king. Before Prince George was born, Andrew was next in line to the throne after Charles, William and Harry. Bump them off and the crown would have been his.

Although Prince Andrew is not a noted Shakespearean scholar, he would have been taught his own family's history, and the history of the monarchy is littered with tales of kindred squabbles, subterfuge, backstabbing and even murder, all with a view to securing the top job. The Royal Family is nothing if it's not about tradition.

Let's not go too far back in time, but the current Royal Family claims lineage of a thousand years from William the Conqueror and the Norman invasion. William was succeeded by his son William Rufus, who died in mysterious circumstances with an arrow through his chest while hunting in the New Forest on the afternoon of Thursday 2 August 1100. It is thought he was murdered. He was rapidly succeeded by his younger brother Henry I, who had been with the hunting party that day. By the evening, Henry was in Winchester, twenty-two miles away, where he seized the royal treasury. The following day, Rufus was entombed in Winchester and Henry was named king by a hastily assembled council. After a seventy-mile ride, Henry was crowned king in Westminster two days later. Historian Duncan Grinnell-Milne, when asked about the expedience of this, concluded: "Only premeditation can account for such speed."

Henry kept another older brother, Robert II of Normandy, in prison for twenty-eight years for claiming the crown of England. This was a promising beginning in the dynasty for ambitious younger brothers.

When Henry died, his nephew Stephen ousted Henry's daughter Matilda, whom Henry had named as his heir and had reigned for a few months. After that, the line straightened out again. By common consent, Stephen was succeeded by Matilda's son, Henry II.

Henry II's son, Richard the Lionheart, was succeeded in 1199 by his younger brother John (nicknamed Lackland) who had already sought to usurp the throne while Richard I was away at the Crusades, as all fans of *Robin Hood* films will know. The Plantagenet kings then succeeded one another in a more or less orderly fashion until 1399 when Richard II was usurped by his cousin Henry IV, blindsiding another cousin in the process. This ultimately led to the Wars of the Roses, where cousins slugged it out over the crown. Eventually, it passed to the fratricidal (and most likely nepoticidal) Richard III who seized the throne in 1483. He was put paid to two years later by distant cousin Henry VII at the Battle of Bosworth, establishing the Tudor dynasty.

Henry VIII came to the throne after his older brother Arthur died, marrying Arthur's widow in the meantime. Mary I, aka Bloody Mary, took the throne in 1553 – a cousin, Lady Jane Grey, losing her head to the axe along the way after reigning for just nine days. Mary also had designs on her sister Elizabeth's life. Nevertheless, Elizabeth I succeeded her in 1558, only to order the execution of her cousin Mary, Queen of Scots, who also had claims on the English throne. This then passed to Mary's son James I of England, VI of Scotland, in 1603, uniting the crowns of England and Scotland. His coronation was in Westminster Abbey, where the three bloodthirsty ladies lay within feet of each other.

James's son, Charles I, succeeded his father in 1625 after his older brother Henry Frederick died of typhoid fever at the age of eighteen. After the minor unpleasantness of the Civil War, Charles was executed in 1649 – a bad augury for Charles III, perhaps. A short-lived republic followed. Then Charles I's son was installed as Charles II. Known as the Merry Monarch, he had his numerous mistresses and a clutch of illegitimate children, so he is hardly a suitable role model for the current, glum and uxorious King Charles III. More of a prototype Prince Andrew, perhaps.

Despite his evident prolificacy, Charles II died without any legitimate heirs, so his younger brother succeeded him as James II in 1685. But Andrew could hardly take comfort from that as James, as a Catholic, rapidly became unpopular and was ousted by the Glorious Revolution of 1688, when his daughter Mary and her husband William of Orange took over. Mary's younger sister Anne became queen in 1702, although her half-brother and her father's legitimate heir, James III and VIII, "The Old Pretender", still claimed the crowns of England, Scotland and Ireland. He had been debarred from the throne by the 1701 Act of Settlement on the grounds that he was a Catholic.

When Queen Anne died in 1714, the rules of primogeniture were ignored again as James refused to convert to Protestantism. Instead, a distant cousin, the Elector of Hanover, became George I of England as he was a Protestant. The lineage then continued in regular fashion from father to son, or grandson, until the dissolute George IV was succeeded by his younger brother William IV. Another steal by the junior bro.

William may also prove an inspiration for Prince Andrew. Also a sailor, he outraged London by returning from Jamaica with a mistress named Wowski and had ten illegitimate children with actress Mrs Jordan.

The often dissipated Georgians ended with Queen Victoria, even though her uncle Ernest, Duke of Cumberland had sought to have her removed from the succession and, possibly, even have her assassinated. With her husband, the high-minded Prince Albert, she established the royal brood as the model family – though her famously libidinous son Bertie who, at his coronation, had pews set aside for his mistresses which were called the "king's loose box", was twice cited in the divorce courts before he acceded as Edward VII. His last mistress, Alice Keppel, was the great-grandmother of Camilla Parker Bowles, now Queen Camilla.

Edward's son George V succeeded due to the fortuitous demise of his elder brother Prince Albert Victor, who was also known as Eddy and was named by the foreign press in the Cleveland Street scandal as one of the patrons of a homosexual brothel there. He is also a candidate for Jack the Ripper.

Even within the living memory of Charles and Andrew's sainted mother, a younger brother has actually succeeded to the throne when, in 1936, Edward VIII abdicated in favour of George VI to marry American divorcee Mrs Wallis Simpson. George overcame his stutter and apparently inspired the war efforts with his speeches, while Edward batted for the other side. It is well documented that he fraternised with Herr Hitler and it is possible that he would have been returned to the throne if the Nazis had won.

So, in short, the family has form. Sibling rivalry, if not outright fratricide, is in their DNA. If Andrew were arrogant and ambitious, and paid close attention to the family history, the possibility of taking the crown himself must have crossed his mind. Instead, he has had to sit back his entire life, watching his older brother preparing himself for kingship – and eventually achieving it – while he himself slipped down the pecking order, rung by rung, into irrelevancy. It is the old, old story of the heir and the spare. And it is a story we are here to tell.

What's more, the story has continued into the next generation. Once good friends, William and Harry have turned their backs on each other and are currently slugging it out in the international popularity polls, particularly in the United States. Meanwhile, a lifelong enmity between Andrew and Charles brews on under the surface in what can be seen as a clandestine "War of the Windsors". Having finally taken the crown, Charles is now top dog. But he is by no means a popular monarch. While the people of Britain held 16,000 street parties for the Platinum Jubilee of Queen Elizabeth II, the number booked for the coronation of King Charles III was just 3,087. Though Andrew has been stripped of all honours and duties, it has been widely reported that he still believes he can make a comeback into public life, if only to spite his older brother who seems determined to exclude him.

And while Andrew may not be a Shakespearean scholar, Charles is. Harry tells us so in his autobiography *Spare*. Charles constantly quotes the Bard and compares himself to Prince Hal in *Henry V* – the wayward youth who, as king, was the victor at Agincourt, wooed the French king's daughter and was adopted as heir to the French throne. His son Henry VI was deposed by Edward IV and died in mysterious circumstances while imprisoned in the Tower of London. Sir Thomas More said that he was murdered by Richard, Duke of Gloucester, who went on to become Richard III. Charles read history at Cambridge, so he may well know that where Andrew is concerned, he may have to be on his guard.

CHAPTER TWO

A MOTHER'S LOVE

At 10.10pm on Sunday 14 November 1948, a proclamation was issued from Buckingham Palace. It read: "The Princess Elizabeth, Duchess of Edinburgh, was safely delivered of a Prince at 9.19pm today. Her Royal Highness and her son are doing well."

The crowd outside the Palace, numbering some four thousand, had to wait in the rain a few minutes more before receiving the news. At 10.23pm, a page in blue livery walked across the courtyard and whispered to the policeman at the gates. A section of the crowd saw what was going on and surged forward. The policeman told a woman standing near him: "It's a boy. Both well."

Word flew round the crowd and a great cheer went up. The policeman closed the gates – just in time to keep the crowd from breaking through. Hats and caps flew in the air and there were cries of "We want Philip!" As if in answer, a man in evening dress appeared in the forecourt. There were more cheers and cries of "Good old Philip!" But it wasn't him and the man quickly retreated.

Prince Philip was not present at the birth. He had been playing squash with his private secretary Lieutenant Mike Parker. They were taking a swim in the private heated swimming pool in the North West

Pavilion of the Palace when Sir Alan "Tommy" Lascelles, the private secretary to George VI, rushed up to tell the two naked men. Hearing that he was father to a boy, Prince Philip quickly towelled himself off, dressed and made his way to the Belgian Suite on the ground floor, overlooking the gardens, where Princess Elizabeth was still unconscious from the anaesthetic she had been given.

The King and Queen were already there. They were in evening dress. Queen Elizabeth embraced Philip and King George shook his hand. They went into the nursery to see the child. Then Philip went back out to his wife's bedside and stood there until she awoke. He had with him a huge bouquet of his wife's favourite flowers – red roses, lilies, camellias and carnations – thoughtfully supplied by Mike Parker. Asked what his son looked like, Philip said: "A plum pudding."

The child's great-grandmother Queen Mary, who had been waiting at Marlborough House, was called. She arrived at Buckingham Palace by car at 10.30pm, wearing an evening gown and white fur wrap. The crowd gave her a tremendous welcome.

Then it was time to break out the champagne. Philip handed out glasses to the doctors and the Royal Household. But the reception committee was depleted. Although the baby had been expected the day before, the final stages happened so quickly that officials, called to the Palace for the birth, were still on their way. For the first time since the eighteenth century, neither the Home Secretary nor any other high government official was present at the birth of a future monarch.

The tradition of officials being on hand is thought to have had its origin in the reign of James II when prominent Protestants alleged that a healthy male child had been smuggled into the bedchamber of his second wife Mary of Modena, a Catholic, in a warming pan. This cast doubt on the legitimacy of Prince James. By his first marriage to Anne Hyde, James II already had two Protestant heirs, Mary and Anne, who succeeded. In future, births were to be witnessed by government ministers to prevent any possibility of a substitution happening again. That ended with the birth of Charles. It was not "a statutory requirement or a constitutional necessity" said his grand-father George VI.

The crowd swelled. At 11.15pm, the police cordoned off the road outside the Palace. By that time, cars were parked in their hundreds on the roads nearby and women in long evening dresses and men in dinner jackets thronged around the Victoria Memorial.

Then at 11.30pm police reinforcements arrived to cut a pathway for Queen Mary's car, which had been waiting in the courtyard to take her home. When she tried to leave twenty-five minutes later the crowd surged around her car, bringing it to a halt. She smiled and waved as the police fought to clear a path for her, though it was reported there were tears in her eyes.

Not yet three hours old, the baby was carefully swaddled in white blankets and taken by the royal midwife Sister Helen Rowe to the vast gilt-and-red-velvet ballroom. It was by far the largest room in the Palace. There, his small cradle was placed at the centre of the room, in front of the two imperial thrones and a massive domed canopy carrying the royal coat of arms embroidered in gold silk thread on the draped red velvet. Then the Palace staff – hundreds of them – filed by the child.

"He seemed perfectly happy even with all the strange faces coming up and staring," said one of the backstairs staff. "But you couldn't help feeling sorry for him. So tiny there in that room, and, of course, he has no idea what's in store for him."

The child was already second in succession to the throne after his mother, the then Princess Elizabeth. Under letters patent issued five days earlier, he would have the title Prince and the style of Royal

Highness. These would be used in preference to the second peerage of his father, Earl of Merioneth, which attaches to the eldest son "by courtesy". He was also born heir-apparent to the Dukedom of Edinburgh and its associated peerages, as well as being heir to his mother. He would also bear his father's adopted surname of Mountbatten, but would not ordinarily be known by it. When he came of age he would sign his Christian name only, followed by P (for *Princeps* – first or foremost) when he became Prince of Wales. At that point, he would also automatically become Duke of Cornwall and Earl of Chester.

Lights in the King's apartments were still burning at midnight. At 12.15am, the megaphone on a police car outside the Palace announced: "Ladies and gentlemen, it is requested by the Palace that we have a little quietness, if you please." But the roar of the crowd drowned out the message.

A squad of policemen marched through the Palace yard and began to clear the crowd from the railings. The police car made another announcement: "There will be no more bulletins from the Palace. You are asked to disperse quietly." But the crowd was too busy cheering to listen and called for "Daddy", "Grandma" and "Grandpa".

Two of Princess Elizabeth's household staff then came into the forecourt, walked along the railings and told those on the other side: "The Princess is trying to sleep. The King and Queen will not be coming out on the balcony. Nor will Prince Philip – he is with the Princess." The news was passed around. The shouting and cheering died down and by 12.30am all was quiet.

News of the birth had been cabled abroad at once. Across the Empire and the Commonwealth, as in Britain, the Union Jack was raised. Bunting was hung out and church bells rang. Radio stations across the United States interrupted scheduled programmes with the announcement. US President Harry S. Truman sent a message saying: "Mrs Truman and I are delighted at the news of the birth of your son and felicitate you and the Duke upon this happy occasion."

Wartime friend General Dwight D. Eisenhower, later US president, sent a message via the private secretary of King George VI saying: "Will you extend to Her Royal Highness the Princess Elizabeth, the Duke of Edinburgh and all members of the Royal Family the personal felicitations of Mrs Eisenhower and myself on yesterday's happy event. We are united with many, many millions in our wish of long years and a fruitful life to the young Prince."

More than four thousand telegrams of congratulation arrived at the Palace, the largest number ever received in a single day. Prince Philip arose early the following morning to begin reading the messages.

Meanwhile the *New York Times* ran a story headlined: "A BABY MAKES THE BRITISH SEEM SOMEWHAT UNBRITISH: A Reticent People Is Not Reticent When It Is a Question of Royal Offspring."

In Trafalgar Square the illuminated fountains sparkled baby blue. The bells of St Paul's Cathedral rang out and at Westminster Abbey, where the Prince would one day be crowned, three bell ringers rang a peal of 5,000 changes that lasted three hours.

Church bells across the nation followed suit. Bonfires, beacons and fireworks were lit. Six guns of the King's Troop Royal Horse Artillery, manned by artillerymen in full dress uniform, fired a forty-one-round salute in Hyde Park. This was echoed by batteries at the Tower of London and at Woolwich.

Warships of His Majesty's naval fleet on station across the globe fired a royal birthday salute. And ships of the US Navy moored in Plymouth harbour joined in with their flags and guns.

The Times of London proclaimed: "The birth of a child to the Heiress-Presumptive is a national and imperial event which can for a moment divert the peoples' thoughts from the acrimonies of domestic argument and the anxieties of the international scene. All can be united in rejoicing as the guns salute and the bells peal. Every newborn child presents to some family the thought and image of the future towards which it moves; this child from the moment of his birth becomes to many peoples the symbol of their common aspirations for an even more splendid realm and Commonwealth than have been handed down to them by the virtue and prowess, of their ancestors..."

On 16 November, loyal addresses of congratulation to the King and Queen, Princess Elizabeth and the Duke of Edinburgh were moved in both Houses of Parliament to be presented by Privy Counsellors of all parties.

Addressing the Commons, Prime Minister Clement Attlee said: "The young prince may have to carry great responsibilities. He is heir to a great tradition and we shall watch him growing to manhood with lively interest, knowing that in his own home he will receive a training by example rather than mere precept, in that courtesy and in that gracious and tireless devotion to the manifold duties of constitutional monarchy which have won the hearts of our people."

This speech was greeted with cheers.

Winston Churchill, then Leader of the Opposition, rose from his place to second the motion.

"Our ancient Monarchy renders inestimable services to our country and to all the British Empire and Commonwealth of Nations. Above the ebb and flow of party strife, the rise and fall of Ministries and individuals, the changes of public opinion and fortune, the British Monarchy presides ancient, calm and supreme within its functions, over all the treasures that have been saved from the past and all the glories we write in the annals of our country. Our thoughts go out to the mother and father and, in a special way today, to the little Prince, now born into this world of strife and storm.

"I have no doubt he will be brought up, as the Prime Minister has mentioned, in all those traditions of constitutional government which make the British monarchy at once the most ancient and most secure in the world. I hope that among those principles that will be instilled will be the truth that the Sovereign is never so great as when the people are free. There we meet on common ground."

Not his finest speech, perhaps, but it was punctuated with cheers.

Even William Gallacher, the lone Communist member, MP for West Fife, said he would make no adverse comment on the celebrations associated with the birth of this baby because, when he was born, there were bells ringing and joyful sounds in abundance. No one mentioned that, for a child not yet two days old, this was a lot to live up to.

A second bulletin from the Palace announced that the Prince weighed 7lb 6oz. This news was duly reported on every front page. Even the left-leaning *Manchester Guardian* felt obliged to inform its readers that the baby's weight was "regarded by gynaecologists as nearly the ideal for an infant boy".

The newspaper went on to reassure its readers: "The absence of an evening bulletin on the condition of Princess Elizabeth and her infant son was an indication that everything is going on entirely normally."

The child's name had not been released. Prince Philip was determined to keep it under wraps so that he could spring it on the world at the christening. There was much speculation on the subject, but it was generally thought that the boy would be called Prince George of Edinburgh.

One of the few let in on the secret was the court's favourite photographer, later Oscar-winning designer Cecil Beaton, who was summoned less than a week after the baby's birth to take the first official pictures of mother and child.

"Prince Charles, as he is to be named, is an obedient sitter," he recorded in his diary. "He interrupted a long, contented sleep to do my bidding and open his blue eyes to stare long and wonderingly into the camera lens, the beginning of a lifetime in the glare of publicity."

The question of the Prince's name would be cleared up at 3.30pm on 15 December in the Palace's domed Music Room on the fifth floor overlooking the Palace Lawns as the Palace's private chapel had been put out of action by a German bomb. Brought in, not by his mother, but by his nurse Sister Helen Rowe, the child wore a christening robe of Honiton lace over a satin petticoat. The robe had been worn by Queen Victoria and her children. Victoria herself had handed it to Queen Mary in 1894. It was worn by King George VI and all his brothers and by the Princess Royal, then by Princess Elizabeth and Princess Margaret.

To the accompaniment of Handel's *Water Music*, played by the organist of the Chapel Royal, the boys of the Chapel Royal choir entered, wearing their Tudor uniforms of scarlet and gold. They were followed by the officiating clergy. After the singing of the hymn, "Holy, Holy, Holy", Miss Rowe handed the baby to his aunt, the Queen's sister Princess Margaret who announced the names of the child – Charles Philip Arthur. She then laid the baby in the arms of the Archbishop, who baptised him with water from the River Jordan using a silver-gilt lily font from Windsor used for the christening of Queen Victoria's children. The Archbishop then handed the baby back to Princess Margaret, who returned him to the nurse.

From the off, there was some concern about the choice of the name Charles. It seemed unlucky as Charles I had been executed and Charles II's reign had encompassed the Great Plague and the Great Fire of London.

Charles was the name by which King Haakon of Norway, the baby's great-great-uncle, was known in the family. Philip was the baby's father's name, while Arthur was the third of the four Christian names of the then king, George VI. It was also the name of Queen Victoria's son, the Duke of Connaught, his son Prince Arthur of Connaught and his grandson the second Duke of Connaught who had died in 1943. There was also, of course, the legendary King Arthur.

In the presence of his parents and eight godparents, including the King and Queen, Prince Charles was admitted to the Church of England and inaugurated into the rites of the faith which, as future sovereign, he would pledge to defend and he could never leave without jeopardising his right to the throne.

In a short address, the Archbishop referred to the religious significance of the ceremony and spoke of the solemn duties undertaken by godparents, which included King Haakon of Norway and Prince George of Greece who could not be there.

Those present included the Princess Royal, the Duchess of Gloucester, the Duchess of Kent, Princess Alice, Countess of Athlone, Admiral Sir Alexander Ramsay and Lady Patricia Ramsay, Princess Marie Louise, the Dowager Marchioness of Milford Haven, Lord and Lady Brabourne, Lieutenant-Colonel and Mrs Michael Bowes-Lyon, and Mr and Mrs David Bowes-Lyon.

A second hymn, appropriately "O, Worship the King", ended the service. Afterwards, members of the Royal Family and their guests moved into the White Drawing Room, where one of the three christening cakes was cut. No expense and no effort was spared in celebrating the arrival of the new heir.

In Buckingham Palace, Charles would sleep in the dressing room adjoining the Princess's bedroom on the second floor. There, he would be cared for by two nurses supported by a staff of maids and footmen. The Prince slept in the same pink satin and lace cot that had been used by his mother in her infancy. He played with her silver rattle and he was taken out across St James's Park and into Green Park in her ancient pram.

The Queen's sister, Lady Granville, reported: "He could not be more angelic looking. He is golden-haired and has the most beautiful complexion, as well as amazingly delicate features for so young a baby." But then, aren't all babies beautiful to their families?

Princess Elizabeth herself was recorded as saying that her baby's hands "are rather large but fine with long fingers – quite unlike mine and certainly unlike his father's. It will be interesting to see what they will become. I still find it difficult to believe I have a baby of my own."

It seems that, from the outset, there was a distance between them.

CHAPTER THREE

NUMBER TWO

The notice of another birth was posted on the railings of Buckingham Palace on the afternoon of 19 February 1960. It said: "The Queen was safely delivered of a son at 3.38pm today. Her Majesty and the infant prince are both doing well." Again, Sister Helen Rowe was in attendance. The boy was the first child to be born to a reigning monarch since Princess Beatrice, the youngest of Queen Victoria's nine children born over a hundred years earlier on 14 April 1857.

Outside the gates, a crowd of nearly two thousand waited patiently in the winter sunshine when the superintendent of the Palace, Stanley Williams, in long black overcoat, walked across the courtyard. There were shouts of "Is it a boy?" When he shouted back, "Yes, it is," there were cheers. People started running, shoving and jostling to read the handwritten notice.

The child was second in the line of succession, as Charles had been when he was born. But by then, with Elizabeth having succeeded to the throne, Charles had already moved up to first in line. Meanwhile, Princess Anne had been demoted to third. Male offspring trumped females in the line of succession until the law was amended in 2011 when Catholics were also allowed to succeed.

The *New York Times* reported: "From taxi drivers shouting, 'It's a boy!' to each other in London's traffic to Edinburgh where a bonfire glowed on Calton Hill in that snowbound city, the strange mystical feeling of kinship with the royal family that periodically animates Britain was evident."

That bonfire in Edinburgh consumed a hundred tons of material. There were more bonfires at Balmoral and along the valley of the Dee. And fireworks were set off on the battlements of Edinburgh Castle.

"Across the Commonwealth in what remains of Victoria's empire, old traditions for celebrating a royal birth were honoured," *The Times* went on. "Guns boomed out on the fortress of Gibraltar and in Accra."

One of the first to congratulate the Queen was Dr Kwame Nkrumah, prime minister of newly independent Ghana. Since Charles had been born, the Commonwealth had replaced the Empire and Britain had changed out of all recognition. A war-ravaged UK crippled by debt and austerity was now a modern nation on the verge of the Swinging Sixties.

At Portsmouth, HMS *Vanguard*, the Royal Navy's one remaining battleship, fired a salute. The crew were also happy. Admiralty had sent the signal to all ships: "Birth of a son to HM Queen Elizabeth. Splice the main brace." That is, issue the ship's company an extra tot of rum. Other Britons resorted to pubs and clubs to wet the baby's head, while a barman at the Savoy came up with "Royal Arrival", a special blue cocktail.

The RAF saluted the birth with a flypast of thirty-six Hunter fighters over the Palace. At the same time, salutes were fired in Hyde Park and at the Tower of London. In the excitement, the armoury of the Honourable Artillery Company in City Road, London, hoisted the Union Jack the wrong way up. This remained unnoticed for about an hour.

Cannons also sounded at Windsor Castle and Cardiff Castle. The bells of St Paul's and Westminster Abbey pealed for an hour. In hundreds of little villages, church bells rang out and flags were unfurled.

The Duke of Edinburgh had attended a lunch at the Guildhall in the City of London that day, but cancelled a visit to the National College of Food Technology in Weybridge, Surrey, that afternoon to return to his study. When Lord Evans brought the news, he visited his wife in the Belgian Suite, its walls hung with cream damask, patterned wallpaper and blue silk taffeta curtains. He told a group of servants: "It's a boy." Again, his name would be kept secret until the christening, though James was tipped. A James following a Charles would have been unfortunate, given the fate of James II following Charles II.

Having toasted the birth with champagne, Prince Philip telephoned the Home Secretary who, by tradition, was the first to be informed. Philip then telephoned Prince Charles, who was boarding at Cheam School in Hampshire and took Princess Anne to see the baby. Charles arrived that evening. Telegrams were sent to the governors general of the self-governing Dominions, while a letter was taken by a police motorcycle dispatch rider to the Lord Mayor of London at Mansion House.

Prime Minister Harold Macmillan was at his desk at 10 Downing Street when Buckingham Palace called with the news. He sent a message saying: "With my humble duty I venture to send my respectful congratulations and best wishes for Your Majesty's health and for that of the new prince."

Now President Eisenhower also sent a message of congratulation: "I know that all Americans join with Mrs Eisenhower and myself in congratulating Her Majesty Queen Elizabeth II and Prince Philip on the birth of their son and are delighted by the news that the Queen and her son are doing well. May the Prince have a long, happy and useful life." Four thousand messages of congratulation were received from all over the world. It was then announced that the baby boy was 7lb 3oz at birth.

After question time on Monday 22 February, the prime minister moved a motion in the House of Commons to send an address to the Queen, conveying their loyal congratulations to Her Majesty on the birth of the Prince. The leaders of the Labour and Liberal Parties supported the motion.

The Lords sent their address of congratulations when they met on Tuesday. The message was handwritten, in a decorative Gothic style. It was taken to the Queen by Lord Scarborough, Lord Chamberlain of Her Majesty's Household.

That same day, it was reported that Parliament had already made financial provision for the new member of the Royal Family under the Civil List Act of 1952: "With the exception of Prince Charles, for whom special provision is made from the revenues of the Duchy of Cornwall, each son is entitled to £10,000 a year at the age of twenty-one (or on marriage if this were to take place earlier), and each daughter £6,000 a year. After marriage the Act provides that each son shall have a further £15,000 a year, and each daughter a further £9,000 a year."

The christening took place on 8 April in the same flower-decked Music Room of Buckingham Palace where the Archbishop of Canterbury again baptised the child using the same silver-gilt lily font from Windsor and water from the River Jordan. The same Honiton lace christening gown was worn.

This time there were only five godparents – the Duke of Gloucester, Princess Alexandra of Kent, Lord Elphinstone (a cousin of the Queen), Lord Euston (whose wife was a lady of the bedchamber) and Mrs Harold Phillips, a friend of the Queen. They stood on one side of the font, which was decorated with white spring flowers, while the clergy and the choir of the Chapel Royal stood on the other.

There were about sixty guests. Among them were the Queen's gynaecologist whom she had knighted half an hour earlier, while her anaesthetist was made a Companion of the Victorian Order.

The child was brought in by his nanny Miss Mabel Anderson until she handed him to the Queen's cousin, Princess Alexandra, who presented him to the Archbishop who asked: "Who names this child?"

Princess Alexandra replied: "Andrew Albert Christian Edward."

Andrew was the name of Prince Philip's father, Prince Andrew of Greece and Denmark, who had twice been exiled from Greece. Estranged from his wife and son – and his daughters who all went on to marry Nazis – he went to live on board his mistress's yacht in Monte Carlo. Albert was the name of the child's louche great-great-great-grandfather Bertie, who reigned as Edward VII, while Christian was the name of his great-great-great-grandfather Christian IX of Denmark, a spurned suitor of Queen Victoria.

The baby was then returned to Princess Alexandra, then Miss Anderson for the remains of the proceedings. He was awake through-out the half-hour service and let out two small cries. Cecil Beaton was again on hand to take baby pictures. The eleven-year-old Charles and Princess Anne, nine, were also present.

The question of his surname had also been settled. It would be Mountbatten-Windsor. The Queen and Prince Philip had decided that this would distinguish their direct descendants from the rest of the Royal Family – Windsor is the surname used by all the male and unmarried female descendants of George V. The new surname had been confirmed by a declaration of the Privy Council. Normally, members of the Royal Family who are entitled to the style and dignity of HRH Prince or HRH Princess do not need a surname, but if at any time any of them do need one – such as upon marriage – that surname is Mountbatten-Windsor. This ruling had been issued in a decree a few days before Andrew's birth. While the Queen herself would continue ruling as Windsor, Andrew's birth had effectively changed Charles's name from Mountbatten to Mountbatten-Windsor.

CHAPTER FOUR

NANNIED

Just for being the first-born son, Charles had already stolen a march on Andrew in all things royal. When Charles was eight months old, his parents moved to Clarence House where he was put in the care of two nannies – Helen Lightbody and Mabel Anderson. In the nursery, Miss Lightbody was an old-fashioned martinet. Her word was the law. Not even the Queen was allowed to interfere with her routine.

The curtains of his nursery were opened promptly at 7am. After breakfast, at 9am, Charles was taken downstairs for the half-hour session with his mother. Then he was returned to the nursery to play until 10.30am when he was taken out for a walk in his pram, accompanied by a royal protection officer.

His mother visited him in his nursery in the evening when he was bathed and put to bed. Though Elizabeth had yet to succeed to the throne, her father's health was failing and she was obliged to take on some of his public engagements. And Prince Philip, still a serving naval officer, was often away at sea.

In October 1949, Philip was made second in command of a destroyer stationed in Malta, headquarters of Britain's Mediterranean fleet. A month later, less than a week after Charles's first birthday,

Elizabeth joined her husband for the first of several lengthy stays. While this meant leaving her infant son behind with the nursery staff for months on end, the Princess revelled in her life abroad, fancying herself as "just another Navy officer's wife", though she had a large retinue of staff. Charles came down with tonsillitis during one of their excursions, but neither of his parents returned to London to nurse their son.

That Christmas, Charles went to Sandringham, the royal estate in Norfolk, where he learnt to bow to the King and Queen. Princess Elizabeth only returned to England in the New Year when she was pregnant with Anne and Philip had put to sea. She stayed in Clarence House to celebrate Charles's second birthday, but almost immediately returned to Philip in Malta, staying there for Christmas.

When the King was diagnosed with lung cancer, Philip was forced to give up his Navy command and return to England to serve as royal consort. His wife had to host a banquet for her uncle King Haakon VII of Norway and take the salute on horseback at Trooping the Colour.

With the King's health failing, Elizabeth and Philip had to undertake a whirlwind tour of Canada and the US, missing Charles's third birthday. They were together for Christmas, but then his parents were off on a tour of the Commonwealth. The only hugs and kisses he got came from his grandmother.

Charles's parents were away when his grandfather, the King, died on 6 February 1952, when Charles was aged just three. The court was plunged into mourning. Charles's mother and father returned from Kenya (then still a British colony) the following day. There was little time for a reunion. On 8 February, the Earl Marshal proclaimed: "The High and Mighty Princess Elizabeth Alexandra Mary is now, by the Death of Our late Sovereign of Happy Memory, become Queen

Elizabeth the Second, but the Grace of God Queen of this Realm and all Her other Realms and Territories, Head of the Commonwealth, Defender of the Faith, to whom her lieges do acknowledge all Faith and constant Obedience."

This had enormous consequences for the infant Charles. He was no longer His Royal Highness Prince Charles of Edinburgh. He was now HRH Prince Charles of the House of Windsor, Duke of Rothesay, Earl of Carrick, Baron Renfrew, Lord of the Isles, Prince and Great Steward of Scotland, and Duke of Cornwall. This also brought with it a huge income from the duchy, making him extremely rich.

There was also another debate over what his name should be. With Elizabeth's accession, it seemed possible that the royal house would take her husband's name, in line with the custom for married women of the time. Lord Mountbatten advocated the House of Mountbatten, the name Prince Philip had taken when he became a British subject. Philip himself suggested House of Edinburgh, after his ducal title. The British prime minister, Winston Churchill, and Elizabeth's grand-mother Queen Mary favoured the retention of the House of Windsor, which the family had adopted during World War I. So Elizabeth issued a declaration on 9 April 1952 that the royal house would continue to be Windsor. Philip complained: "I am the only man in the country not allowed to give his name to his own children."

Charles was dispatched to Sandringham during his grandfather's funeral and interment in St George's Chapel at Windsor Castle. The court was still in mourning when, soon after Easter, Queen Elizabeth and family moved into Buckingham Palace, while the Queen Mother and Princess Margaret moved to Clarence House.

Elizabeth and Philip occupied the second- and third-floor apart-ments on the north side of the Palace, while Charles, Anne and their nannies were given a six-room apartment on the floor above. This had one well-lit day nursery and two night nurseries, as well as a bathroom and a kitchen. All these changes were a puzzle for a small boy.

"If his mother was a mystery to Prince Charles before," Martin Charteris, the Queen's former private secretary, observed, "she was much more of a mystery after she became Queen and could spend even less time with her children."

But the new Queen did make one concession. Although her own mother and sister were required to bow or curtsy in public, Charles and Anne were not obliged to do so.

"It's silly. They're too young to understand," she said.

As head of state, the Queen now had a coronation to plan. When she was in London, Charles's audiences with his mother were cut down to fifteen minutes, morning and evening. However, he and Anne did get to watch as their mother walked up and down the bedroom practising balancing the five-pound St Edward's Crown on her head. It had been made for the restoration of Charles II by Sir Robert Vyner, a leading slave trader.

Charles received a special, hand-painted invitation to his mother's coronation. Wearing navy-blue shorts and a ruffled white satin shirt pinned with a medal, his dark hair plastered down with pomade, Charles waited in Westminster Abbey for his mother to arrive through cheering crowds in the Gold State Coach. He sat next to his grandmother. With no clear idea of what was going on, he fidgeted throughout the ceremony. Afterwards on the balcony of Buckingham Palace, looking down on the vast crowds and soldiers below, he first began to realise how different he was from other children. This perturbed him, though his sister grew to relish it.

As his fifth birthday approached, his toys disappeared from one room in the nursery apartment. In came a desk, a blackboard and a governess, a stern Glaswegian named Catherine Peebles – Miss P, or

Misspy for short. She found that he had a fragile ego and was lacking in self-confidence.

"He was not terribly good at arithmetic, to say the very least," she said. If corrected, he would mope for the rest of the day. She found him, if not a dullard, an uninspiring pupil. "He was very responsive to kindness," she said, "but if you raised your voice to him, he would draw back into his shell."

The Queen and Prince Philip were rarely there to advise or encourage. Misspy soon found that history was Charles's thing. Over the next three years, she used the magnificent sculptures, paintings, tapestries, suits of armour and illustrated books at Buckingham Palace, Sandringham and Windsor Castle to bring history – and the history of his own family – to life. Charles was particularly taken by Anthony van Dyck's *Triple Portrait of Charles I*, showing the King full face and both profiles, which hung in the Queen's Drawing Room in Windsor Castle.

"King Charles lived for me in that room in the castle," he said.

He must have discovered, too, of his forebear's gruesome fate at the hands of the axeman.

Charles hoped his parents would stay in London for his fifth birthday. Instead they took off to Sandringham. They returned for a flying visit before setting off on a seven-month tour of the Commonwealth countries where she was now head of state.

The children caught up with their parents briefly in Malta, shipped there on the newly commissioned royal yacht *Britannia*. But their time there was taken up by naval displays and military parades. Their job, it seemed, was to look cute for the cameras.

When the Queen returned to England, Charles had to wait twenty minutes at the end of a line of dignitaries greeting her. He then got a handshake, like the rest of them, instead of a hug. Then she continued along the line, greeting her new subjects.

During one of her daughter's long absences, the Queen Mother sat down and wrote a letter to her daughter, saying: "You may find Charles much older in a very endearing way. … He is intensely affectionate. And loves you and Philip most tenderly."

It was as if Elizabeth had become a stranger to her own son. There was further estrangement in the family when the Queen forbade Charles's beloved aunt Princess Margaret to marry Group Captain Peter Townsend as he was a divorcé. The controversy dragged on for two years. The Queen, Margaret argued, had been allowed to marry the man she loved, even though he was not British nor a member of the Church of England – that is, until he naturalised, changed his name and converted from the Greek Orthodox Church to wed – but Princess Margaret was to be denied the love of her life. It was another example of the rivalry between an heir and their spare.

Charles himself was to face further alienation around the same time. Formerly, princes of the blood had traditionally been taught privately by tutors. But the decision was made that Charles would no longer be educated at home.

"The Queen and I want Charles to go to school with other boys of his generation," Philip said, "and learn to live with other children, and to absorb from childhood the discipline imposed by education with others."

In fact, Philip was concerned that Charles was getting too much coddling with hugs from Mabel Anderson and the Queen Mother, and wanted to toughen him up.

"He wanted his son to have an experience that would build character," said Mike Parker. "I suppose he thought Charles was still soft – not like his sister at all."

It was Anne who was the apple of Philip's eye – loud, rowdy, fearless.

"She had a much stronger, more extrovert personality," said Mabel Anderson. "She didn't exactly push Charles aside, but she was the more forceful child. He was, basically, a rather shy little boy."

When the Queen put Charles on horseback at the age of four, he was terrified and begged to be taken down. At the same age, Anne tried to grapple the reins from the stable hand and take off on her own.

The Queen Mother encouraged Charles's interest in the arts – particularly music and ballet – the things that his father considered soft. Philip clearly favoured the daredevil Anne.

Charles was kind and eager to share his toys with other children. If Philip had a cross word to say to Charles, he would dissolve in tears. While Mabel Anderson was not above administering a spanking, she took the time to comfort and reassure Charles. She became his surrogate mother. Charles called her "a haven of security, a great haven".

"At least," he later said, "she was there for me."

Indeed, she was the centre of his daily life from the moment she woke him in the morning until the time she tucked him into bed at night.

As for his real mother: "It's not that she was distant or even cold," explained Martin Charteris. "But she was very detached. And she believed Philip was in charge. She would never have interfered with his authority. Even if he was being very tough on Charles."

Charles was hardly prepared for school. When told of the plans for his education, he asked: "Mummy, what are schoolboys?"

The press were informed of the new arrangement. The Queen's press secretary wrote to the Newspaper Proprietors Association, saying: "A certain amount of the Duke of Cornwall's instruction will take place outside the home; for example he will visit museums and other places of interest. The Queen trusts, therefore, that His Royal Highness will be able to enjoy this in the same way as other children without the embarrassment of constant publicity."

However, when Charles turned up at Hill House preparatory school behind Harrods in a limousine wearing a velvet topcoat over his school uniform on the first day of Lent term 1956, he was greeted by Fleet Street photographers.

The *Manchester Guardian* reported: "On his first day at school the Duke of Cornwall painted a picture." It showed *Britannia* going under Tower Bridge.

It was impossible for Charles to experience the life of a normal schoolboy when he was greeted by the headmaster's wife every morning and seen off by the headmaster himself at the end of the school day. As it was deemed inappropriate for the heir to the throne to use a public swimming pool, two black cabs were hired each week to ferry Charles and his classmates to the pool in Buckingham Palace. However, he did travel on a bus with the other children to play football at the school games field, which were in the grounds of the Duke of York's Headquarters, a military depot in the King's Road.

But Charles was no sportsman. He was not physically robust and was prone to colds, flu and bouts of tonsillitis. As a consequence, he was often away from school, which did little for his education or his self-confidence. Things improved when he had his tonsils removed in 1957, though neither his mother nor his father were by his bedside. Visiting Buckingham Palace, the former First Lady of the United States Eleanor Roosevelt remarked that her hostess was as "calm and composed as if she did not have a very unhappy little boy on her mind".

In a further attempt to toughen him up, at the age of eight, Charles was sent to Cheam, a boarding school in Hampshire. Its regime was said to be "spartan and disciplined". Prince Philip had been sent there after he had been abandoned by his parents. His fees had been paid by one of his uncles, George Mountbatten, the Second Marquess of Milford Haven.

The Queen appeared to do nothing to mitigate Philip's decision, though she was worried that Charles would be exposed to too much publicity.

A newsreel crew recorded Charles arriving in a Jaguar with his ma and pa. He emerged dressed in the school uniform, only with a black tie rather than the school's blue one. The court was in mourning as King Haakon of Norway had recently died.

"He will be the first King of England to be educated as a boy among other boys –admittedly, a boy with a rather special destiny," the newsreel commentator said. "But his rank will count for little in the rough-and-tumble democracy of playground and dormitory, which is exactly how his parents and his future subjects would wish it."

Their duty done, mum and dad sped off. Although he had his teddy with him, Charles did not take his abandonment well. The first few nights in the dorm he shared with seven others, he apparently stifled his tears in the pillow. It was soon noted that he did not mix easily with the other boys.

"I'm not a gregarious person so I've always had a horror of gangs," he said.

The other boys did not find it easy to approach him. For fear of embarrassment, he sought to be unobtrusive. Otherwise he would spend his time in the dorm, writing to his mother and grandmother, begging to be allowed to come home. Even on the rare moments he got away from the school grounds, there was still no respite. Photographers followed him everywhere and journalists pestered the staff for details of the young Prince's school life.

While his parents had asked the school to treat Charles like any other boy, some masters handled him with kid gloves. Others, endeavouring to flaunt their democratic credentials, cracked down on him hard. The other boys were much the same. While some toadied to the heir to the throne, others seized the opportunity to bully their future king. Others sought to ignore him completely.

Foreseeing that his son might have trouble at school, Prince Philip got two of his military aides to give Charles some instruction in self-defence. During his five-year stay at Cheam, he twice had a fight in the dorm, only to be thrashed afterwards by members of staff, who seemed to enjoy meting out the punishment.

After the second time, Charles said: "I didn't do it again. I am one of the people for whom corporal punishment actually worked."

But conflicts were rare. Charles was completely unsuited to the unruly life of a boys' boarding school, and kept as low a profile as possible.

Though his maths did not improve, he did well in English and learnt to recite long passages from Shakespeare. Reports of his progress dribbled out in the press until the Queen threatened to remove him if they did not stop.

But still, she ignored his pleas to be allowed to leave Cheam. After the Christmas holiday, she wrote to Prime Minister Anthony Eden, saying: "Charles is just beginning to dread the return to school next week."

There was no way he could fit in. Things got worse. One Saturday afternoon in July 1958, Charles and a group of other boys were summoned to the headmaster's study. Alerted by a phone call from the Palace, they were to watch the closing ceremony of the British Empire and Commonwealth Games from Cardiff.

The boys sat on the floor to watch the fuzzy black-and-white images on the screen of the headmaster's small television set. The Queen was supposed to have been there, but had been kept home after an operation on her sinuses. Prince Philip had stepped in, but the Queen had decided to make her contribution via a recorded message.

"To my total horror," Charles recalled, "I heard my mama's voice."

"The British Empire and Commonwealth Games in the capital… have made this a memorable year for the Principality," she said. "I have therefore decided to mark it further by an act which will, I hope, give as much pleasure to all Welshmen as it does to me. I intend to create my son Charles Prince of Wales today. When he is grown up, I will present him to you at Caernarfon."

Charles was painfully aware that all eyes were upon him.

"All the other boys turned around and looked at me," Charles recalled.

His headmaster noticed the look of acute embarrassment that flashed across his face. Charles now saw the awful truth. He had been dropped in it. There was no way out. The nine-year-old was now, in state documents, His Royal Highness Prince Charles Philip Arthur George, Prince of Wales and Earl of Chester, Duke of Cornwall, Duke of Rothesay, Earl of Carrick, Lord of the Isles and Baron of Renfrew, Prince and Great Steward of Scotland. That was quite enough titles for anyone, but, throughout his life, he would go on acquiring more.

Schoolmates of the new Prince were not impressed. Though the monogram HRH appeared on his school bag, he was known among the boys as fatty. Mysteriously, he was made captain of the school football team. The results were disappointing. The *Cheam School Chronicle* reported: "Prince Charles seldom drove himself as hard as his ability and position demanded."

The people of Wales were more accommodating. A fortnight after the announcement, Charles was to visit the Principality for the first time when the royal yacht moored off Anglesey en route for Scotland and he was greeted by cheering crowds.

Although the movement for home rule in Wales was growing, *The Times* recorded "the spontaneous warmth of feeling in the hearts of Welshmen that after twenty-two years they are to be represented by a Prince of their own". The last Prince of Wales had been David, later Edward VIII, then the Duke of Windsor. Again, it was not a good precedent.

In his time at Cheam, Charles came down with a particularly virulent strain of the flu, then chickenpox. Then he later fell down stairs and broke his ankle. But on no occasion did his mother or father visit. Only when he came down with measles did his grandmother step in, allowing him to recuperate in the Royal Lodge in Windsor Great Park where she then resided. Later, when he was rushed by ambulance at night the sixty miles to Great Ormond Street Hospital for an emergency appendectomy, the Queen remained in bed in Windsor.

An aide recorded that the Queen "knew that his first few years at Cheam had been a misery to him", though offered him no comfort.

Charles said: "We were made to do things you didn't want to do, which we were told were 'jolly good for you'." For example: "We were made to make polite conversation, to put people at their ease, not just sit there because it didn't suit you." He rose to become head boy, no doubt on merit. Asked whether he had enjoyed his five years at Cheam, he said: "I loathed it."

But there was one high spot in his career at Cheam. He was cast as understudy to play the Duke of Gloucester – the future Richard III – in the school production of *The Last Baron*, written by David Munir. He studied for the part by listening to Laurence Olivier's performance in *Richard III* over and over again. At the last minute, the principal was unavailable, so Charles got to play the role. The Queen and Prince Philip were, as usual, unable to attend, but the Queen Mother and Princess Anne came to watch his performance.

There was tittering when he intoned a line "And soon may I ascend the throne", but otherwise, the *Cheam School Chronicle* said:

"Prince Charles played the traditional Gloucester with competence and depth: he had a good voice and excellent elocution, and very well conveyed the ambition and bitterness of the twisted hunchback."

When the final curtain fell, the headmaster stepped out on stage to announce that the Queen had just given birth to another boy, Prince Andrew. Charles had been upstaged by his younger brother already.

CHAPTER FIVE

THE AGE GAP

If Philip had grown distant from Charles, things did not promise to be much better with Andrew.

"People want their first child very much. They want the second almost as much. If a third comes along, they accept it as natural, but they haven't gone out of their way to try and get it," he said.

However, the Queen had wanted another child. She had once confided to a close friend that, when she was married, she wanted a family of four – two boys and two girls. Then nearly ten years after the birth of Princess Anne, Andrew came along. In the meantime, Elizabeth had been getting used to her role as Queen, while Philip, if the newspapers were to be believed, had been having trouble adjusting to his new, secondary, position – not the captain of the ship, but the man who had to walk two steps behind.

Philip complained to a friend: "I'm nothing but a bloody amoeba. I am the only man in the country not allowed to give his name to his children." He once remarked: "Constitutionally I don't exist."

Along the way he had lost his name, his nationality and his religion.

"When King George died, there were plenty of people telling me what not to do," he said. "'You mustn't interfere with this.' 'Keep out.'

I had to try to support the Queen as best I could, without getting in the way. The difficulty was to find things that might be useful."

But the period of adjustment was over. Philip had taken two long trips on the royal yacht *Britannia*, visiting distant outposts of the Empire. The Queen missed him. When he finally returned, she ordered a car to go and meet him. After long weeks at sea, he was lean, tanned and athletic. Soon she was pregnant. During the pregnancy, she got her royal duties out of the way, undertaking a nine-week tour of Canada which included the official opening of the St Lawrence Seaway.

Asked whether he wanted a baby brother or baby sister, Charles plumped for a brother. So did Anne. With Charles away at school, she needed another brother to go riding with. When the public were finally let in on the Queen's secret, they were told that Her Majesty would be undertaking no further public engagements in the foreseeable future. She also gave up horseback riding, driving and wine.

The arrival of the new baby called for the rearrangement of the nursery. When Charles came home for Easter, he had been moved out of his room – which had views out over the Mall and the changing of the guard in the forecourt – to a room around the corner to make way for the new baby. Andrew was to have Anne's old night nursery, while Anne was moved into Charles's room.

Andrew slept in the same cream-painted cot used by Charles and Anne before. He also inherited some of Charles's toys and the day nursery was stocked with some of the Queen's hand-me-downs, including a rocking horse which had long since lost its tail. A fresh crop of wooden toys would be supplied by Charles, which he made for his baby brother in the workshop at Cheam.

There was a miniature armchair that Charles had outgrown. Andrew now sat in it to watch *Champion the Wonder Horse*, his favourite

TV show. And there was a cuckoo clock on the wall that had been there since Charles was a baby. When an attempt was made to remove it, Andrew kicked up such a fuss that it had to be returned.

According to staff, Andrew was a handful from the beginning. His nanny, Mabel Anderson, called him "Baby Grumpling" for his temper tantrums. He called her Mamba and led her a merry dance. She was spared the task of teaching him to bow or curtsy as Charles and Anne had been until the Queen put a stop to it.

While the Queen had been away on official business for many of the key moments in Charles's and Anne's childhoods, when Andrew came along, she had been on the throne for eight years. She was no longer a raw young monarch and could get through the red boxes containing state papers in half the time. Nor did she have to spend hours listening to the advice of the aides she had inherited from her father.

Other time-consuming chores, such as sitting for a royal portrait, were behind her. She cut out evening engagements altogether and took a year off from state visits and Commonwealth tours so she could spend time with her new young son.

No longer did she dash off to her study to get to work in the morning. The first half-hour after breakfast was devoted to baby Andrew. The boxes could wait. She spent another half an hour with him when Mabel Anderson brought him downstairs mid-morning. At lunchtime, the Queen would head up to the nursery. Afternoon engagements were kept to a minimum so she could wheel him out into the garden in his ageing pram to see the flamingos in the lake.

At teatime she would go up to the nursery again. And, if Mabel Anderson had an evening off, the Queen would take over the running of the nursery, giving Andrew his evening feed, his bath and tucking him in at night – all things that Charles had routinely been denied.

The Queen, at last, embraced the pleasures of motherhood – laughing, smiling and chuckling with the infant. In the evening, Prince Philip would stop by for a few minutes while on his way out to some event. On one occasion, Andrew smeared chocolate pudding down the front of Philip's snowy-white dress shirt, sending him back downstairs for a quick change.

Prince Philip called Andrew "The Boss", as he was wilful and self-possessed. Once, after a mock boxing match at bedtime, Andrew whacked him in the eye. That night, Philip was on his way to a film premiere, where he was asked how he got the shiner.

"That was the boss," he said. Everyone thought he meant the Queen.

The infant Andrew was protected from the press, so much so that rumours spread that he was in some way malformed. Philip was determined to put paid to this. After the Trooping the Colour in 1961, the Queen appeared on the balcony of Buckingham Palace with the sixteen-month-old Andrew in her arms. It was the first time he had heard the cheering of the crowd. Overhead was the roar of a squadron of RAF Javelin fighters giving the royal salute.

Far from there being anything wrong with the child, Andrew, unlike Charles, was unusually sturdy and healthy. The Queen put this down to the time of year that he had been born.

"I think children always do better if they are born with the spring and summer ahead of them," she said.

Andrew might also have benefited from the absence of the forbidding Helen Lightbody, who had retired. With time to spare, the Queen was now able to bring up the baby in accordance with her own ideas – regular meals, few sweets, early to bed, light clothing, plenty of fresh air and, when he was a toddler, plenty of exercise.

She cast aside the old wives' remedies, believing that prevention was better than cure. The Queen was one of the first mothers to have her children immunised against poliomyelitis. By the age of six months, Andrew had also been vaccinated for smallpox, tetanus, whooping cough and diphtheria. Just to be on the safe side, the royal paediatrician, Sir Wilfrid Sheldon, visited Andrew once a month to give him a check over. In his early years, Charles, by contrast, had not benefited from his expertise.

In accordance with his mother's firm belief in the benefits of fresh air, Andrew spent long hours in the garden every day, warm or cold, wet or fine. If it was raining, the pram would be parked with its hood up in the shelter of the canopy of the Palace garden entrance. Policemen patrolling would act as stand-in nannies. If Andrew cried for any reason, a telephone call from the police lodge would bring Mabel Anderson hurrying down from the nursery.

While the public saw few photographs of the infant, his proud mother would show him off to distinguished guests. Former US President Dwight D. Eisenhower called at the Palace one day and the Queen invited him to stay for lunch. She had Andrew brought down from the nursery when they were having coffee and sat him on her lap for Ike to admire. Andrew was already old enough and active enough to scramble on to the table and help himself to a handful of sugar.

"A fine little boy you have there, Ma'am," said Ike.

For Elizabeth, the days of Andrew's babyhood passed all too quickly. Her year sabbatical was over all too soon. She regretted being away on a seven-week tour of India, Pakistan and Nepal when he said his first words and took his first steps. However, his grandmother, the Queen Mother, was there for the occasions.

When the Queen returned, she found Andrew was no longer a baby, but an adventurous little boy. While Charles and Anne had never been allowed to come into her study during the day while she was working, with Andrew she dovetailed her work with the joys of motherhood. She had missed out with the first two, but she was now determined not to miss any more precious moments of her third child's infancy.

Royal aides, visiting her room on official business, were not surprised to find Andrew playing with his toys on the floor next to the desk where the Queen was dealing with state papers. A stash of toys – building blocks, balls, toy trucks and wooden soldiers – were kept in the bottom drawer of an antique bureau. Indeed, they would sometimes find the Queen, conscientious as she was when it came to work, on the floor playing with Andrew while the corgis scampered around.

One day, a page came in, stood on one of Andrew's wooden balls and almost fell into the Queen's lap.

"Andrew, you really must learn to put your toys away when you've finished with them," she chided.

While Andrew was not versed in the art of bowing, he was taught to be polite. "Please" and "thank you" were a must. And while the Queen addressed the staff by their Christian names, Andrew was told to address them as Mr, Mrs or Miss. They were told to call him Andrew. The "Prince" could come later.

On fine days, the Queen would spend afternoons in the Palace gardens with Andrew. She got the staff to build him a sandpit and a climbing frame. A knotted rope was slung from one of the trees and a miniature caravan served as a den.

When her lessons were over, they would be joined by Anne, who showed him how to make sandcastles. Though she would later find his impish, mischievous ways irritating, she doted on him as an infant. So much so that, when he fell down while running around a garden path and began to cry, she cried herself.

He soon got acclimatised to royal ways. At the age of twenty months he began waving to a crowd of well-wishers who had gathered on Aberdeen station when they were on their way back from Balmoral. Still too young to join the traditional Christmas dinner at Sandringham, when he was brought in after the meal by Mabel Anderson, he clambered up on the Queen's lap and joined in pulling the crackers. When they went back to London, he marched along the platform in a cream coat and gaiters and joined the rest of the family, shaking the hands of the dignitaries lined up to greet them. He also copied Anne, waving to the crowds when they visited Charles in Great Ormond Street Hospital after he had had his appendix removed.

At the age of two, he greeted visitors to the nursery with "hello" and "goodbye". One visitor was photographer Lisa Sheridan who came to take his portrait. She found him "pliant and intelligent", with "a vital, happy disposition" and full of "quicksilver activity". He could not have been more different from Charles.

His education started at two. The Queen was his first teacher. The family's private dining room was equipped with a counting frame, a clock face and a small blackboard. When Prince Philip had disappeared in the direction of his study after breakfast, Andrew would sit on the Queen's lap while she taught him the alphabet, how to count and telling the time.

She also taught him to ride, taking him to the royal mews beside the Palace for his first lessons. Hoisted on to the back of a small Shetland pony, she walked him round the yard. Later, he would get his own pony, Dinky.

As a youth, Andrew was taught ballroom dancing, though this ill-fitted him for the dance floor at Tramp. The Queen thought it improved a boy's deportment, so arranged for him to join his sister's weekly dance classes. Philip taught him to swim in the Palace's private pool. They played cowboys and Indians in the Palace gardens and football in the Palace's red-carpeted corridors, which Andrew also used as a racetrack for his pedal car. During a visit, Philip's ageing mother was drawn into a game of indoor cricket, bowling underarm.

"Every now and again a pane of glass got broken, but I don't think we ever broke a piece of Meissen or anything like that," Andrew recalled.

When Charles was back from school, he joined in. At Sandringham, on the snowy Boxing Day when Andrew was nearly three, the three children had a snowball fight and made a snowman, complete with hat and pipe.

While the Queen was away on a tour of Australia and New Zealand on his third birthday, she did not forget to phone Andrew to wish him many happy returns. There were responsibilities too. The Queen put him in charge of feeding the dogs and making sure they always had drinking water – it was a job, as a dog lover, she had always done herself rather than trust to servants.

His royal education continued when he was sat in Charles's miniature armchair in the nursery to watch his mother on horseback Trooping the Colour on TV. But he soon realised that it was better to watch the ceremony from the window. Beyond this, he loved television, though his mother tried to curb his viewing.

He had just turned three when the Queen Mother commissioned sculptor Franta Belsky to make a bronze bust of him.

"I want it done before he loses the look of babyhood," she said.

It took eight sittings with Andrew distracted with toys, picture books and chocolate to nibble on. He also got to play with the offcuts of clay which Belsky showed him how to model into shapes.

"I have never seen such sustained concentration and excitement of discovery in a child," the sculptor said.

Belsky thought that Andrew took after the Queen Mother and the Windsor side of the family generally. But Philip's mother thought that he resembled Philip as a child with his impish grin, tousled hair and the prolonged shrug of the shoulders when something amused or intrigued him. When Philip's sisters visited from Germany they found him, like the younger Philip, "Sometimes naughty, never nasty."

Andrew played practical jokes on the staff, swiping the knives and forks when a footman was laying the table and hiding, giggling, behind a chair with the stolen cutlery. Sentries guarding Buckingham Palace had their shoelaces tied together. In the nursery, he took a radio to bits, then he went missing, only to be found asleep in the airing cupboard. Using a tea tray, he tobogganed down the stairs in Buckingham Palace.

When Andrew was three, Princess Anne went off to boarding school at Benenden in Kent, and the Queen was concerned that Andrew would be alone in the nursery.

"It's time we thought about having a little playmate for Andrew," she told "Bobo" MacDonald, her personal maid and long-time confidante.

To cushion Andrew against sibling rivalry, the Queen told him early in her pregnancy that he was going to have a baby brother or baby sister. Andrew misunderstood. He told Mabel Anderson excitedly: "I'm going to have a baby brother *and* a baby sister."

Soon after Andrew's fourth birthday, the Queen gave birth to Prince Edward. Princess Margaret, the Duchess of Kent and Princess Alexandra all had sons by then, and Margaret and the Duchess were pregnant again. So Andrew would have plenty of playmates. And with his mother and father at home much more often, Andrew grew up in a much more secure family atmosphere than Charles had ever experienced.

Approaching five, Andrew had lost the baby look that his grandmother had cherished. It was time for a new portrait. This one was to be an ivory miniature that his mother wanted for her collection.

The commission would go to the Australian artist Stella Marks who had made her name as a miniaturist in the US. Prince Philip had got Marks to paint his new wife. Since then, she had produced miniatures of Philip, Charles and Anne. Now it was Andrew's turn.

He was a restless child, so Mrs Marks distracted him with a story about two baby rabbits whose mother had brought them along to the studio to have their portraits painted.

"Did the baby bunnies sit still?" Andrew interrupted, a trait he had inherited from his father.

"Not as still as Prince Andrew," Mrs Marks replied.

He asked to see the miniatures she had painted of the bunnies. Of course, they did not exist, so she parried this by saying that she would give him the preliminary drawings she had done and duly handed over some hastily prepared sketches at the next sitting.

While Charles had taken his lessons in the Palace alone until Anne was old enough to join him, the Queen arranged for two boys and two girls to join Andrew in the nursery's school room. Female company at that early age made Andrew at ease with women, while Charles remained shy and awkward.

Their teacher would, again, be Catherine Peebles, who had given Charles his early lessons. She found teaching Andrew easier, as his mother had already given him a grounding in reading, writing and arithmetic. Miss Peebles introduced scripture, history and geography. This was a particular favourite of Andrew's, as he would follow his mother's tours on the map. French was added to the curriculum as the Queen was fluent in the language. The dancing lessons continued and Andrew was taught to play the piano.

While his fellow pupils were also from the upper crust, Andrew was to be given a taste of ordinary life by being enlisted in a local cub pack, the 1st St Marylebone. They were known as the Fighting First as so many of their number in an earlier generation had lost their lives in World War I. To avoid publicity, Andrew was not allowed to join them at their weekly pack meetings. Instead, the pack would be ferried to the Palace in a minibus. They played games like British Bulldog. Andrew enjoyed the rough and tumble. They also taught him woodcraft and how to identify various wild birds and flowers – much more his brother's sort of thing.

Most evenings, Andrew, Edward and their parents would spend time together. Before a state banquet, the Queen would visit the nursery in her evening gown and tiara, and sit on the piano stool reading to Prince Edward, while the Duke of Edinburgh, in white tie, would chat to Andrew about the day's events.

"They were just like an ordinary family," recalled a former royal servant.

Nevertheless, Andrew had to be prepared for official duties. At the age of six, he handed out rosettes to junior contestants at the Windsor Horse Show. Otherwise, he was smuggled back and forth to the Brigade of Guards sports ground where he trained and played football with other small boys. Once an enterprising photographer tracked him down, but Andrew dodged behind his royal bodyguard and yelled: "You can't catch me."

His fellow pupil Katie Seymour's parents had a holiday home on the Isle of Wight. Andrew was allowed to join her family there, where he could play on the beach with the reasonable assumption of privacy and it was there he learnt to sail a dinghy. Another of Andrew's early playmates was Lady Diana Spencer whom he met at Sandringham. As a youngster, she always said she was going to marry him. At boarding school, she hung a photograph of him over her bed. They exchanged letters and there was talk of romance throughout their childhoods.

Andrew and his younger brother Edward were taken to Lord's to be taught how to play cricket by the MCC's chief coach Len Muncer, Wimbledon for tennis coaching from former champion turned commentator Dan Maskell, who had taught other royal children, while figure skater Roy Lee gave them private lessons in Richmond rink after the other skaters had been cleared off the ice by security staff.

In the spirit of the sixties, Andrew's parents aspired to give him an ordinary upbringing. This was impossible when he lived in a six-hundred-room palace and holidays were spent in a Disney-style castle in Scotland or on a luxury yacht half the size of an ocean liner, with liveried footmen bowing and scraping, policemen saluting and sentries snapping to attention every time he walked by.

There would be visits from famous people, such as Neil Armstrong after he walked on the Moon. And there would be no queuing to buy tickets at the cinema. He and his companions would automatically be ushered to the best seats.

There were other perks. Veteran clown Charlie Cairoli entertained at Andrew's eighth birthday party. He was taught salmon fishing by the Queen Mother and driving by former Formula One world champion Graham Hill, and he was given a miniature version of the gadget-laden Aston Martin DB5 driven by James Bond in *Goldfinger* said to have cost £4,000 (£65,000 today) to build. It had a top speed of 40mph, but the Queen banned it from the Palace grounds as it distracted him from his lessons.

There were sailing lessons at Cowes. The Bishop of Norwich took him to see Norwich City play Chelsea. He was given a guided tour of New Scotland Yard with an Iranian prince and, during a visit to King Olav of Norway, sailed up the coast to visit Prime Minister Per Borten at his farmhouse near Trondheim Fjord. Always on the go, one of the newspapers dubbed him "Action Man".

As a girl, the Queen had been shy – and her father painfully so. So it was with some pride that she announced to friends: "Andrew isn't a bit shy."

Indeed, he was often pushy, demanding and domineering.

"He's his father all over again," said a friend of the family. Philip was proud that at least one of his sons was a chip off the old block. But he was also conscious of the dangers.

"Don't let him have all his own way," Philip admonished Roy Lee before Andrew's first skating lesson.

But often he did get his own way. At Sandringham the men would walk across the park to church on a Sunday, while as a child Andrew went in the car with the women.

"Why can't I walk to church with Papa – like Charles?" he demanded to know. After that, he did walk to church and, like Papa, he did so with his hands clasped behind his back.

Andrew grew up boisterous, self-willed, extroverted, confident and active – everything Charles was not. He sprung a whoopee cushion on the Queen Mother, sprinkled itching powder in his mother's bed and once climbed on to the roof of Buckingham Palace to turn the TV aerial so that when the Queen sat down to watch the horse racing from Sandown Park, there was no picture. The Palace maintenance man had to be called in to do something about it or she'd have missed the 3.30. Meanwhile Andrew hid away laughing before telling his mother what he had done.

A garden party was disrupted when he switched signs, leaving guests bewildered. He smashed the greenhouse windows with a football and poured bubble bath into a fountain at Windsor. Boisterous and energetic, Andrew spent his days chatting to housemaids and favoured visitors such as the Queen's lady-in-waiting Susan Hussey, who popped in regularly from her nearby office.

Wherever they went, the skylarking continued. At Balmoral, on the occasion of a formal changing of the guard, the guard commander would salute and ask the Queen her permission to proceed, to which she gave her consent. It was a mere formality.

"I do wish Mummy would say 'no' for a change," said Andrew on one occasion.

While many considered him a sturdy, lively youngster, energetic and full of beans, Andrew did not always endear himself to the butt of his pranks, or those who had to clear up afterwards. Even his mother conceded that he was "not always a little ray of sunshine" when she found a hat laid out for a formal occasion had been used for football practice.

Anne began to find her younger brother's constant larking about a little wearing. Charles was more phlegmatic. "Just wait until you go to school," he told Andrew. "Then you'll have to knuckle down."

For Andrew there would be no breaking-in period of day school that Charles had been given. But while Charles dreaded being sent off to boarding school, Andrew looked forward to it. At the age of eight and a half, Andrew was sent to Heatherdown, a prep school in Ascot, just seven miles from Windsor where the Queen spent her weekends. It did not have the stern regime of Cheam. The Queen had vetoed Philip sending him there. She wanted her favourite son closer to home.

Sending a royal child to school was no longer a novelty, so there was little interest from the press. He was not trailed by photographers wherever he went. As he was not the heir to the throne, Andrew got an easier time and took to it like a duck to water. He loved wearing the same grey uniform and red cap as the other boys.

An extrovert, competitive and sometimes aggressive, Andrew did not submit to bullying. At Heatherdown he developed into a boisterous bruiser. Sharing a dormitory with six others, he complained that TV watching was restricted.

"All the best programmes come on after we've gone to sleep," he said. "I'm allowed to watch them at home."

There were clashes with authority as well. Some of the teachers found him a bit of a handful. Andrew was spanked following a school outing to the Natural History Museum in London where there was a brawl with a group of teenagers who they claimed approached them and demanded money.

At school he organised midnight feasts and, continuing his practice of practical joking, mixed up everyone's shoes in the dorm. He was blamed when a shirt appeared flying from the top of the school flagpole. There was only one problem. Whatever his achievements in acting, swimming and sailing, the conscientious and hard-working Charles would have done it first and usually better. Andrew now became Action Man 2, a soubriquet he resented.

And, despite efforts to give him an upbringing that was as normal as possible, there were privileges that skewed his experience of life. While boys were only allowed to travel home for one weekend a term, if there was nothing else going on at school, his parents would sometimes drive over at the weekend and take Andrew and his schoolmates to tea at Windsor Castle.

Unlike other boys, of course, he had a royal protection officer on hand at all times. In the spring term of 1971, extra guards were laid on as there was the threat of a kidnap plot against Prince Andrew. This came to nothing, but one of the guards at the time did teach him how to handle a pistol.

Tuition in handling a shotgun was left to his father, who also taught him how to handle a boat. Soon, he bagged his first pheasant on the moors at Balmoral and took part in the Britannia Club races at Cowes on a yacht his father had borrowed for the occasion.

Out and about, he watched his sister Anne come third in the three-day event at Badminton and drove through cheering crowds with his granny, the Queen Mother, to attend Trooping the Colour. The crew brought in to film the *Royal Family* documentary were pestered with questions.

Occasionally, Prince Andrew's arrogance revealed itself. One evening, the Queen and Prince Philip arrived as Andrew and Mabel Anderson were watching the long-running TV soap opera *Coronation Street*. Blowsy barmaid Bet Lynch was in the midst of a rowdy argument at the Rover's Return pub when Prince Andrew commented disdainfully: "Oh God, look at all those common people."

His father reprimanded him immediately. He gave the royal teenager a clip around the ear and told him sternly: "If it wasn't for people like that you would not be sitting here." For once, the usually talkative prince fell silent.

Clearly, Andrew did not think he was going to be mixing with common people. Early on, his name had been put down for Eton. This was his mother's choice as, again, it was close to Windsor. The Queen herself had her only formal schooling there. She had been sent to Eton for weekly lessons on constitutional history from the Vice-Provost. But Philip overruled her. He was determined that Andrew would go to his old alma mater, Gordonstoun in Scotland, a fate Charles had already suffered, and one that would cement their diverging fates even further.

CHAPTER SIX

COLDITZ IN KILTS

Both Charles and Andrew were sent to Gordonstoun, a tough boarding school on the remote, windswept north coast of Scotland that Philip had been to. For Charles, it was another attempt to toughen him up so that he would be fit to be heir to the throne.

There, the sensitive youth would have to endure freezing temperatures. The classrooms were unheated and, in the belief that fresh air was good for you, the dormitory windows were left wide open while the boys slept, winter and summer. Charles was assigned to Windmill Lodge, a long, narrow, stone-and-timber building with a green asbestos roof and bare wooden floors. It was a temporary building supplied by the RAF which had never been replaced. There were fourteen hard wooden beds to a dorm and bare light bulbs hung from the ceiling.

Charles's bed was under a window and, in winter, he often woke to find his bed covers encrusted with frost or even snow. When it rained, he would have to gather up his bedding and sleep on the floor in the centre of the room. Each day there was a pre-dawn run, through the countryside – shirtless and in short trousers even when it snowed – to "shake the sleep out of them", followed by an icy shower.

"Charles was a very polite, sweet boy – always incredibly thoughtful and kind, interested in art and music," Elizabeth's cousin and confidante Margaret Rhodes said. "But his father interpreted this as weakness, and the Queen believed he knew what was best. Gordonstoun was supposed to 'make a man out of him', although I never really understood what that meant."

Charles himself had wanted to go to Charterhouse, where the few friends he made at Cheam were headed. But he did not have a say. Philip believed that Charles was too soft to be king and something had to be done about it. Gordonstoun was supposed to draw him out of his shy and reticent disposition. He would become more self-assertive. And, of course, Philip had been happy there.

But Philip had been an obscure foreign prince, not heir to the throne, and anyone who befriended him would not be seen as a boot-licking sycophant. When Charles walked down the corridors, he would be greeted with loud sucking sounds.

And there was bullying. Once, after taking a shower, the thirteen-year-old Prince was pounced upon, tied up and shoved into a large wicker laundry basket which was hoisted on a hook on the wall and blasted with freezing water. Once his tormentors had had their fun, they left him hanging there, naked and shivering, for sometimes half an hour until a staff member heard his plaintive cries.

At night he would be pummelled in the darkness with pillows, shoes and fists until he dreaded going to bed.

"The people in my dormitory are foul," he wrote in a letter home. "Goodness, they are horrid. I don't see how anybody could be so foul."

He told his mother: "I hardly get any sleep in the House because I snore and I get hit on the head all the time. It's absolute hell."

The headmaster was a sadist who encouraged the older boys to pick on the younger ones, extorting money and food from them. After the housemasters had gone to bed it was a free-for-all. The custom was to haze new boys by taking a pair of pliers to the flesh and twist them until the skin tore. The worst of it occurred at Windmill Lodge and Prince Charles got the worst of the worst.

Having been told not to pick on the heir to the throne, the boys enjoyed it all the more. It was open season on the rugby field, with boys boasting that they had punched the future King of England. On one occasion he ended up with a broken nose. Despite what his father had taught him, Charles did not put up a fight.

"Maybe once or twice he made the effort," a former teacher said, "but I never really saw him fight back."

Nor did he complain about the bullying, for fear that it would get worse. Charles sought solace, taking long walks in the countryside of Morayshire. Otherwise, he sought refuge in the art room, but this hardly helped. He was shunned.

"How can you treat a boy as just an ordinary chap when his mother's portrait is on the coins you spend in the school shop, on the stamps you use to mail your letters home, when a detective trails him wherever he goes?" said one schoolmate. "Most boys tend to fight shy of friendship with Charles. The result is that he is very lonely. It is this loneliness, rather than the school's toughness, which must be hardest on him."

Another contemporary said: "Charles was crushingly lonely for most of his time there. The wonder is that he survived with his sanity intact."

His health suffered too. He spent ten days in a nursing home in Aberdeen with pneumonia.

Getting off campus did not help either. On a school trip to the Isle of Lewis, he was spotted by a crowd and sought sanctuary in a bar. When asked what he wanted to drink, he did not know what to do. Then he remembered that he once had a cherry brandy while out shooting at Sandringham and asked for one. Charles was fourteen at the time. The next day the press was full of tales of his underage drinking. Charles was mortified, terrified that he had embarrassed the Queen. In tears, he called her. But she was unruffled.

"It will do him good," she said. "He learnt the hard way."

But things got worse when his protection officer carried the can and was sacked.

"I have never been able to forgive them for doing that," Charles said, "because he defended me in the most marvellous way, and he was the most wonderful, loyal, splendid man... It was atrocious what they did."

Nor was he safe from the press even when he was on the premises. Someone stole his exercise book of essays and sold it to the German magazine *Der Stern*, prompting another apology to Her Majesty.

A family friend, Sir Iain Tennant and his wife Lady Margaret had an estate nearby and invited him over to play the cello, which he had been learning at Gordonstoun. He was fairly awful and it was embarrassing for all concerned, but these visits gave him some respite from the school. Even so, the Tennants heard him sobbing his heart out in his room at night.

The Queen Mother took the trouble to stay at Birkhall, her fourteen-bedroom home on the Balmoral estate. But even that was a two-hour drive from the school.

Charles hated Gordonstoun even more than Cheam, calling it "Colditz in kilts" after the notorious German prisoner-of-war camp in Colditz Castle in Saxony.

Again, the letters he wrote home, begging to be released, fell on deaf ears. The Queen was now lavishing her affection on his younger siblings, leaving Charles feeling isolated and unwanted.

"The Queen treated Andrew and Edward very differently than she did Charles and Anne," said the Queen's cousin. "She was very affectionate towards the two younger ones, especially Edward. Perhaps by that time she felt more comfortable in her role as Queen."

Another confidante said that it was as if a switch had been thrown: "There she was, a loving, caring mum. Too late for Charles and Anne sadly."

When Charles returned home for the holidays, he'd rush to the nursery to spend time with Andrew and Edward, and his beloved nanny Mabel Anderson. Then, when it was time to return to school, he vanished. Footmen were sent to seek him out. He would usually be found crying in his room or reading a bedtime story to Andrew whom he then doted on. It was leaving Mabel that upset him most.

"He said goodbye to his mother as a courtesy," said a footman, "if she gave him the time and wasn't busy doing something more important. But he loved Mabel, and when he said goodbye to her, he was genuinely sad."

The stickler was, of course, Prince Philip who was hell-bent on stiffening his son's spine. He would hear none of his complaints about his treatment at school and urged him to be steadfast. Now trained as a pilot, Philip sometimes flew the reluctant Charles up to the RAF airbase just miles from the school and drove him the rest of the way. There was no escape.

They had always had a difficult relationship. There was nothing Charles could do to please his father. When, at the age of thirteen, Charles proudly announced that he had killed his first stag, Philip upbraided him in front of guests at lunch for some minor infraction. One visitor remembered "tears welled into his eyes with a whole table of people staying there... And I thought how could you do that?"

Another accused Philip of "belittling" his son and realised that the Duke thought his son was "a bit of a wimp… and Charles realised what his father thought, and it hurt him deeply".

The "rough way" Philip treated his son was "very bullying… which would have the effect of driving Charles back into his shell". Asked how Charles felt about his father, a senior courtier told *The Times*: "Simply put, Charles was frightened of him."

His hunting endeavours did not endear him to some of his future subjects. When it was reported that Charles had ridden with the West Norfolk Hunt, the chairman of the National Society for the Abolition of Cruel Sports wrote to the Queen saying: "This news, we venture to suggest, will dismay a great number of your Majesty's subjects since, as your Majesty is no doubt aware, there is continually increasing evidence of public resentment against cruelty in the hunting field. … May we respectfully suggest that the mere presence of Prince Charles at the hunt implies approval of this so-called 'sport', and he find sufficient opportunity for his enjoyment of riding, for exercise and his love of animals, by attending drag-hunts and point-to-point meetings rather than in patronising events wherein cruelty so manifestly enters."

These country pursuits were very much part of Charles's nature. He longed to be at Balmoral, as it gave him a chance to get away from his father and wander the moors and hills.

"I cannot tell you how much I miss Balmoral and the hills and the air," Charles wrote in a letter home from school. "I feel very empty and incomplete without it all… I hate coming back here and leaving everyone at home."

But even then, home offered few comforts. Apart from being mocked by his father, he failed to match the exacting standards of his sister Anne in horsemanship and the equine arts, much to the amusement of others. He would withdraw to the library where he would sort out treasures to be put on display for visiting dignitaries. At Windsor, these included the drawings of Leonardo da Vinci. A horsey lot, the rest of the family were unimpressed.

Then there was the matter of the size of his ears, which he was ceaselessly teased about at school. The Queen and Prince Philip would have nothing done about them, despite the urgings of Charles's trusted mentor, Lord Mountbatten. But even he made it worse by once telling Charles: "You can't possibly be king with ears like that."

When the school put on a production of *Henry V*, Charles failed to get the title role he coveted. Instead, he played Exeter, who gets the immortal Shakespearean line: "Tennis-balls, my liege." Next, he got to play the lead in the tragedy *Macbeth*, who kills a king and in turn gets killed. It was a role close to his heart. His beloved grandmother, the Queen Mother, had been brought up in Glamis Castle, Macbeth's home and the setting of the play. Prince Philip laughed during the performance of the tragedy and likened Charles's acting to *The Goon Show*, an idiotic radio comedy show.

Just as Charles was making some headway with his peers, he was picked out again. This time he was to attend the funeral of Sir Winston Churchill, alongside a hundred world leaders, while his schoolmates watched on TV. Other boys could hardly compete on the national stage and, again, he was given the cold shoulder.

Philip was not impressed by his son's interest in the arts, nor the comfort he got from religion – sitting in a pew reading a book on naval tactics throughout the sixteen-year-old's confirmation service in the chapel at Windsor; he regarded these as symptoms of his son still being a weakling. He must be toughened up at all costs. Charles would be sent to Timbertop, the wilderness survival programme run by Geelong Church of England Grammar School a hundred miles north-east of Melbourne in the foothills of the Great Dividing Range.

"It will put some steel in him," Philip said, "or I simply give up."

Charles had no say in the matter. The whole thing was cooked up between Philip and Sir Robert Menzies, prime minister of Australia, as there were questions of protocol to be ironed out.

The Prince travelled with his father's equerry, Squadron Leader David Checketts. He was greeted at the airport by Bob Menzies, the governor general and over three hundred members of the press.

"However, I did nothing as foolish as to fall down the steps and land on my face at the bottom," he wrote to his great uncle, Lord Mountbatten. "I'm dreading the day when I do that!"

The greeting from the crowd of well-wishers who waited in the rain was warm.

Although the creation of Timbertop drew its inspiration from Gordonstoun, it was free of the bullying and sadism. The boys were taught self-reliance, chopping firewood and cooking for themselves. They went on long hikes into the outback where they had to contend with poisonous snakes and venomous spiders and ants.

There were 140 boys housed in nine huts at Timbertop. Prince Charles was put in charge of three of these compounds, though he was housed in a flat which he shared with another boy selected to keep him company. While the nights were cold as they had been at Gordonstoun, during the day the temperature hovered in the nineties Fahrenheit.

After a month, Charles was allowed to go and stay with the Checketts family in a small farmhouse in a village 120 miles away. Although he was given the option to go home to Britain after one term, Charles stayed on to go on a school trip to New Guinea where he danced, feasted and threw spears with the Papuans. There were other side trips and he made over fifty public appearances, at last overcoming his fear of crowds.

The Prince was also guest of honour at dozens of dinners, galas and parties, some attended by people his own age. At a school dance in Melbourne, he met Dale Harper, the spirited blonde daughter of a printing magnate. Nicknamed Kanga by Charles because of her bouncy personality, Dale – later Lady Tryon – would one day become his mistress and confidante. When Charles left Australia, he was scarcely recognisable. He was fit, tanned and confident.

Much to Philip's surprise, his son had returned home a far more formidable foe on the polo field, having practised with some of the leading players in Australia. The Duke had given him his first polo pony before he went to Gordonstoun, though constantly criticised his performance.

"He was just brutal," a teammate said, "singling Prince Charles out at every turn."

But now Charles found himself on the winning side against a team captained by his father.

"Was Prince Philip finally proud?" a teammate was asked.

"Hard to tell," he replied. "Never heard him say it if he was."

After Timbertop, Charles found himself better suited to life at Gordonstoun. He worked his way up to "Guardian" – the title the school gave head boy – though he proved inept at imposing the discipline on miscreants that was required. He was too kindly.

The position gave him a private study-bedroom which he filled with wild flowers. This was next to the flat occupied by his art teacher, who further encouraged his interest in music. They duetted with Charles on the cello and his teacher on the piano.

The first heir to the throne to have his academic abilities tested at A level, Charles got a B in history and a C in French. Before leaving Gordonstoun, as Guardian, Charles had one last duty to perform.

"There is a dance here in a fortnight's time," he wrote, "which fills me with horror as I have to arrange most of it. The idea is so awful as thirty girls are being transported from an Aberdeen school to provide material for dancing. I shall do my best not to dance or become involved, but will no doubt be required to search every nook and cranny for enterprising dancers."

In fact, it was not as awful as he feared, writing afterwards: "They were pretty hardy lasses with an equally hardy bespectacled mistress in charge of them. I danced with quite a lot of them and in the end there was only one left without a partner – and so was I, so all was well for the last five minutes. Fortunately, nothing ghastly happened and I wasn't head-hunted!"

Prince Charles would leave Gordonstoun without a tinge of regret. But freedom did not beckon quite yet. On 22 December 1965 the Queen hosted a dinner at Buckingham Palace to decide what he should do next. Among the guests were Prime Minister Harold Wilson, the Archbishop of Canterbury, Lord Mountbatten (technically representing the heads of all the armed services) and Philip – though not, of course, Charles himself.

Charles's mentor Mountbatten took charge. Clearly, the heir to the throne should go into the armed services. Mountbatten and Philip, both Navy men, agreed that it should be the Navy. Other members of the ad hoc committee urged that Charles should be allowed to go to university first. The choice was simple – Oxford or Cambridge. No red-brick would get a look in.

Neither the Queen nor Prince Philip had any experience of university. They depended on the judgement of Robin Woods, the Dean of Windsor, who favoured Cambridge. The Queen dispatched the Dean to sound out six colleges – King's, Magdalene, Selwyn, Corpus Christi, Churchill and Trinity.

After discreet lobbying by its master, former Chancellor of the Exchequer Lord Richard Austen "Rab" Butler, Trinity College was chosen. It had been founded by distant relative Henry VIII in 1546. Charles was going to be the first heir to the throne to graduate. Then it would be on to the Royal Naval College in Dartmouth, following his father. Charles himself was not consulted.

CHAPTER SEVEN

THE SNIGGERER

Andrew's experience of Gordonstoun was very different. Like Charles, Andrew did not shine academically and said of his alma mater: "The beds are hard and it's all straw mattresses, bread and water – just like a prison."

But Andrew was made of sterner stuff. Philip said: "He'll settle down at any school once he finds out a smile and a bit of charm won't always get what he wants."

Besides, the regime had loosened up considerably since Charles's time. The early morning run was now more of a saunter and there were hot showers as well as cold. The rooms were centrally heated and there were carpets on the floor. Corporal punishment had been curtailed. Discipline was taken on trust. Punishment was measured in minutes – two minutes for talking after lights out, three for being late for assembly, ten for smoking behind the bike sheds. The accrued time must be spent on cross-country walks thinking "pure" thoughts rather than on any preferred leisure activity. The punishment was not supervised and pupils were on their honour to do it. But it was understood that if you had any sense you'd skive off.

Andrew got his fair share of stick. Other pupils called him "boast-ful" and "big-headed". One said: "He had a bit of the 'I am the Prince' about him when he arrived. He soon had it knocked out of him. The ribbings he got were unmerciful. He soon caught on." Andrew was gifted with a thick skin.

To endear himself to the other boys, he regaled them with blue jokes. One classmate said: "By the time he's finished a joke he's laugh-ing so much you can't understand the punchline." This earned him the nickname "The Sniggerer".

His sense of humour and easy charm soon made him friends, though his high spirits sometimes got him into trouble. In a dormitory frolic, he bashed his head. In the morning he went to matron with a headache and a large lump on his cranium. No serious damage was detected by an X-ray at a local hospital.

Both Charles and Andrew joined the school's coastguard service. When they heard short blasts on a siren, they would have to tumble out of bed, throw on their navy-blue duffle coats and race to the cliff top as lookouts. Both had to make their own beds and muck in at mealtimes. And though their mother was one of the richest women in the world, they had the same paltry pocket money as everyone else.

"He was always hard up," said a schoolmate of Andrew's. "He was always hard up like the rest of us."

However, there was a gulf between Andrew and other boys. Occasionally, a royal jet was sent to collect him from Gordonstoun and return him to London – for the wedding of his sister, Princess Anne, to Mark Phillips, for example. But rather than be a loner like Charles, he joined in and became the leader of the pack.

"He has no time for sycophants and if anyone tries to take the mickey out of him, he fights back," said a master. "He's just as good with the verbalistics as with his fists."

Andrew was good at engineering and woodwork, and shared a propensity for pottery. He made two glazed vases as a birthday present for his grandmother.

Charles and Andrew were also both proficient seamen. Charles paddled a canoe from Hopeman Beach to Findhorn Bay. This was twelve miles in a direct line, but double that distance if you allowed for wind and tide. In deteriorating weather, it took all day. Andrew was chosen to crew the school's sixty-three-foot yacht *Sea Spirit* on a trip around the treacherous north coast of Scotland. After battling through a Force 8 gale, he landed at Oban and took refuge in a local hotel.

And, of the two, it was Andrew who was the sportsman. He played hockey, cricket, football and rugby for the school team. Shortly before his brother's thirtieth birthday, Andrew broke his foot and hobbled into the ballroom with a stick doing a Charlie Chaplin walk and waltzed as best he could. His mother had also taught him to be a skilled card player and he excelled at backgammon.

During the holidays, he learnt to ski in Switzerland, stayed with his cousins in Germany and visited the North Sea rigs on the royal yacht *Britannia*. He even had a walk-on part when the Queen pressed the button that started the oil flowing into British Petroleum's Grangemouth refinery.

His parents had learnt a lot since Charles first took to the slopes and was besieged by the press. They smuggled Andrew out to the ski resorts in almost total secrecy, while Philip personally flew him out to see his German relatives.

He took a three-week school trip to France to brush up his French under the name Andrew Edwards. Charles would never have got away with such anonymity. Even Andrew's tutor at Le Caousou Jesuit College in Toulouse didn't know who he was. Asked about his parents, he said: "My father's a gentleman farmer and my mother... she does not work."

His tutor said his French had improved, adding: "He is a lively boy with the good and bad points of any fourteen-year-old."

At Gordonstoun, Andrew achieved a royal first. Joining the school's Air Training Corps, he learnt to fly a glider at nearby RAF Milltown – something neither his father nor brother had done while at school. To get his wings, he had to perform a solo circuit of the airfield. He had to wait to do this until he was sixteen, the legal age limit. As soon as he was old enough, he made three four-minute circuits. When he landed he gave a thumbs up to the waiting photographers. He had got one up on his brother. To a point.

By that time Charles was already flying helicopters from the deck of the HMS *Hermes* and was sporting a beard in the tradition of sailing royals. Newspapers reported rumours that the Queen became concerned about the dangers involved and ordered that Andrew be prepared as a possible successor. However, courses on how to be a monarch were not on the curriculum at Gordonstoun.

On the stage, Charles was still out ahead on the dramatic front, but the Queen came to watch Andrew perform in the farce *Simple Spymen.*

"Charles is a better actor. Better at dramatics," he said. "I like to make a comedian of myself."

Another major change that Gordonstoun had undergone since Charles's day was that it had become co-educational. When Andrew arrived, age thirteen and tall for his age, he immediately made for a striking blonde, engaging her in conversation to the evident envy of the other new boys. The girl concerned was sixteen-year-old Amanda "Mandy" Knatchbull, granddaughter of Lord Mountbatten. That is, his cousin.

A woman's magazine called her "gorgeous", while the girls at school called him "dishy" and "super". His popularity with the girls provoked jealousy among the other boys who began to call him "bumptious" and "something of a show-off".

At sixteen, he went with his parents to the Montreal Olympics where Canadian girls began to take an interest in him. Most of the family were staying on the royal yacht *Britannia*, though Anne, who was competing in the equestrian events, was staying in the Olympic village with the rest of the team. Prince Charles got leave from the Navy to join them, bringing Prince Edward with him.

But it was Andrew who stole the show. He was now as tall as his father and Charles was forced to concede that Andrew was the "one with the Robert Redford looks" – after the famously handsome Hollywood actor. To others he was a pin-up alongside tennis player Bjorn Borg and footballer Kevin Keegan.

One Canadian newspaper called him "six foot of sex appeal", another the "Royal Redford". He was bombarded with requests for dates, invitations to parties and telephone numbers. This boosted his already dizzying self-confidence. He flirted with the female competitors in the Olympic village and took a shine to a bubbly blonde named Sandi Jones, who was assigned to mind him, saying: "Call me Andrew, not your Royal Highness."

Charles could only look on awkwardly. Having lived a near monastic existence at school he was still not at ease with women. At university, one girl dubbed the eighteen-year-old Charles "naïve and old fashioned". He was twenty when another called him "a sweet virgin boy".

Andrew returned to Canada at the beginning of 1977 to attend Lakefield College School near Toronto. This was arranged by Canadian Premier Pierre Trudeau. When he arrived, dozens of young girls turned out at the airport. They screamed, blew kisses and chanted: "We want Andy." As his official car pulled out of the airport, he wound down the window to chat to some of them. Asked about the girls in the subsequent press conference, he said: "I like them as much as the next chap."

However, the press took against him, calling him "boorish and a snob" after he asked: "Do you do Shakespeare here?" Jumping on Charles's coat-tails, perhaps. The *Toronto Sun* said: "What we don't need is some young prince in expensive blue suits sipping ginger ale and claiming he'd like to be 'an ordinary schoolboy'. Yes, it's cold here. It is also, despite what the British like to tell each other, civilised… I hope he brought his woollies."

Lakefield was run much along the lines of Timbertop with an emphasis on outdoor life. There were sports, canoeing, kayaking, rock climbing and cross-country skiing. This suited Andrew. But it was a single-sex school, which did not. Nevertheless when he played rugby at Lakefield, girls turned out on the touchline to cheer his every move, wearing sweatshirts emblazoned with the slogans "I'M AN ANDY WINDSOR GIRL" and "ANDY FOR KING".

At school, the teachers addressed him as Prince Andrew, while the governors called him "sir" and the chairman of the board of governors "your Royal Highness". The boys called him just plain "Andy", though his popularity with girls earned him the sobriquet "Randy Andy". Like Charles at Timbertop, Andrew was also assigned a room-mate. Two years earlier he had been an exchange student at Gordonstoun and introduced Andrew to ice hockey, which unleashed a vicious streak.

Andrew also proved popular across the border when the school's hockey squad went to play in Pittsburgh.

"He sure attracts the ladies," said one of the Lakefield team. "Some of the Pittsburgh guys were getting worried."

He invited Sandi Jones to the school dance. At first, she thought that she was the victim of a practical joke and insisted on a formal invitation from the headmaster's wife.

"I was flabbergasted when I received it," she said. "Although I guess we took a shine to each other when we met at the Olympics, I had not expected to hear from him again so soon."

They danced and shared doughnuts and non-alcoholic punch. She also taught him to do the Bump, the dance craze of the time which involved the couple bumping their hips together, sometimes suggestively.

"The ball was great and we danced cheek to cheek quite a bit," said Sandi. "He learnt the Bump pretty fast. Most of the time he wiggled and squirmed on the dance floor like any other teenager."

This did not go down well with the other girls. Schoolgirl Patricia Foy complained: "It was unfair that he had one girl all the time. A lot of us wanted to dance with him."

The following day on the ski slopes, he managed to ditch his protection officer, a Mountie, so he could spend time alone with Sandi. He drove her to the station afterwards.

"Luckily, I don't think anyone recognised him," said Sandi. "We talked about seeing each other again and it was left that he should write first. He's absolutely great and we get on together fabulously."

They met up later at a jazz concert in Toronto and had dinner together at the Harbour Castle Hotel after the show. But for Sandi this was a bit of a disappointment.

"There sometimes wasn't much romancing under the eye of Andrew's bodyguards," she said, "though we managed to give them the slip on occasions. Andrew can be extremely resourceful. He's just an ordinary guy who wants to have a fun time with his girlfriend."

Sandi's mother was quick to pour cold water on the idea that young love was blooming.

"They are both only sixteen," she said – though Andrew had already turned seventeen. "So any talk of true love would be absolute nonsense."

However, she visited him regularly and spent a few happy week-ends at a remote log cabin in northern Ontario. On one summer's evening as they sat in the silence of the wilderness, he asked her to marry him and run away with him to Gretna Green – a village just over the Scottish border where, traditionally, an eloping English couple could marry without parental consent.

They both realised in their hearts that it was an impossible dream, but that did not prevent their teenage romance developing into a long-distance friendship. When he returned to the UK they corresponded regularly.

In a school production of George Bernard Shaw's *Passion, Poison and Petrifaction (or the Fatal Gazogene)*, Andrew played Adolphus, a dandy who is poisoned by a jealous husband. And in *Oliver!*, as Mr Brownlow, he tries to revive the stricken Nancy. "My heartbeat shot up to about a hundred miles an hour when he put his fingers on my wrist," said Gillian Wilson who was playing the martyred ingénue. He had a similar effect on the teenage Linda Sergeant who bumped into him while jogging on the college playing fields. "He was a real charmer," she said. "I really fancied him."

Andrew found time to visit Prime Minister Pierre Trudeau and his wife Margaret and go skating with their three children. Then he had to return to England for his mother's Silver Jubilee.

His memento of his time in Canada was an oil painting which went on a Jubilee exhibition of royal painting at Windsor Castle. One art critic said it revealed "an adventurous sense of abstraction and composition beyond the admirable amateurism of royal performance". Charles, of course, was a devotee of the watercolour. They were oil and water.

Andrew's other duties included lighting the bonfire in Windsor Great Park that touched off a chain of beacons across the country, attendance in St George's Chapel for the annual re-dedication of the

Knights of the Garter, which he would join in 2006, and taking his turn accompanying his mother on her progress around the provinces. His travels included a controversial trip to Northern Ireland which it was thought was too dangerous for the Queen to visit.

Mairead Corrigan, who helped found the Northern Ireland Peace Movement, said she found him "absolutely dishy".

"He is a really handsome young man with charming manners and I was swept off my feet," she said. "Betty Williams [co-founder of the Peace Movement] embarrassed me by asking him if he was spoken for as I was still single and available if asked."

When he asked what the conditions in Northern Ireland were really like, Corrigan said he should come out on the streets with some of their youth groups.

"I'll have to ask my mother about that," he said.

After the Jubilee, Andrew flew back to Canada for a brief reunion with Sandi Jones and a tour of wildlife parks. At a party given for him at Government House in Ottawa, Andrew spent the night dancing with star figure skater Lynn Nightingale. In Vancouver for the celebration of Canada Day, marking the 110th anniversary of the founding of the Dominion that year, the Algonquin Indians invested him with the title *Soya Hun* – "Heir of the Earth". This could be seen as senior to heir to the British Crown.

Andrew and Prince Philip attended the bicentennial celebrations in Victoria, British Columbia, for Captain Cook who had put into Nootka Sound with George Vancouver on his third voyage to the Pacific. It was inevitable that these should include a bevy of grass-skirted Polynesian girls. Father and son exchanged a smirk. At a state dinner given by Premier William Bennett at Government House, Andrew was presented with a salmon-fishing outfit. One of the lures that came with the outfit was named "Strip Teaser".

Everywhere he went, Andrew was besieged by teenage girls. One said: "He's cute, even better than Prince Charles."

America's *People* magazine put him in their list of the top ten best-looking men and the American Bachelor Women's Society named him one of the world's most eligible bachelors alongside Warren Beatty, John Travolta, John McEnroe and Woody Allen – possibly a bad choice, in retrospect. The society's president, Rhonda Shear, agreed: "He's much better looking than Prince Charles."

Andrew went sailing, fishing and partying with Lise Owen, the nineteen-year-old granddaughter of the lieutenant governor. This was followed by a boring round of public engagements. The beds in the halls of residence of a new college were a bit hard, he complained as he bounced on one for the photographers, before enquiring whether the accommodation was co-educational.

At the Calgary Stampede, he met up with Charles. But they needed someone to explain the technicalities of rodeo to them. "Who better than a couple of pretty girls?" Andrew suggested. "He was a real Prince Charming," Gillie Newman, one of the girls, said.

Andrew moved on to Resolute Bay in the Arctic Circle. Two years earlier Prince Charles had been dunked through the ice in a wetsuit there for a half-hour dive. Andrew declined the invitation. He flew on to Beechey Island where Sir John Franklin and his expedition perished in 1846. A cairn there commemorated the visit of Prince Charles.

He also followed in Charles's footsteps to a small settlement on Ellesmere Island in Grise Fiord where an Inuit showed him how to make a kayak out of the skin of a polar bear. However, he did go one better than Charles – and even Prince Philip – when he flew on to Cape Columbia, the northernmost tip of Canada, just four hundred miles from the North Pole. Neither elder brother nor father had ventured so far north into the polar region. To mark the occasion, a cairn was to be built for Prince Andrew on the top of a glacier.

The Deputy Commissioner had come fully prepared to erect the cairn, which would be similar to the one set up on Beechey Island for Prince Charles. However, there was a major snag – how to get the monument up the icy slope of the glacier. The Deputy Commissioner explained: "We scaled the almost vertical hill to erect the monument. The original intent was to back-pack the equipment and monument up the hill ourselves. However, once we viewed the hill, we quickly changed our minds. Coincidentally, at that moment, we picked up the radio conversation of a helicopter talking to a geological survey group in the area. We asked the pilot if he could drop by and sling our equipment to the top of the hill, which he did. Can you imagine sitting almost at the top of the world, thousands of miles from civilisation, and discovering a helicopter just happening to pass by and offer a helping hand?"

On one side there were the flags and arms of Canada and the United Kingdom, along with Prince Andrew's portrait. The other side bears a plaque that reads:

THIS CAIRN WAS ERECTED
BY
HIS ROYAL HIGHNESS PRINCE ANDREW
TO COMMEMORATE HIS
VISIT TO CAPE COLUMBIA,
THE MOST NORTHERLY
LAND MASS IN CANADA
83° 12' NORTH LATITUDE
70° 25' WEST LONGITUDE
HIS ROYAL HIGHNESS IS THE
FIRST MEMBER OF THE ROYAL

FAMILY TO PENETRATE THIS
FAR INTO THE POLAR SEAS
CAPE COLUMBIA, NORTHWEST TERRITORIES
JULY 12, 1977

Not many people are ever going to see it, being in so remote and isolated a setting. After further Canadian adventures, he returned to school in Scotland.

Both his father and elder brother had been made head boy, or Guardian, at Gordonstoun. Andrew was pipped at the post by Georgina Houseman, the first girl to become Guardian. This failure bothered him. However, he was still a success with the girls and a resounding one at that.

One visitor noted: "Andrew was already tall and well built – he certainly was very handsome. He appeared to be benefiting greatly from Gordonstoun's bracing and progressive atmosphere. There was one female for every two young males at the school, although the evidence suggested that Andrew would have thrived even if the ratio had been less enticing."

The girls he took out became known as Andy's Harem and he retained the nickname he'd acquired in Canada, Randy Andy, for his effortless conquests.

"Whose turn is it on the royal rota today," girls would ask. One said: "He's a great dancer."

"I've danced with him many times," she boasted, "and he's one of the best."

"He's not a bit wet," said another, "which is a nice change. He knows how to make a girl feel special."

Yet another noted that he also knew "how to spread himself around".

"One minute he's making you feel really great… that you're the only one that matters," she said. "The next minute, just as you really think you're getting somewhere, he's off with someone else."

Georgina Houseman's sister Lucilla or "Lulu" reported: "He had several girlfriends at Gordonstoun as well as many friends who happened to be girls. His girlfriends were quite good for him because he took them fairly seriously and serious relationships are a steadying influence."

The first was Clio Nathaniels, the daughter of an architect who lived in the Bahamas. Andrew took her home to meet mother. That is, he got his parents to invite her to Windsor Castle one weekend. And he took her to watch brother Charles take part in a cross-country riding event organised by the North Warwickshire Hunt. Charles was accompanied by Lady Sarah Spencer, Diana's sister. This was the nearest the brothers came to double-dating.

Clio left school unexpectedly and fled back to Nassau after he dropped her. The school authorities denied that this was the reason, but her mother said: "Andrew was very embarrassed about the whole affair. Clio was only one of his friends. She decided to leave the school after talking to me and her father."

He then turned his attentions to Clio's school friend, eighteen-year-old Kirsty Richmond. They shared a love of tennis and skiing, and wrote to each other during the holidays. She was a hit with the Queen and was invited to spend a week at Balmoral and Christmas at Sandringham two years running. There, she went to church with the family and was officially listed as "a guest of the Queen".

She was "just a good friend," the Palace explained. "He brings friends home with him every holiday. Naturally, like any other boy of his age, he wants his family to meet them."

However, at the end of the Christmas holiday, she spent a night in Buckingham Palace on her way back to Gordonstoun from her home in Suffolk. Staying there made it easier for her to catch the early morning train to Inverness, a Palace spokesman explained.

Andrew did not accompany her. He and Edward, who was now at Gordonstoun, were flown back to school.

The other girls dismissed the affair, saying: "It was just Kirsty's turn." Besides, Andrew was involved with another girl at Gordonstoun, an American beauty named Sue Garnard. According to school friends: "She is Andrew's long-term girlfriend. She doesn't mind Andrew taking Kirsty home because she knows she is just a friend." He also took Sue home to meet the Queen during the vacations.

In London, he spent time with Julia Guinness, usually in the posh nightclub Annabel's.

"He is a bit of a flirt but the most charming person you could hope to meet," she said.

He also hung out at Tramp and Tokyo Joe's in Piccadilly. Newspapers began carrying pictures of him emerging from night-spots with various blondes. However, his activities were inhibited by his police minder. "He's a real passion killer, if you will pardon the phrase," said one of his escorts.

During the school holidays, society mothers would lay on society functions for their debutante daughters and invite him along. He was seen with Sarah Gordon Lennox, granddaughter of the Duke of Richmond and Gordon, at her coming-of-age party at Goodwood House. But not all invitations were accepted.

"Who wants a chap who suffers from dandruff?" said one disappointed deb.

Generally he shunned the "tiara mob". Prince Harry said in his book *Spare* that these girls suffered from "throne syndrome" – she would be "visibly fitting herself for the crown the moment she shook my hand".

Comparing himself to his brother, Andrew said: "Because I haven't been the centre of attention, I've been able to lead my own life."

There was trouble at school when one of his detectives reported some of the pupils for smoking cannabis. Five boys and a girl were expelled. There was no implication that Andrew was involved. But his father was asked in an interview: "If Prince Charles was in a country where one could legally take drugs, would you object to him taking them?"

"It is not really a question of whether they are legal or illegal, but whether it is sensible or not," Prince Philip replied. "I would rather he did not."

Before Andrew left school, there were exams to take. Few expected much from him. Lulu Houseman said: "He didn't shine at anything. He loved having a good time. In fact, the story that went round the school was that he failed some O levels because he spent all his time reading trashy magazines and comics. Having started school in the top stream, he gradually slipped down the rankings in all subjects except in French, which he was very good at. He gave up Latin and went down a set in maths. This was partly because he was very talkative. If there was laughter in the refectory Prince Andrew was bound to be the centre of it."

Nevertheless, he passed six O levels – English language, English literature, French, history, general science and maths. He also got three A levels – taken under an assumed name to avoid accusations of bias – one more than the ostensibly intellectual Charles.

At the age of eighteen, he received his first handout by the state when Parliament granted him £20,000 a year, worth £100,000 now. However, his mother considered that he was still a schoolboy and that £600 a year (£3,000 pa) should cover his needs. The balance would be held back and invested for him by the Royal Trustees. His £20,000 would be increased to £50,000 when he got married.

But he was a pauper compared to Charles, who had inherited the Duchy of Cornwall which, from the age of three, gave him £90,000 a year (£2.3 million pa). This was raised to £220,000 (£3 million), tax free when he was twenty-one. After that, the entire income of the Duchy was made over to him, but he elected to forgo half of it in lieu of income tax when the top rate was 90 per cent.

Charles had wanted to go to university, though with only a B and a C at A level, he hardly deserved a place on merit. The accusation was that he only got a place through "a blatant use of royal prerogative". Though there was talk of Andrew going to Clare College, Cambridge, the Royal Family wanted to avoid another furore about privilege. Nor was Andrew keen. And Prince Philip did not push him.

"I'm one of those stupid bums who never went to university," Philip said, "and it hasn't done me any harm."

Besides, Andrew had some catching up to do.

CHAPTER EIGHT
UNIVERSITY CHALLENGED

For Charles, Trinity College was the least worst option, as Cambridge was only an hour's drive from Sandringham. But first there was to be his eighteenth birthday at Windsor Castle, where he would rub shoulders with the sons and daughters of the aristocracy. His birthday also meant another pay rise. He was still at Gordonstoun when he heard that he had been appointed Counsellor of State, which meant he could take over as regent if the Queen was incapacitated.

"The first thing I knew about being a Counsellor of State was from the 6pm news," he said. "However, I assumed there was nothing for me to do and didn't rush to pack my bags."

The following year, he attended the State Opening of Parliament for the first time and was sent to represent the Queen at the funeral of the Australian Prime Minister Harold Holt, who had been presumed dead when he disappeared while swimming in a rough sea.

"I am so glad to be able to do something like that for Mummy," he wrote.

Charles flew to Australia with Harold Wilson and Leader of the Opposition Edward Heath. Among the heads of state he met there was the murderous President Ferdinand Marcos of the Philippines and the US President Lyndon Johnson, then embroiled in the Vietnam War.

In October 1967, Charles arrived at Trinity in a Mini Minor to be greeted by the press, a crowd of well-wishers, the master of the college Lord Butler and the statue of Henry VIII above the Great Gate. Four "pool" reporters, six photographers and three TV camera crews followed him while he was given a tour of the college.

"We were absolutely determined that Prince Charles was going to live in college and share as far as possible in the everyday life of the ordinary undergraduate," said Lord Butler.

Of course, this was impossible. To start with, the solid wooden gates of the college had to be closed behind him to keep the crowd out. "It was like a scene from the French Revolution," he wrote.

While other freshers shared cramped dormitories and the communal toilets in the basement, Charles had a second-floor suite with a bedroom, sitting room, kitchen and private bathroom. This had been hastily installed by workmen from Buckingham Palace after the Queen had paid a covert tour of inspection before he arrived.

Interior decorators had supplied curtains and rugs, and a tartan comforter had been brought from his bed in Balmoral. A private telephone had been installed and there was a security cabinet for his mail.

Like other Trinity students, he had a maid. But also on call were his equerry David Checketts and his royal protection officer, who had their own rooms next door to Charles's apartment. The detective would be responsible for his laundry, a precaution against trophy hunters who might seek to steal his underwear. Just in case the accommodation was too small, Butler slipped Charles a key to the Master's Lodge.

His tutor drew up a list of college societies he was not to join. These included Amnesty International, the Fabian Society, the Marxist Society, the Buddhist Society, the Heretics and the Society for Anglo-Chinese Understanding. It was also made clear that he could not be a member of the Conservative Association or the Labour Club. As future monarch, he could not be seen to be partisan.

Neither was Charles allowed to pick his own courses. Lord Mountbatten and Prime Minister Harold Wilson had drawn up a list of subjects he should study. These included history, constitutional law, economics and foreign affairs – just in case they became useful in future. Charles insisted that his curriculum was broadened to take in both anthropology and archaeology. They were equally valuable, he argued, especially if he were to rule a multiracial society.

"To get on with people of other races and countries," he said, "you've got to know how they live, eat, work, what makes them laugh – and their history."

He also insisted that his studies were scheduled on the understanding that he could zip off to Sandringham for polo matches and shooting parties if needs be. While other students were not allowed cars on campus, Charles could park his MGB in the college. This means of escape was vital, as his shyness had not left him.

"I'm trying to beat it," he said. It would be a lifelong struggle.

While the student body, at the time, was approaching a thousand, Charles spent most of his time with four or five fellow students whose families had some connection to the Palace. They would walk with him to his lectures, dine with him in his rooms and accompany him to the cinema and concerts. He avoided social functions, or would leave early, and he steered clear of girls.

According to Checketts, Charles "didn't really mix with anybody. He lived for the weekends." During those weekends, he would go to Sandringham where, Charles explained, "You really had the crème de la crème of wild birds. They are beautifully driven. Everything is perfect."

Such statements alienated him from his contemporaries. This was the 1960s. Other students grew their hair long, wore T-shirts and jeans and took to the streets to protest against the Vietnam War, while Charles could hardly appear at a demo, bedecked in corduroy and a tweed jacket, with highly polished shoes and his hair cut short back and sides.

Even Lord Butler found Charles a little out of touch. He said that it was rather regrettable that Charles's "cronies tended to be conventional huntin' and shootin' Army types from public school". Other students dismissed Charles as "stuffy" and "a snob", while he found them "dirty", "smelly", "noisy", "misguided" and "pathetic". In the Swinging Sixties when a new generation was changing everything, he defended tradition. "Tradition is really the basis of everything," he said. "Change for the sake of change, from my point of view, is pointless."

Meanwhile he began on his quest of "finding the inner self" with the Dean of Trinity, Harry Williams, a monk and theologian who combined psychoanalysis with the Book of Common Prayer. After Communion, Charles would retire to the Dean's room for breakfast and a talk. Williams said he was impressed by the "spiritual potential" he saw in the young Prince.

"I always thought he was a deep person; that he wasn't taken in by the surfaces of life," he said. "He had an interest in the deeper things of life, in the source of life, an openness of mind, a readiness to evaluate ideas, not taking things off the peg but thinking them out for himself... It may sound absurd, but I always thought that he had the makings of a saint when he was young: he had grace, humility and the desire to help other people."

The other person Charles shared deep discussions with was Hywel Jones, a scholarship boy from Wales and amateur rock musician whom Charles met on the stairs below his own apartment. Jones was a member of the Conservative Association, the Labour Club and the Marxist Society – to get a rounded view, he said. Over mugs of coffee, they discussed politics late into the night. Beyond this, the revolutionary spirit of the 1960s passed Charles by.

When he did well in the exams at the end of his first year, Charles noted a volte-face in the press. Previously, they had tried to have all members of the Royal Family "look rather dim". He had now "shown them in some small way, at least, that I am not totally ignorant or incompetent. The tables will not be turned, and I will be envisaged as a princely swot."

Not that he found studying easy. Reading history for the second part of his tripos, he said: "It appears there are hundreds of lectures, all clashing with each other, all in different places at once and all packed solid with hairy unwashed student bodies. At the moment, I'm wrestling with George III's problems, faced with a boggling choice of six books and no apparent prospect of completing the essay by Friday."

Charles told the tale of how he was almost killed during his first year at Cambridge in a speech at the Fitzwilliam Museum marking its bicentenary.

"Quite how I survived being run over by a bus when I was on a bicycle just outside here I don't know," he said.

Had he died then, Prince Andrew would now be king – a thrilling, and chilling, prospect.

Even as a student there was no way out of royal duties. In 1968, he was invested as a Knight of the Garter, attended his first Buckingham Palace garden party and went on an official visit to Malta. A guest at a garden party there wrote to Mountbatten, saying: "This is a young man who reminds me very much of you; he's immensely interested in humanity and the details of human suffering... Anyone can have brains but a warm heart is rare among the young today."

In his second year, Charles tried to reach out to other students by returning to the stage. He took the role of the padre in a Joe Orton comedy *The Erpingham Camp*, where he had pork pies thrown at him as part of the script. He had hoped that making a fool of himself might endear him to others. It didn't work.

"When I come here and try to go around with people, it is a pretence," he wrote, "and the awful thing is that I feel they can feel it. However, I must try and improve myself."

The invisible barriers between him and the rest of humanity would always be there. Charles said: "I am a single person that prefers to be alone. I'm happy just with hills or trees as companions."

However, he did at last show some interest in female companionship. Rab Butler's wife Mollie introduced him to her husband's research assistant, twenty-five-year-old Lucia Santa Cruz, daughter of the Chilean ambassador. With short skirts and model good looks, she was "a most charming and accomplished girl," said Mollie. "I am confident she will find favour with Prince Charles."

She was right.

"Prince Charles was totally smitten with Lucia – and she with him," she said.

Lucia was a Roman Catholic, so marriage was out of the question. But Mollie reasoned that she was a "happy example of someone on whom he could safely cut his teeth, if I may put it thus".

Whatever went on behind closed doors, Charles was still public property. In 1969, the BBC approached the Palace to make a documentary about him. Instead, the Queen wanted the whole family to be included. She allowed the TV cameras in to make the wide-ranging fly-on-the-wall documentary *Royal Family*. It begins with Charles being described as heir to the "thirteen thrones" of the Commonwealth. In it, the Queen is caught saying that the American ambassador "looked like a gorilla". Charles was shown waterskiing, riding a bike and studying for his finals.

When it was shown on the TV, the Queen realised that the whole thing had been a mistake and, after its first run, it was locked away for good.

After four terms at Trinity, it was decided that, as Prince of Wales, Charles should spend a term at the University College of Wales at Aberystwyth. As well as facing "the same long-haired, bare-footed and perspiring variety" of students he'd met at Trinity, he now risked riling the extremists demanding home rule for Wales.

"As long as I don't get covered too much in egg and tomato I'll be all right," he said.

Within a week of his arrival, a bomb went off outside the police headquarters in Cardiff. Prince Charles was named as a target by the Free Wales Army and a crack bomb disposal squad was moved to Aberystwyth, where there were protests about his presence.

From the comparative luxury of his suite in Cambridge, Charles was now confined to a tiny room in a granite-wall hall of residence where he spent nine lonely weeks.

"No one can make any real friends in nine weeks and we just don't have the more aristocratic type of person here," he confided to his cousin James Buxton.

Charles made an effort to learn Welsh and gave his maiden speech at the National Eisteddfod. There were demonstrations by Welsh nationalists.

"I was grateful," he said, "because they were distracting people in the audience from my terrible pronunciation. The Welsh language is impossible – I felt as if I had a mouth full of marbles!"

Next came his investiture at Caernarfon Castle. Again, there were security concerns. Two hundred and fifty extra policemen were drafted in. Roadblocks were set up and the area was searched for bombs. There were four; two went off.

The investiture had only taken place once before in modern times, in 1911, when Charles's Great-Uncle David, later Edward VIII, had donned white satin breeches and purple satin robes trimmed with ermine to be crowned by his father George V. The spectacle had been cooked up by the then Prime Minister David Lloyd George, a Welshman, to cement Welsh ties to Britain.

Charles's investiture was designed by his uncle, Lord Snowdon, the celebrated photographer Antony Armstrong-Jones and husband of his Auntie Margaret. The satin breeches were dispensed with in favour of the uniform of the commander-in-chief of the Royal Regiment of Wales. The robe was retained.

As Charles rode to the castle in an open coach, a bomb went off in the distance. In the courtyard of the castle there were three slate thrones under a Plexiglas canopy. Three thousand ceremonial troops were assembled, along with choirs, military bands and banners bearing the red dragon of Wales and royal crests. A crowd of thousands looked on. Millions more watched worldwide. Some failed to be impressed by the arrangements.

"He is to be turned into a puppet, publicly in front of all our eyes and ears," said the *Daily Mirror*'s columnist Cassandra (aka Sir William Connor). "He is dressed up in daft clothes. He's presumably trained to speak a few glib words in the Welsh form of Gaelic." Cassandra condemned the whole thing as a "stunt" and a "pantomime" where Charles was the "plaything of outmoded politicians".

Presiding at the ceremony, the Queen was accompanied by Prince Philip in full dress uniform, only to be outshone by the elaborate outfit of the Garter King of Arms. There were speeches in English and Welsh. Then Charles knelt as his mother presented him with the symbols of office – a ceremonial sword, a gold rod and a gold ring symbolising his marriage to Wales. Then came the crown, which was too big and slid down to rest on his over-large ears.

"For me," Charles wrote in his diary, "by far the most moving and meaningful moment came when I put my hands between Mummy's and swore to be her liege, man of life and limb, and to live and die against all manner of folks – such magnificent medieval, appropriate words, even if they were never adhered to in those old days."

The whole thing cost £200,000 – £2.8 million at today's prices. And there was a slip-up. At his investiture, Charles sought to be a man of the people. Despite his odd regalia, he mingled with the crowd and astonished a mother, who had brought her two small children along, asking her: "Are you their nanny?"

The Queen and Prince Philip bailed out back to London, leaving Charles to tour Wales in a bubble-topped Rolls-Royce in a sweltering July. The crowds turned out, but great-uncle Lord Mountbatten offered a word of caution: "I'm sure you'll keep your head. Your Uncle David had such popularity that he thought he could flout the government and the Church and make a twice-divorced woman Queen. His popularity disappeared overnight. I am sure yours never will, provided you keep your feet firmly on the ground. Well done and keep it up." Wise words.

Reassured, Charles replied: "I, myself, cannot believe that I have really had an effect on people, particularly young ones, but several people have been writing to me recently saying very flattering things. The immediate problem is to remain sane and sensible and I try hard to do that. As long as I do not take myself too seriously, I should not be too badly off."

He confided to his diary: "I now seem to have a great deal to live up to and I hope I can be of assistance to Wales in constructive ways. To know that somebody is interested in them is the very least I can do at the moment."

His duty to Wales done, Charles promptly returned to Cambridge. The downside was that "in Cambridge, I feel as though I am in a zoo". But then at weekends he could leave "to pursue other people's pheasants". He also left to attend concerts and galas or make speeches. In November, he addressed five thousand Indians, in the presence of the prime minister and Lord Mountbatten, to mark the centenary of the birth of Mahatma Gandhi. In it, he stressed the virtues of "will-power and discipline".

"Some would have us believe that these are out-of-date concepts, but as long as man has an ounce of humanity left, they will survive," he said. His diary was soon filling up with public duties where he stood in for the Queen and royal tours abroad. This gave him his first opportunity to get to know the Saudi Royal Family – they had diffi-culties talking to the Queen as she was a woman. He also attended his first Privy Council meeting, relishing the fact that in this body, the monarch retained the last vestiges of power.

Now at the age of twenty-one he received his full whack from the Duchy of Cornwall, which comprised (and still comprises) 135,000 acres spread out over Cornwall, Herefordshire, Somerset, Dorset, Wiltshire and Gloucestershire, and almost all of the Isles of Scilly. It includes farmland, forests, waterfront property, London real estate, Dartmoor Prison, tin mines and the Oval cricket ground.

To celebrate Charles's coming of age, the Queen threw a black-tie party for him at Windsor. For music, Charles asked for a Mozart recital by Yehudi Menuhin. His mother gave him a Seychelles-blue Aston Martin DB6, which he later converted to run on wine and cheese to make it sustainable.

He graduated with a 2.2. It was a mediocre degree by normal standards, but it was a royal first. Others had attended university, but no one in the Royal Family had graduated before.

CHAPTER NINE

ALL AT SEA

During his second year at Cambridge, Charles had taken up flying. Before he entered the Royal Naval College, Dartmouth, he went to RAF Cranwell to learn to fly jet fighters. He also made his first parachute jump. After being awarded his wings, it was on to the Navy.

"I am beginning to pale at the thought of what Dartmouth is going to do to me," he wrote to a friend. "Whatever it is, it's going to be far worse than the most excruciating tortures they could ever dream up at Cranwell."

It was worse than he expected.

"It was exactly like being locked up at school again and we weren't allowed out, except at rare weekends," he said.

Up at 6am each day, he was to be fast-tracked through a twelve-week course in six weeks. "Papa wrote and said I could console myself with the thought I was serving 'Mum and country'," he wrote.

While his contemporaries were intimidated by him at first, they soon warmed to his genial lack of competence. "If it was anyone else, we would have thought: 'What a nice man. What's he going to do for a living?'" said a fellow officer in training.

When he graduated, he was posted to the destroyer HMS *Norfolk* at Gibraltar. But his itinerary would have ruled out a day's shooting at Broadlands, Lord Mountbatten's estate, so great-uncle had a word with the Vice-Chief of the Naval Staff and his flight was delayed.

While the captain of the *Norfolk* told him that he would be treated like any other sub lieutenant, special security arrangements had to be made and, if he was going to do anything remotely dangerous such as diving or waterskiing, a doctor had to be on hand. His permission also had to be sought if officers were to remain seated during the loyal toast.

At Toulon, he was taken on a tour of the bars of the red-light district, though emerged unscathed. During various NATO exercises, he maintained regular correspondence with Mountbatten, whom he now considered his adopted grandfather. Mountbatten also sought to make a reconciliation between the Royal Family and the exiled Duke of Windsor, the former Edward VIII. The Queen Mother was intransigent, but Charles went to visit his Great-Uncle David in Paris. He died eight months later. At his funeral in St George's Chapel, Charles was "deeply moved".

Having led a wide-ranging love life himself, Mountbatten encouraged Charles to sow his wild oats. He even told Charles that, after he was married, as Prince of Wales he would be expected to keep a mistress, as long as he was discreet about it. After all, in the 1960s, rumours of his father's extramarital activities abounded.

On a visit to Washington, President Nixon's daughter Tricia was lined up. She had attended his investiture as Prince of Wales and was designated to accompany Charles to events, both official and informal. In the White House, the President would make himself scarce, leaving them alone together. It didn't work. Tricia said that she found her father's attempts at matchmaking "embarrassing", while Charles found Tricia "plastic and artificial".

What irked him most was being treated as an ordinary young bachelor, not the heir to the throne of Great Britain. He was not being given the deference he thought he deserved.

"Protocol and decorum mean a great deal to Prince Charles," a former equerry said. "He asks himself if his mother or his father would stand for this sort of treatment, and then his blood starts to boil."

When he returned to the White House thirty-five years later, Charles was asked about his first visit.

"That," he said, "was the time they were busy trying to marry me off to Tricia Nixon."

Mountbatten planned some matchmaking of his own. He hoped to pair Charles off with his granddaughter, Lady Amanda Knatchbull, who was also Charles's cousin. But that would have to wait on the back burner for the moment. Nine years younger than Charles, she was only fourteen at the time. By sixteen, she would catch the eye of Prince Andrew.

Lucia Santa Cruz stepped in. She said that she had found "just the girl" for Charles – one Camilla Shand. Famously, she was the great-granddaughter of Edward VII's last mistress Alice Keppel and introduced herself as such. Though not of the aristocracy, she was from the traditional rural squirearchy. They shared a love of riding and hunting, and hit it off immediately.

For Charles, she was a dream come true. He had already confided to friends that he could not conceive of anyone he might hope to marry that would want to marry him. But Camilla put him at his ease and they spent time together in London and at Broadlands.

Then duty intervened. Charles was due to sail for the Caribbean on the frigate HMS *Minerva*. He would be gone for eight months. They spent their last weekend together at Broadlands and he gave her a tour of the ship before he set sail, leaving her waving from the quayside.

The Navy had been at a bit of a loss about what to do with Prince Charles. They could not keep shuffling him around training courses. Never good with figures, his navigation was unreliable and, on board the *Norfolk*, he had failed to achieve his bridge watchkeeping certificate. So, on tour with the *Minerva* his main duty was to attend cocktail parties ashore.

Aboard he was an acting sub lieutenant; ashore he was an HRH. This caused all sorts of wrangles over protocol, with the Ministry of Defence under instructions that he was to be treated as an ordinary junior officer while the Foreign Office insisted that he was a representative of the monarchy and the British government, so the red carpet had to be rolled out. Polo matches were arranged and, in Cartagena, he was taken to a Colombian brothel where one of the denizens momentarily placed a hand on his thigh, adding, he recorded, "yet another of life's essential experiences to my collection. Not literally, I hasten to add."

In Venezuela, he was much taken with the wife of a polo player.

"Never in my life have I had such dances as I had with this beautiful lady," he wrote to a friend. "She is unbelievable is all I can say and I danced with every conceivable part of her. I fell madly in love with her and danced wildly and passionately, finally doing a Russian dance at one stage which cleared the floor because I was wearing my mess boots."

Elsewhere there were other innocent encounters: "I tried a belly-dancer last night at a hotel where we were having dinner! She came up to me and wobbled everything at me and so I ran my fingers up her tummy (rather hot and sticky!) and she hit me on the head with her castanets! I think she rather liked it…!"

While he was away, news came that Camilla was to marry Andrew Parker Bowles, a Guards officer who had been a suitor before Charles met Camilla.

"I suppose this feeling of emptiness will pass eventually," Charles wrote.

Then came the news that Anne was to marry Captain Mark Phillips.

"I can see I shall have to find myself a wife pretty rapidly, otherwise I shall get left behind and feel very miserable," he said.

After a break at Balmoral, he flew out to Singapore to join HMS *Jupiter* – as seaman officer, relieved of any navigation duties – for a tour of the Pacific, returning via the Americas and Bermuda. Again, there were junior officer duties on ship, receptions and garden parties on land. There, he said, he deployed "the old eye-flashing technique".

In the South Pacific, Charles was a magnet for every unattached woman, including a few erring wives. Fellow officers rued that he was always the centre of attention. In his journal he noted that he had been to a party at the Yacht Club, where he danced with "gigantic lady after gigantic lady, around all of whom I was incapable of putting my arms! The third amazon finally finished me. She announced in halting English that she had been wanting to dance with me since she was twelve and now she had finally 'got me'. Apart from the fact that she was like dancing with several tractor inner tubes mounted on top of each other and vibrating slowly in different directions, she began to feel me all over with a wild look in her eye… It wasn't so much her eye that I minded, but what she was going to do with her teeth! I thereupon left the steaming, sweating Yacht Club and headed back for the ship, past bushes which kept saying 'Psst! Hello, sailor,' and appeared to be occupied (as it later transpired) by off-duty policemen."

Not that he was always so successful. In Acapulco, he went to a discotheque with the other officers.

"While the Captain and I sat pensively in a corner fingering a gin and tonic, the others immediately set off like dogs into every dark recess of the club and soon appeared on the dance floor armed with some lady who had been whisked off her feet! Not being accustomed to the art of 'picking up' a girl in a discotheque, I could bear the suspense no longer and finally plucked up the courage to go across and ask a lonely-looking girl if she would come to join us at our table. 'No thanks,' replied this paragon of beauty and virtue in a terrifying American accent – and so I shrank back to our table, and immediately sank into a gin and tonic-induced reverie."

The heir to the throne did not always meet with such summary rejection. In Samoa, he met a beautiful girl "with superb black hair down to her waist and with a devastating smile". In half an hour he said he "must have shattered all the illusions she had had about me through excessive reading of *Woman's Weekly*".

At a cocktail party in Hawaii he met "two spectacular blonde ladies" whom he invited out to dinner: "They were incredibly keen and purred that they would give me an evening I would never forget...!"

They invited him back to a small apartment that belonged to one of them.

"Left alone with these two blonde bombshells wondering what on earth was going to happen – I must be very naive!" he wrote. "However, after a long time it transpired that all these girls wanted to do was 'to get the Prince loaded' as they put it. In other words, they wanted me to smoke the rarest, most expensive form of marijuana, which comes from Thailand. They showed me this large cigarette thing in a plastic bag, which is known as an 'Elephant', but I refused to try it and said I did not like smoking for one and secondly had no need of artificial stimulation... Both my policemen and the two locals were outside in the car and so as soon as I could, I made a retreat; rather reluctantly because they were great fun."

Despite these risqué adventures, Charles was still the innocent abroad.

Then in San Diego, he was smitten by "a tall blonde lovely in a shimmering green dress" who had mesmerised everyone at a cocktail party on board. Arranging to meet her again, he went to the wrong address and had to be redirected. Eventually finding the right apartment, he duly serenaded her over a lingering drink.

While in the Caribbean, Charles had stayed briefly on the small island of Eleuthera with Baron Brabourne, who was married to Mountbatten's daughter, Patricia. Their daughter Amanda Knatchbull had been there. She was now fifteen.

"I must say Amanda really has grown into a very good-looking girl – most disturbing," Charles wrote to Uncle Dickie – Lord Mountbatten.

The following year, Mountbatten wrote to Charles, saying that, during their Caribbean idyll, Amanda had fallen for him and he hoped that one day his granddaughter and great-nephew would be betrothed.

"I believe in a case like yours, a man should sow his wild oats and have as many affairs as he can before settling down," he advised. "But for a wife he should choose a suitable and sweet-charactered girl before she meets anyone else she might fall for."

While Charles was tempted, he said he "couldn't possibly get married yet"; though he was now twenty-five and he knew the pressure was on.

While in the Navy, Charles also served as Britain's unofficial representative in the US. Staying with Walter Annenberg, America's former ambassador to the UK, he played golf with Bob Hope and Ronald Reagan, then governor of California. That evening Frank Sinatra dropped in for a drink. Then in Hollywood, he met Charlton Heston, Ava Gardner and Barbra Streisand – "my only pin-up" he called her.

When Turkey invaded north Cyprus in 1974, the *Jupiter* was put on standby. Charles was on leave and sped from Balmoral to Rosyth to join the rest of the company.

"I was rather keen to be sent to Cyprus," he said. "I had a yearning for some sort of action – some sort of constructive, *useful* naval operation where perhaps a medal could be won and I could supplement the one I have (for supreme gallantry at the Coronation!) with a proper one."

Instead, the *Jupiter* was to join a NATO exercise in Scapa Flow.

That autumn, Charles transferred to the Fleet Air Arm. After a helicopter course in Yeovilton, Somerset, he joined 845 Naval Air Squadron as a pilot on board the aircraft carrier HMS *Hermes*. The two helicopters he had been assigned to fly were maintained to the dizzying standards of the Queen's Flight (the Royals' private airline) – though again, it was said he was being treated as any other officer. There were also certain restrictions placed on his flying which did not apply to others.

On leave, he flew back to Eleuthera before making an official visit to Canada. Then in February 1976, Charles took command of the HMS *Bronington*, the last of the wooden-hulled minesweepers, at Rosyth. When his father visited, Charles was to introduce him to his officers, but forgot their names. For the next nine months, he undertook boring patrols in the comparative safety of domestic waters, constantly terrified that he would run aground or have a collision. There were a couple of minor mishaps. In one he had to jettison an anchor after it threatened to separate the telephone cables linking Britain and Ireland.

After an exercise in the Baltic where *Bronington* was shadowed by East German patrol boats, they encountered seas so rough that the Prince was stricken with seasickness, but remained on the bridge with a bucket between his knees.

Before Andrew flew out to Canada to attend Lakefield, he visited Charles who had then completed his five-year stint with the Royal Navy. For the benefit of the press, he had sailed the *Bronington* from Rosyth to London for his farewell. Andrew went on board there and was unimpressed. The ship was twenty years old and only 153 feet from stem to stern, less than half the length of the royal yacht *Britannia*. Charles's cabin was a cubby hole wedged between the ship's refrigeration and the toilets.

In December 1976, Charles left the Senior Service in true Navy fashion. He was escorted ashore in a wheelchair with a black lavatory seat round his neck.

CHAPTER TEN

ALL THE NICE GIRLS
LOVE A SAILOR

Prince Andrew had already earned his wings as a glider pilot at Gordonstoun, while older brother Charles had, by then, trained on jet fighters and helicopters. In 1978, Charles had been appointed colonel-in-chief of the Parachute Regiment and invited Andrew to join him on a parachute jumping course.

But first, there was some groundwork to do. He had to land and roll without breaking any bones. Then you had to learn how to pack your own parachute and there were safety checks to memorise. The first jump was from a static balloon, then from a Hercules aircraft flying at a thousand feet. As Andrew jumped, he got tangled in the parachute rigging and fell nearly two hundred feet before he managed to spin and twist clear, as he had been taught.

Charles had experienced something similar the first time he made a parachute jump in 1972. The drop zone had been at Studland Bay in Dorset.

"As I had been clever enough to say I wanted to jump and the press had said I was going to jump, I was going to," said Charles. "It was a curious sensation standing in the doorway and just waiting.

I was certainly nervous, but I was longing to experience the sensation of launching myself out of the door... I kept having morbid reflections on wrapping myself round the tail plane or hitting my head on the side of the aircraft, or even dropping out of the harness before I reached the water."

When his turn came, Prince Charles was so keen that he jumped almost before the green light came on. He felt a "tumbling, unreal sensation", but as he came out of the slipstream and the parachute opened, he found himself upside down with his feet tangled in the rigging lines: "I thought how stupid of them not to warn me of this, but I was extraordinarily calm and in command of the situation and quickly removed my feet... There was only a short time to admire the view and enjoy the sensation before my feet touched the water and I was trying to get free of the harness."

He described the situation as "a hairy experience". Later he admitted that he had to be fished out of the water by the Royal Marines.

Andrew was less sanguine.

"Of course I was nervous," he said once he was safely on the ground. "If you're not nervous, you do something stupid. But I'm dead keen to do it again. Parachuting is an experience I would never have wanted to miss."

On his second jump, he carried a fifty-five pound Army pack on his back. As a result, he qualified for his parachute badge. With it came a framed certificate that he hung on the wall of his room at Gordonstoun, another one up on his brother.

With Edward now old enough to join in, all three went to the Farnborough Air Show together, though it was just Andrew and Edward who attended the London premiere of the film *International Velvet*.

They were together again at Cowes for the yacht races. Charles had taken up windsurfing, which Andrew had also mastered at

Lakefield. However, at the Isle of Wight, Charles's sporting activity was hampered by Andrew who, in a speedboat with the inevitable pretty girl, sped round him in ever-decreasing circles.

It was Charles's thirtieth birthday that November. Andrew and Edward got special leave from Gordonstoun to attend his birthday party at Buckingham Palace. This was when Andrew had broken his foot and appeared with a Chaplinesque cane. Though his injury meant he had to wear slip-ons rather than formal shoes, he managed to get around the dance floor with numerous partners.

Now he was leaving Gordonstoun, Andrew could look back at a successful career there on the sports field at least. He had played cricket for the school First XI in 1976, 1978 and 1979, becoming, like his father before him, team captain. He would have made the eleven in 1977 as well if he had not been away at Lakefield. Andrew also played for the First XI at hockey in 1978 and got his Gold Duke of Edinburgh's Award.

This cut no ice with Prince Philip. Asked whether he was proud of the Duke of Edinburgh Award Scheme, he said: "I've no reason to be proud. It's satisfying that we've set up a formula that works but I don't run it. It's all fairly second-hand." He had not even wanted his name to be attached to it. "That was against my better judgement," he said. "I tried to avoid it but I was overridden."

Later, when he was asked if the Duke of Edinburgh Award Scheme would be more popular if it wasn't named after him, he said: "Whatever you call it, some people will think it is rubbish while some people would not be worried about the connection with this cantankerous old sod up here."

That December, Andrew went to Biggin Hill to take an aptitude test to see whether he could become a Navy pilot. This involved a written test, an interview and a thorough medical examination. He passed all three.

The following Easter he went to RAF Benson, the headquarters of the Queen's Flight in Oxfordshire, to train on a de Havilland Chipmunk. After ten forty-five-minute lessons with a Royal Navy flying instructor, he flew solo for the first time.

"He went solo much earlier than normal and appears to have been well above average," said instructor Lieutenant-Commander Sandy Sinclair, a World War II fighter ace.

There followed a royal tour of Africa where he was greeted by bare-breasted dancing girls in Botswana. Andrew lowered his eyes and appeared deep in conversation with local officials.

In Dar-es-Salaam, a group of British wives unfurled a banner saying: "Hi Andy, come and have coffee." Everywhere he was in demand. Visiting Blantyre in Malawi, a man bet his wife £5 that she would not dare ask Andrew for a dance.

"The next thing I knew I was in his arms, looking up into his eyes, such fabulous blue eyes," she said.

When other women there made it clear they expected the same privilege, he beat a retreat.

At the Commonwealth Conference in Lusaka, as part of the Save the Rhino campaign, Prince Philip made reference in his speech to a "nameless" country where rhino horn was in demand for "purposes which are popularly believed to bear some relation to what St Paul described as the desires of man's lower nature".

"Considering that the population of that country was well over 500 million, either the rhino horn was spectacularly successful or patently unnecessary," he added. He meant China, of course.

In September 1979, Andrew followed his father and elder brother into the Royal Naval College in Dartmouth to begin two years' training in seamanship. The first thing that happened was that the training officer Lieutenant-Commander Jack Eglen ordered him to have his hair cut. Andrew's response was to mutter "a few things I don't want to repeat". He was shorn of an inch or so.

"Now you look smart," said Eglen, admiring Andrew's Charles-style short back and sides.

On his first day, he had lunch with the head of the college, Captain Nicholas Hunt. "Once this small ceremony is over, the Prince will be treated like any other midshipman," a college spokesman said. This was hardly the case and other recruits resented his privileges.

"He played the big 'I am the Prince' routine all the time and seemed rather arrogant," said one midshipman.

The wife of one of the instructors said: "Prince Charles is still remembered with tremendous affection, but Andrew isn't popular with either the staff or his fellow cadets. His brother was a great practical joker, but Andrew walks away from anything like that. He never lets you forget who he is."

Nor could he forget that he had a royal protection officer, Inspector Steve Burgess, with him at all times. Shortly before, Lord Mountbatten had been blown up by the IRA, demonstrating that the Royal Family was a terrorist target. So Inspector Burgess was joined by a bodyguard from Special Branch. The two of them had to slog it out beside Andrew on the twelve-mile route marches that were part of the basic training for Navy cadets. There were tougher tests. He had to swim several lengths of the college pool fully dressed and dive to the bottom to retrieve a brick. With all the hiking, running and swimming, Andrew had lost seven pounds during the first month's basic training.

There were some high jinks though. War games were staged against the Royal Naval Engineering College from Manadon, Devon – aka HMS *Thunderer* – in aid of the Royal National Lifeboat Institution. Dartmouth's task was to smuggle several firkins of beer through opposition lines to a tiny Dartmoor village named Milton Combe. Things got out of hand. Cadets trespassed on private land and set up illegal roadblocks. Cars were stopped and searched. There was even a minor traffic accident. It was said that cadets "behaved like drunken louts".

Local councillor Lieutenant-Colonel Ian Greenlees wrote a letter of complaint to the Ministry of Defence, saying: "It was just a grown-up version of cops and robbers with a total lack of responsibility. It made not one hoot of difference as far as I am concerned whether Prince Andrew took part or not. I would say of all of these men that they must learn to behave."

Other recruits were not allowed to have a car for the first four weeks of training. "They're too busy to touch one," said Lieutenant-Commander Eglen. An exception was made in Andrew's case on the specious grounds of security. He arrived in a brand new black Escort RS2000.

"You can't park there," he was promptly told. "Get it stowed somewhere else."

At college he spent much of his time trying to avoid press photographers and he would race out of the college gates with the paparazzi soon in hot pursuit.

"I remember we were reversing up narrow lanes at forty miles an hour and doing handbrake turns round corners to shake them off," Andrew said. "It was great fun but they were very persistent."

Sometimes their persistence paid off. One pressman managed to get a picture of Andrew with naval architecture student Kirsty Robertson having a drink together in a remote pub before the landlord set the dogs on him.

As a midshipman, he was paid £2,400 a year – £11,000 pa now. Although he had a substantial income from the state he did not donate his Navy salary to charity as Charles had. So at least he had the cash to show a lady a good time.

To mark the end of basic training there was an informal passing out parade with cadets in weird and wonderful attire – perhaps only a jockstrap and a bowler hat. Prince Andrew chose to wear pyjamas. Those who had been tipped off wore swimming trunks as the parade ended with the recruits being doused with fire hoses.

The official passing out parade was a more spit-and-polish affair as it was attended by the Queen. A sly smile was exchanged between mother and son as she inspected the graduating cadets.

While Andrew was on leave from the Navy, he was still on duty as a royal. As the "spare" and second in line to the throne he was given a quick course in legal and political matters in preparation should he ever become king. Twice in the twentieth century the second son of the reigning monarch had ascended to the throne. The possibility was always borne in mind and Buckingham Palace did not like to take chances.

He also sat in on a murder trial at the Old Bailey and visited Prime Minister Margaret Thatcher in 10 Downing Street. At the age of twenty-one, he too would become a Counsellor of State, replacing the Duke of Gloucester. This would allow him to handle state papers in the absence of the Queen.

He made his first public speech as the guest of honour at the century dinner of the Varsity rugby match between Oxford and Cambridge. It was a boisterous affair and most of the audience were drunk. The following September, he flew out to Florida with nineteen other young midshipmen for a three-week tour of duty on board the aircraft carrier HMS *Hermes*, where his brother had served before.

Immediately Andrew hit the headlines, having been photographed in Trader Jon's Club Pigalle in Pensacola. The club was situated in a sleazy area of the dockland and had the reputation in the area of being the naughtiest nightspot in town. It was famous for two things – a collection of military souvenirs and its topless go-go dancers.

Club owner Martin Weissman said: "We were amazed when he came to see us, but he seemed to have a wonderful time looking at our pretty girls."

It seems he had other interests.

"When he wasn't looking at the girls, he was asking me about the military memorabilia," said Weissman. "He stayed for two hours and really enjoyed himself."

Weissman's wife Elizabeth was also delighted.

"It was a real treat having the Prince here," she said. "But Lord knows what his mother would have thought."

One of the topless dancers, Lindy Lynn, said: "He couldn't keep his eyes off us. Now I know where he gets his Randy Andy nickname." She later renamed her act the Randy Andy Eye Popper.

Another topless dancer, Sonia Larren said: "He was a real prince charming. I didn't feel embarrassed at all. But I would imagine that the Queen would not be amused."

The Royal Navy were unconcerned. A spokesman said: "When sailors go on the town, it's only natural they want a bit of fun."

The switchboard at the US Navy base in Pensacola was inundated by southern belles asking to speak to the English prince. However, on board the ship, he was not so popular. Charles had also served on board the *Hermes* and the inevitable comparison was made.

"Andrew is very likeable, but he's very conscious of being a royal," said one senior officer. "He's a bit of a mummy's boy. You could never say that about Charles. Charles would never need encouragement to join in the fun. And he certainly wouldn't talk about girl conquests."

While in Florida, Andrew took time off to visit Disney World. He donned one of the staff's blue coats as a disguise and even guided one visitor to the exit. He was also seen taking a spin in a toy racing car with a pretty young Disney World guide.

"It was magic," he said, though it was not clear whether he meant the ride or the young woman's company.

Back in England, he was sent on the ten-day Royal Marine endurance course at Lympstone, which involved tackling the Marines' gruelling assault course, a thirty-mile route march, wading fully equipped up to the waist through icy water and sleeping rough out on Dartmoor in sub-zero temperatures in winter.

"We've put him through hell, and he's come up smiling," said a commando training officer.

Completing the course earned him the green beret of the Royal Marine commandos, though he wore his blue Navy uniform at the passing out parade.

Making the presentation, Lieutenant-General John Richards, Commandant-General of the Royal Marines, said: "He is strong, physically fit, but more important, he has determination."

This must have pleased his father, who was Captain-General of the Royal Marines – the ceremonial head of the regiment. He was succeeded by Prince Harry, who was then stripped of the post when he left his royal duties and the country in 2022. After that, Charles appointed himself to the position, as if being king he did not have enough on his hands.

Andrew went on the survival course at Seafield Park, Portsmouth. This involved ten days roughing it in the New Forest with only a parachute for shelter. The idea was to simulate the conditions of being shot down behind enemy lines. Andrew's long-suffering royal protection officer had to accompany him, roughing it too.

Sent into the wilderness with only the knowledge of how to kill a rabbit, skin it and cook it, Andrew set traps and collected wild berries. He also scavenged in litter bins for orange peel or sandwiches discarded by day trippers.

"Andrew was spared nothing," said another midshipman. "He had to do everything we did and proved himself quite tough. It was as though he had something to prove – that he could do anything just as well as the next man."

While on leave, Andrew was seen with nineteen-year-old beauty queen Carolyn Seaward, then Miss England, Miss UK and runner-up to Miss World. In those days, contestants in beauty pageants were introduced by the "vital statistics". Hers were 35-24-35 and she was five feet nine inches tall. They had a candlelit dinner together in Buckingham Palace. A footman spotted her leaving early one morning.

"Prince Andrew was very charming, witty and amusing," she told the newspapers. "After dinner we just relaxed, listened to music and chatted."

When asked if they had kissed, she said: "That's a question I'm not answering, but I did tell my mum afterwards."

The Prince was more tight-lipped. "We are not prepared to confirm, deny or comment on such a story," a Palace spokesman said.

Carolyn was next seen in the company of tennis player Ilie Nastase who had just split from his wife Dominique. She went on to become a Bond girl, appearing in *Octopussy*, while Andrew was next spotted approaching a pretty blonde at Cowes.

"He really laid on the chat for a good half an hour," she said. "Then he realised I was married and toned down the yo-ho-ho stuff. He certainly likes to flirt with the girls. He knows he's good-looking, but he's not conceited. He listens to what you have to say. He's interested in what you are and who you are. I suppose that's the secret of his chatting-up technique. He's genuinely interested in you as a person.

He's a bit of the wholesome boy-next-door type. Really sweet but very fanciable and lots of fun. He likes to laugh as much as anyone."

He turned up at the Ritz for Princess Margaret's fiftieth birthday party with twenty-two-year-old Gemma Curry. Her father had taught Andrew to fly at RAF Leeming in Yorkshire, where Andrew was nicknamed Golden Eagle for his habit of dropping clangers in theory classes. The affair foundered when he was sent to the Royal Navy air station at Culdrose in Cornwall to learn to fly helicopters.

After eighteen weeks, he had mastered the Gazelle. Unlike Charles, Andrew was not restricted in what he could fly. At Dartmouth, Charles had pleaded to fly the College Wasp, but was forbidden because of its poor safety record. Later, he was not allowed to fly single-engined helicopters over the sea, while flying in fixed-wing aircraft was "strictly circumscribed and is not normally to be permitted".

Prince Philip had arranged long in advance to attend the passing out parade at Culdrose for Andrew's twenty-first birthday in 1981. He turned up in the uniform of an Admiral of the Fleet and was not disappointed. Andrew won the silver salver for the midshipman with the highest marks and was only a whisker away from winning the character and leadership trophy.

Making the presentation, Philip told his son: "Congratulations, good luck and happy landings."

At his belated twenty-first birthday party, Andrew kept his promise to his colleagues at Culdrose. "It's going to be a hell of a party," he said inviting them. Five hundred guests entered the historic Windsor Castle under a spectacular canopy of laser beams. There were more lasers inside. There was no Mozart recital for him. Music was provided by Elton John and DJ Kenny Everett, who played everything from waltzes to punk. Guests included Prime Minister Margaret Thatcher, Prince Edward and Prince Charles with his new fiancée Lady Diana Spencer, who had actually once set her heart on Andrew when they were younger. Also, there were several of Andrew's young lady friends, including his old flame Sandi Jones.

Carolyn Seaward was present, along with the current royal favourite, twenty-two-year-old cover girl and model Kim Deas, who had taken over from her cousin Gemma Curry. Kim later dined alone with Andrew at Windsor Castle.

Soon rumours circulated that Kim had jilted the Prince when she flew to New York on a modelling assignment. Countering comments that he was a male chauvinist pig after he got Kim to wash his car, she said: "He isn't at all. He's a lovely man. I don't want to say anything bad about him because he's still my friend. People think that because he's so good-looking he's not a nice person. But he's extremely sensitive and kind. He certainly doesn't live up to his nickname of Randy Andy at all. He's simply a good friend."

Pressed on the details of their split, she said: "I went to Buckingham Palace to see him and found him on his own watching television. He was happy that I was going to New York for the first time because it was something he couldn't do. He doesn't put on the Prince bit at all although I'm sure he wouldn't like me to say it. He's just a very nice young man under a lot of social pressure."

Andrew was best man at Charles's wedding and encouraged his brother to kiss Diana on the balcony of Buckingham Palace. That autumn, Andrew trained on the large Sea King helicopter. During an exercise in the Firth of Clyde, he rescued a sailor who had been swept into the water. Wearing a full beard, he joined 820 Naval Air Squadron at RNAS Culdrose. The following February he went on a NATO exercise along the coast of Norway.

The orderly hierarchy in the Senior Service seemed to suit his temperament. On board he was known as "H", for Highness, sang the praises of service steak and kidney pie, and joined in the easy affability and insular techno-speak of the modern wardroom.

The institutional life aboard ship, where the parameters of responsibility and enterprise are laid down and logged, suited Andrew's personality which, at that time at least, craved order and a settled routine.

"You can ignore all that is going on in the rest of the world and get on with one's job," he said. "When I'm at sea I feel about six inches taller."

CHAPTER ELEVEN

GOING SOUTH

When Argentina invaded the Falkland Islands in April 1982, Andrew was sent to the South Atlantic with 820 Squadron on board HMS *Invincible* after first hosting a dinner for the squadron at Buckingham Palace. He invited his fellow fliers and their wives and girlfriends back for a meal at "my place".

Before the twenty-two-year-old sub lieutenant left on active service, he had to get permission from, essentially, his mum. Clearly, as first in line to the throne, Charles would not have been allowed to go. But Andrew was merely a spare. As the son of the Queen, the Argentines would be gunning for him. By then, though, the Royal Family already had another spare in the form of Prince Edward and it had been announced that Princess Diana was pregnant the previous November, so Andrew was about to make another step down the ladder.

He was adamant that he would go, particularly after Charles had been so cotton-woolled. There were reports that he threatened to resign his commission if he was not allowed to go. Prince Philip visited him in Culdrose. As a former Navy man himself who had seen action in World War II, Philip backed his son. Andrew, it was decided, was expendable.

Although she had a war on her hands, Prime Minister Thatcher took time to drive out to Windsor to consult the Queen. When she returned to Downing Street, permission was granted and Buckingham Palace issued a short statement on behalf of the Queen, saying: "Prince Andrew is a serving officer and there is no question in her mind that he should go."

Andrew made a flying visit to his parents. Then on the morning of 2 April, he packed his bags and headed back to Cornwall in his blue 2.8 Ford Granada. With him, as always, was his royal protection officer – though he could offer little protection in the South Atlantic.

The following day, Parliament held a rare Saturday sitting where Mrs Thatcher told the House of Commons: "The Task Force will leave on Monday with HMS *Invincible* in the lead." So, Andrew would be in the thick of it.

With forty-eight hours to go, he managed to get some leave. Sub Lieutenant Leslie Taylor, a chum since training days, was about to leave on the *Hermes*, the flagship of the Task Force. But first he was getting married. Andrew raced to North Leigh in Oxfordshire to attend the reception.

The following day, 5 April, he was standing to attention on the flight deck as *Invincible* headed out into the Solent. The Queen watched on TV. For those watching in the Casa Rosada in Buenos Aires, it was clear that there was only one thing they had to do – sink the *Invincible*. If Andrew was lost, Britain would crumble, or so they thought. Admiral Jorge Anaya spelt out his plan to throw the entire weight of Argentina's air power against the *Invincible* to the three-man junta headed by General Leopoldo Galtieri. For Andrew, this was going to be no quiet voyage around the Caribbean or the Pacific, or an eventless patrol of domestic waters.

As the Task Force made its way to the South Atlantic, Andrew was confined to a private cabin, just eight foot by six foot. In it was a bunk, a washbasin, and a desk and chair. It was on Deck 2, directly below the spot where the Sea Harriers landed day and night.

On board, the facilities were rudimentary – a barber, a laundry and a shoe-mender. There was a galley where you could get a burger and chips, and other fast food. Andrew was a fan of pizza and a regular at Pizza on the Park in Belgravia. Stewards served other more fancy fare under portraits of his mama and papa in the officers' wardroom which doubled as the ship's cinema three nights a week. Andrew was normally the first to grab a front row seat there. Gin and tonics were also available at 14p (45p now) though, like most fliers, Andrew chose to go dry for the duration. Nevertheless, he was a firm favourite in *Invincible*'s wardroom, buying his round of drinks and settling his monthly mess bill from his sub lieutenant's annual salary of £5,950 (£19,500).

Otherwise, to pass the time there were fitness exercises on the flight decks when it was cleared of planes and helicopters. Below decks, there was table tennis, darts, table football, TVs and a well-stocked library.

Such was the patriotic fervour of the time, the officers and men of the *Invincible* made every effort to welcome him on board. He made his first guest appearance on the ship's own TV station shortly after the ship sailed for the Falklands. Plans were made for him to host his own show, provisionally titled: "A dose of Andrews" – after the proprietary brand of liver salt.

Andrew had the guest spot in *Invincible*'s version of *What's My Line?* Lieutenant Nick Bradshaw, the station controller, said: "The Prince was a mystery guest and the crew phoned in asking questions to identify him. Nobody guessed – and when Andrew showed his face, the ship was delighted. He's a great sport and a very interesting bloke. He realises the popularity of this type of programme and suggested the idea himself."

When 820 Squadron – one of the more boisterous groups of Navy fliers – let their hair down after a strenuous day's duties, Andrew was at the front of the squadron's choir as the men crowded around the ship's piano and belted out some rousing version of bar-room classics. It was reported that Andrew received more than his fair share of good-natured ribbings in the wardroom, but his 820 comrades appeared to be delighted that they had a Prince among their ranks. Beyond that, the only thing that picked him out was the "HRH Prince Andrew" on his name tag.

Andrew's commanding officer, Lieutenant-Commander Ralph Wykes-Sneyd, explained: "I think the Prince relishes his time at sea. It's probably the only place where he can be left alone. He gets no favours – and would be annoyed if he did. People can't believe that he's just another officer, but that's how we play it. The only people who find it unusual are strangers who come aboard."

Once *Invincible* had left harbour and headed out to sea, Andrew could lead a life as near normal as he could ever hope for. His personal detective, who was constantly at his side on land, was left on the quayside. Photographers were not hiding around every corner to snap the young prince and there were no crowds jostling to see the Queen's son.

There was a serious task at hand. As the giant British fleet assembled at the start of its eight-thousand-mile voyage, the men on board began to prepare for action. Two days out of Portsmouth, as dusk descended, the captain opened up the flight deck so that those on board could witness the awesome power of the Harrier's US-built Sidewinder air-to-air missile.

One Harrier swept in low alongside the carrier's port beam and dropped a parachute target. Seconds later, another of the jump jets screamed in low and unleashed the Sidewinder. The missile, its tail glowing red in the darkening sky, sped through the air and blasted the target to bits.

Prince Andrew stood with his comrades who watched, mesmerised, by the demonstration. It was impressive enough, but as they trooped silently back inside from the chill sea air, everyone was only too aware that the next target for a Sidewinder might be an Argentinian Mirage or Skyhawk.

While the Sea Kings did not carry anything like that firepower, the helicopter crews' role was no less important. Their task was to be the eyes and ears of the Task Force, on constant lookout for the enemy. Day and night, in every weather, the Sea Kings were fanned out in front of and around the fleet trying to spot enemy ships, planes and, most importantly, submarines.

The Mark V Sea King was crammed with sophisticated anti-submarine sonar equipment to detect an underwater adversary. For hours on end, Prince Andrew and his crew would skim the waves at virtually zero feet, dropping sonar buoys and listening for a tell-tale ping.

Andrew was the co-pilot of his Sea King. The senior pilot on board during the Falklands campaign was Sub Lieutenant Chris Heweth. The navigator was Lieutenant Ian McAllister with Leading Aircraftman Tom Arnull making up the four man. If an enemy submarine was detected, the Sea Kings were to attack it with depth charges.

On Good Friday, the fifth day of the voyage, Andrew's crew undertook a practice drop. Minutes after his helicopter lifted off *Invincible*'s deck, more spectators lined the railings. Andrew's helicopter approached the mother ship from astern along the port side. Then it dropped its load and soared skywards. Seconds later, the depth charge exploded, shooting a huge plume of water into the air.

The first week at sea had been spent getting the ship into a state of constant readiness. On Easter Sunday the *Invincible*'s Captain Jeremy Black gave the men a day off. Most went to the flight deck to sunbathe. Now in the tropics, white shorts and shirts had replaced the heavy-duty navy-blue uniforms. Prince Andrew stripped down to shorts and sunglasses, and soaked up the sun.

However, nobody was able to relax fully. The following day, the blockade of the Falkland Islands began officially with the introduction of a two-hundred-mile Total Exclusion Zone. Any Argentinian shipping within it would be sunk.

Aboard *Invincible*, mock Action Stations alerts were sounded. The exercise was designed to close up the ship, making her watertight within minutes. Once the klaxon sounded, every man donned white anti-flash masks and long white gloves to prevent burns. To add a note of realism, Captain Black had thunderflashes set off, their blast reverberating through the ship's hull.

Andrew and the other airmen were spread out, each given a separate post at times of attack. The ship's damage control officer, Lieutenant-Commander Andy Holland explained: "No ship can afford to lose all its fliers with one enemy direct hit." Andrew would spend alerts at 820's briefing room or would remain alone in his cabin.

While the ship's crew prepared to face the Argentinian enemy, Andrew's old adversaries were already on board. A select group of national newspaper reporters had been allowed aboard the *Invincible* to cover the war. When they were told by a representative of the MoD that "Prince Andrew is just another member of *Invincible*'s crew", they smiled. They would have Andrew at close quarters for the entire voyage.

The problem for the pressmen was that they were forbidden to approach him. For the first week of the voyage, the Prince and the press exchanged wary glances. But they were bound to bump into each other in the gangway, galleys and the crowded wardroom.

While playing cat and mouse, Andrew had always rather enjoyed the attention of the media. So he bowed to the inevitable and bought the press corps a round of drinks.

"It's about time we introduced ourselves," he said. "What are you having?"

From then on, he cultivated the press, sometimes wandering into the makeshift press office to offer hints and angles for stories. Andrew was at ease because he knew that anything written about him would have to be passed by the censor before it was transmitted back to London via satellite. The captain, too, would have a final say.

Consequently, Andrew felt free to laugh and joke with reporters, and even dined and debated with them. Over dinner one night, he told Mick Seamark of the *Daily Star* that he and Charles compiled a hit list of those in the press corps they would like rubbed out. And he laughed out loud when he recounted how he had given Fleet Street photographers the slip in frantic car chases in narrow Cornish lanes near the Culdrose air station in his racy Escort RS2000.

Now big brother Charles had been safely married, Andrew realised the spotlight would fall on him and the two brothers had already discussed how best to keep his love affairs off the front pages of Britain's newspapers. According to Andrew, Charles has used false names, addresses, false titles, even false noses, to give Fleet Street the slip.

"Charles has told me what to expect from you lot," he said. "I will be on my guard."

It appeared that Andrew shared his brother's sense of fun and liked to play practical jokes on reporters. He confided to one reporter the story of the ship's gyroscopically-stabilised pool table.

"It's remarkable," he explained. "However much *Invincible* heels, the table stays level and the balls don't roll around."

Once the hapless reporter had left the group, Andrew burst out laughing and said: "I hope his newspaper doesn't print that story. Any sailor reading that will know it's a spoof. It's the oldest joke in the Navy. I should know, I fell for it hook, line and sinker, soon after I walked aboard."

Andrew enjoyed playing the court jester, but sometimes he was merely an overgrown schoolboy. Writer Roald Dahl's daughter Tessa would tell the tale of a dinner party hosted by the Duke and Duchess of Westminster. "At the end of the meal," she said, "Prince Andrew showed us what a sport he is by chucking endless bread rolls around the table."

Back then Andrew enjoyed seeing his picture in the paper, but sometimes found it confusing when the tabloids linked his name with that of more than one pretty woman at a time. He was also an avid reader of the newspapers that were occasionally airlifted out to the Task Force and showed a particular interest in the pictures of topless beauties then published in the *Daily Star* and the *Sun*.

While he was at sea, the story of his candlelit supper at Buckingham Palace with topless model Joanne Latham came out in the press. He was ribbed endlessly about it, but he claimed he had never met her. When she revealed all to the *Daily Star*, he examined her from every angle and said: "No, I've never seen her. Mind you…"

In fact, the dinner date had never happened. Joanne later admitted she had made the whole thing up.

Although there were Soviet planes overhead tracking the Task Force and Russian shipping at sea, there are some maritime traditions that cannot be broken. As they crossed the equator, Captain Black gave everyone another day off. Every sailor crossing the line for the first time must go through a traditional ceremony before King Neptune before being dunked in water.

Prince Andrew, with a gold-coloured crown perched jauntily on his head and the words "H – The Real Prince" stencilled on his waistcoat, tried to make a run for it when he was summoned before the 'throne' of King Neptune. But five burly petty officers – King Neptune's "bears" – were having none of it. To the delight of *Invincible*'s crew, they grabbed Andrew, carried him unceremoniously across the crowded flight deck and dumped him at the feet of the mythical master of the deep.

Andrew listened as the indictment was read out. He was accused of "positioning himself in front of TV cameras so your mum will see you on television". He pleaded not guilty – to no avail. He was daubed with red, green and blue dye and was tossed backwards into a canvas pool of salty seawater. Then he was tossed high into the air and back into the water three times.

One of the bears, wardroom chef Harry King, said: "It's not every day you get to throw a member of the Royal Family about. If I did this in Civvy Street I'd be thrown in jail."

Andrew took it well, particularly when the reporters who were writing up the story for their newspapers got the same treatment, allowing him to have the last laugh.

At Ascension Island, the Sea Kings ferried in large amounts of ammunition and supplies out to the warships. Prince Andrew was one of the few from *Invincible* allowed to set foot on the island.

"What's it like?" said Andrew rhetorically. "Red, dusty and very boring."

This brief landfall lifted morale, particularly because the crew received their first mail from home. But Andrew got none. The royal mail had let him down, it was pointed out.

"I shall have to send a sharp message home about this," he said.

However, when the next mail arrived a couple of days later, it included a large batch for the Prince, including several from his sister-in-law Princess Diana, who kept Andrew up to date with the latest family news.

After they had left Ascension Island, the ship was moved on to a war footing. Pictures and mirrors aboard were stowed and anything that could move was tied down in case of attack. The colourful insignia on Andrew's helicopter had been blacked out for the sake of security. Even the time those aboard spent undressed was kept to a bare minimum. Every sailor was ordered to sleep fully clothed and be ready for action day or night.

Invincible was now operating a twelve hours on/twelve hours off work routine for every crewman. They received their war orders posted on the ship's noticeboard, reminding all sailors of their duty to reveal only name, rank and serial number if they fell into enemy hands.

Prince Andrew and other crewmen were handed personal supplies of morphine-filled hypodermic syringes with instructions to stab them swiftly into the thigh to lessen pain if wounded. Like all airmen, Andrew was now carrying a Browning automatic pistol and ammunition when he took off on search-and-destroy missions.

As they neared the Falklands, the bitter South Atlantic winter was rapidly approaching. The waters in this part of the world saw waves as high as tower blocks, freezing fogs and howling gales, and it was the icy ocean that claimed the Task Force's first casualty.

A Sea King from the flagship *Hermes* ditched in freezing seas in the black of an evening. In the driving rain, Prince Andrew's helicopter was immediately dispatched to locate and rescue the two-man crew.

In a scene that was illuminated by occasional flashes of lightning, Andrew's helicopter edged forward a little above the massive waves searching for survivors. After several minutes, the beam of their searchlight caught an inflatable life raft bucking wildly below them.

Leading Aircraftman Tom Arnull, on his first ever emergency, swung out from the tail of the helicopter and was winched down into the blackness as Senior Pilot Chris Heweth battled to keep the aircraft level.

Arnull said: "There were flashes of lightning and sheets of rain as I was trailed thirty yards through the water towards the survivor. After three attempts he was just out of reach. But then he managed to grab my wrist and pull us together."

They were then winched back inside the Sea King. The shocked survivor said his fellow crewman was still inside the ditched helicopter. But despite further searches, only pieces of wreckage and the flotation bag from the Sea King undercarriage were spotted. Later, in the cold light of dawn, the dead crewman's helmet was found, gently floating in the South Atlantic swell.

It was a tragedy every helicopter crewman with the Task Force knew might happen after they had been flying long, tiring hours in the most atrocious conditions. But for the Royal Family it was the spare that was in danger, not the heir.

CHAPTER TWELVE

ACTION STATIONS

The island of South Georgia had already been retaken by the time the Task Force reached the Falkland Islands. The action began there on 1 May, when a Vulcan bomber from Ascension Island bombed the runway at the capital Port Stanley. *Invincible*'s klaxon sounded a genuine "action stations" for the first time and Commander Tony Provost announced over the tannoy: "Hostile aircraft approaching from the southwest."

While the Harriers engaged the enemy, Andrew and the crew of the *Invincible* waited, sealed in the hull in their anti-flash gear.

"To be told to lie down on the deck of a ship is the most lonely feeling I know, waiting for a bang, or the all-clear," said Andrew.

They were there for nine terrifying hours. But the Sea Harriers were more than a match for the Argentinian Mirages and, by the end of the first day, three enemy fighters and one bomber had been shot down. As darkness fell, the danger abated and Andrew and his comrades emerged to gather in the wardroom where they heard the Harrier pilots recount tales of their dogfights in the biggest British air battle for decades.

The Argentinian air force did not resume the attack the following day and Prince Andrew and his crew lifted off to search out the enemy. Andrew was back on the *Invincible*, relaxing in the wardroom, when a young airman from 820 Squadron dashed in and announced: "We've sunk the *Belgrano*."

The British nuclear submarine HMS *Conqueror* had torpedoed the ageing cruiser *General Belgrano*, with the loss of 321 Argentinian sailors and two civilians. Andrew joined in the cheering.

The Argentinian response came on 4 May, when a Super Étendard fighter flew within thirty miles of the British fleet and, from over the horizon, launched an Exocet missile. This skimmed over the waves at 700mph and hit the British destroyer HMS *Sheffield* which was on picket duty protecting the two carriers *Invincible* and *Hermes*. The crew had just twenty seconds warning before the missile hit. The *Sheffield* caught fire. Twenty British sailors died in the inferno, while another twenty-four were badly injured.

Prince Andrew was airborne at the time of the attack and watched in horror as a thick black pall of smoke rose from the burning ship.

"For the first ten minutes after *Sheffield* was hit, we really didn't know which way to turn or what to do. I was fairly frightened," he said. Meanwhile the ships of the Task Force weaved back and forth, fearing another missile attack.

The following dawn, Andrew saw for himself the terrible consequences of war when he flew over the still burning hulk of the *Sheffield*. The twisted wreckage was black and charred. Landing back aboard the *Invincible*, he said: "It was a dreadful sight. It's something I never thought I would ever see – a British warship devastated."

The Argentinian junta was jubilant but Prince Andrew was still in navy chief Admiral Jorge Anaya's sights. A military spokesman in Buenos Aires duly announced: "*Invincible* is our priority target.

It is a symbol, and if we destroy it, it will prove that Britain is not invincible."

Morale was struck another blow on board the *Invincible* when two of Andrew's complement were killed. In the early hours of 6 May, Harrier pilots Lieutenant-Commander John Eyton-Jones and Lieutenant Al Curtis had been scrambled to intercept a mystery radar contact, possibly an enemy aircraft, near the hulk of the *Sheffield*. The weather was appalling, with rain, freezing fog and low cloud. Radio contact was lost with the two jump-jets shortly after take-off. The two men were never seen again. A mid-air collision was suspected. Andrew joined the other men for a memorial service in the *Invincible*'s hangar.

Over drinks in the wardroom, Prince Andrew met members of the SAS and SBS. They were airlifted off the *Invincible* and landed on Pebble Island, where they knocked out eleven enemy Pucara fighter-bombers, vital radar installations, ammunition and supplies.

On 18 May, the troop-carrying fleet led by the requisitioned ocean liner *Canberra* arrived. Andrew and his crew then spent their time ferrying men and supplies from ship to ship ready for the landings. The following day, Captain Black announced to the men that the invasion would begin on the 21st. While the Harriers would give air cover, the Sea Kings of 820 Squadron would look out for submarines.

It would be the longest day of the war. Two Gazelle light helicopters and one Sea Harrier were shot down, while HMS *Ardent* was sunk. On 24 May, HMS *Antelope* was hit by a bomb that failed to explode. However, an attempt to defuse it failed, resulting in the death of the bomb disposal officer and the loss of the ship.

The following day, the *Sheffield*'s sister ship, HMS *Coventry* was set ablaze and seventeen crewmen were killed. HMS *Argonaut* and HMS *Brilliant* were damaged. But these attacks were feints. The real target was the *Invincible* and Prince Andrew.

Andrew and his helicopter were on Exocet decoy duty that day. The missile locked on to its target from about twenty miles away, over the horizon. The idea was for the Sea King to place itself between the ship and the Exocet and lure it off course. The helicopter would hover twenty-seven feet above the waves – thought to be the maximum height of Exocet's trajectory. Then when the missile changed course and locked on to the helicopter, the Sea King would rapidly soar skywards and the Exocet would pass harmlessly underneath it. Or that, at least, was the theory.

"The helicopter hovers near the rear of the carrier, presenting a large radar target," said Prince Andrew. "But on the day *Sheffield* sank, one Exocet was seen to fly over the mast of the ship – and that's well over twenty-seven feet."

While Andrew hovered dangerously above the waves, every ship in the vicinity fired shells or Sea Dart and Sea Wolf missiles at the Exocet to try to knock it out of the sky before it reached its target. At the last minute, one fired at the fleet veered off course. Moments later, the MV *Atlantic Conveyor* was hit and ripped apart. The giant container vessel had been hired by the government to ferry vital helicopters and supplies to the Task Force, as well as maintenance facilities, runway construction equipment and tents.

Tragically, twelve men died. It is not known whether the Exocet that hit the *Atlantic Conveyor* was originally bound for the *Invincible*, but an early report said that the missile had been "successfully decoyed away from another ship".

While Andrew's Sea King was on station, there was nothing he could do but look on in horror.

"I was airborne when the *Atlantic Conveyor* was hit," he said. "We saw the odd 4.5-inch shell come pretty close to us and I saw *Invincible* fire her missiles. Normally, I would say it looked very spectacular but from where I was it was very frightening. I think the moment really sticks in my mind. It was horrific and terrible and something I will never forget. It was probably my most frightening moment of the war."

Andrew had to put his private feelings aside and get on with the job he now had to do. Within minutes of the attack, his Sea King was scouring the freezing waters for survivors from the stricken ship. Twelve were killed in the attack, while twenty-year-old merchant seaman Michael Chapman found himself with others in the water.

"The weather was dreadful," Chapman said. "It was very cold and the waves were about twenty feet."

He was hanging on to the grab-handle of a fluorescent orange life raft when he saw a Sea King helicopter above his head. There were more than twenty other seamen in or around the inflatable. Many were burnt or suffering from other injuries.

"We were like sardines, one on top of the other," Chapman said. "There were four or five lads hanging on to the side of the raft because there was no room. They were suffering from hypothermia."

Chapman was one of the last to be winched up.

"When I got inside the helicopter, one of my pals pointed to the co-pilot and said: 'Look, it's Prince Andrew.' At first I thought he was joking. But I looked up and sure enough, it was the Prince. He was very cool, like all helicopter crew. And he asked me how many more men were still in the life raft. I told him there were a couple more and they were safely winched up. He and his crew did a great job."

In Buenos Aires, the jubilant media reported that the *Invincible* had been sunk. One headline read: *"El Aplastante Al* Invincible" – "A Crushing Blow to the *Invincible*". It was accompanied by a photograph purporting to show the *Invincible* on fire.

Opening the Kielder Dam in Northumbria that day, the Queen told the crowds: "Before I begin, I want to say one thing. Our thoughts today are with those in the South Atlantic, and our prayers are for their success and safe return to their homes and loved ones."

Although the main action was now taking place on land, the Queen heard repeated claims from Argentina that the *Invincible* had been sunk and her son killed. Attending her local church near home in Gatcombe Park, Gloucestershire, Princess Anne heard the local policeman, who was leading the prayers, say: "We continue to pray for all those involved in the Falklands, especially remembering Prince Andrew, and all who wait at home for news of relatives and friends."

While the land forces were making their way westwards towards Port Stanley, the Argentinians staged one last attack on the fleet. They hit the Royal Fleet Auxiliary *Sir Galahad*, with the loss of fifty Welsh Guardsmen. Her sister ship *Sir Tristram* and HMS *Plymouth* were also hit, but with no fatalities.

The last British offensive began on 11 June. HMS *Glamorgan* was providing artillery support when it was hit by an Exocet, killing nine. The Argentinian forces surrendered three days later.

"When the end came, there was no cheering and shouting, no celebrating," said Andrew on board the *Invincible*. "We could not really believe that was the end of it. Everyone just looked at each other and said: 'It's over then.'"

In fact, it wasn't over. Although Argentinian dictator General Galtieri was forced from power, Argentina would not accept defeat. Mrs Thatcher was warned that one defiant member of the discredited junta might launch one last desperate attack. That meant, for Andrew, tireless helicopter surveillance continued and, with winter descending, the dangers for the fliers had hardly decreased.

On tour in Denver, Colorado, Princess Anne was asked about her younger brother and said: "He is still flying missions in terrible weather. In many ways the weather is a more difficult enemy than Galtieri."

Four days after the Argentinian surrender, Prince Andrew and his helicopter crew got the chance to visit the island they had risked their lives for. On 18 June, their Sea King touched down on the muddy playing field across the road from Port Stanley's tiny hospital with its Red Crosses emblazoned on the rooftop.

His visit to the Falklands was supposed to be a private affair but the islanders recognised him. They were grateful to see him. It was the first royal visit since Prince Philip, then a serving naval officer, had stepped ashore in 1957.

Andrew was provided with a military jeep requisitioned from the Argentines. Along with his CO, Lieutenant-Commander Ralph Wykes-Sneyd and 801 Harrier Squadron's leader Lieutenant-Commander Nigel "Sharky" Ward, he was taken on a conducted tour of the island. This had its dangers. The battlefields around Port Stanley were still strewn with enemy mines and few roads on the island were safe.

Everywhere Andrew went, he was confronted by line after line of dejected Argentinian troops, waiting for ships to take them home. The young conscripts were a pitiful sight. They had fought a war many never wanted against British troops who were better equipped and better trained. Some of them had been shot through the foot by their own officers to stop them running away.

As for many men who fought there, Andrew found the Falklands campaign was a turning point in his life. The brush with death, acting as a decoy for Exocet missiles and rescuing survivors from the *Atlantic Conveyor* left an indelible mark. The misery and chaos of the conflict, especially the dejection on the faces of the Argentinian prisoners of war, inspired an interest in photography. It was a passion which, for some time, would dominate his spare time. He later converted his bathroom at Buckingham Palace into a darkroom.

At the blitzed and flattened Stanley airfield, Andrew saw for himself the result of countless days of continual naval shelling and bombardment from the air. Crippled enemy jet fighters and their rockets were strewn the whole length of the windswept runway. The Falkland Islands might be in a desperate state, but they were once again British.

The islanders joyfully thanked their royal visitor for his part in their liberation, while Andrew shook hands with the Falkland Islanders and posed for pictures.

Asked what he thought of Port Stanley, he said: "It's really a nice little town – a bit muddier than I expected. I am only sad that I had to visit under these circumstances. But at least there's peace now and you can start thinking about the future." Then he added: "It's a perfect place to bring my bride on honeymoon." Fergie was, in the end, spared that.

After the fall of Port Stanley, one of the first British ships to enter its tiny harbour was the Royal Fleet Auxiliary *Sir Bedivere* which carried a Marisat satellite-telephone communications system. Weary soldiers queued up for hours outside *Sir Bedivere*'s tiny radio shack for the chance to make a phone call home. After his guided tour, Prince Andrew also walked up *Sir Bedivere*'s gangplank, marched up to the bridge and asked where the radio room was. Once there, he asked the operator to put a call through to the Queen at Buckingham Palace. They chatted for fifteen minutes.

"My mother was in – it was about the right time in the evening," he said. "She was quite surprised to hear from me."

He told his comrades that among her first words was praise for the men of her armed forces.

"She asked me to pass on how proud she was of everyone and to say how marvellously all the troops had done," he said.

Andrew was modest about his own contribution.

"I didn't do a great deal," he insisted. "I have been at sea. But we did do quite a lot of flying in the last month and a half, when it really got intensive. We have done our little bit and the lads have done extremely well."

His closest brushes with death, he said, came not from the Argentinians but from British missiles. Several times in the heat of battle, the automatic British Sea Wolf anti-missile systems mistakenly had his helicopter in their sights during an Exocet attack.

"Sea Wolves locked on to our helicopter three times while we were hovering," he said. "It's not much fun having one of those fellows pick you out as a target. It really makes the hair stand up on the back of your neck."

He heaped praise on 820 Squadron.

"My squadron has been absolutely fantastic," he said. "The spirit has been there all the time and I think the squadron really pulled everything out. I can only say it is a great squadron and I am glad I served with it.'

But it wasn't all plain sailing.

"I have been frightened,' said Andrew. "It was an experience, but I would not say I would not have missed it."

Before strapping himself back into his Sea King and flying back to the *Invincible*, Andrew said ruefully: "If I had the choice, I would not want to go through it again."

Andrew faced two more months of flying in the freezing weather before *Invincible* finally headed home. The helicopter and Harrier patrols continued in the skies around the islands. This was all the more galling as the other ships they had sailed down with were disappearing. It seemed that the *Invincible*, the first out, was going to be the last back.

On 21 June, news that Princess Diana had given birth to Prince William came through.

"Congratulations on your demotion," shouted one officer at Andrew as he walked into the wardroom. The birth meant that Andrew had dropped one place in the line of succession. Nevertheless, Andrew came off the wagon, briefly, to wet the baby's head with champagne. There was another cause for celebration. In the light of its service in the Falklands War, plans to sell the *Invincible* to Australia for a knock-down price were shelved. The Aussies would get the *Hermes* instead, which was a delight to the crew of the *Invincible*.

By this time, the *Invincible* had been at sea for four months and boredom had set in. So the MoD sought to boost morale by sending an entertainment concert party – complete with three bikini-clad girls in a dance troupe called Dream. They were flown out from Stanley by helicopter. Andrew was particularly captivated by one pretty dancer, twenty-eight-year-old Carole St James. Gazing into her eyes, he sang a chorus of "You made me love you".

He was photographed with Carole on one side and the equally attractive Carol Hungerford on the other with his arms around both of them.

"Andrew's pulling again," yelled a shipmate.

Naturally, the pictures made their way to the British press.

"He gave us a squeeze and a lovely cuddle," said Carole St James. Randy Andy was making the headlines even at sea.

After 145 days, *Invincible*'s station was taken over by her sister ship HMS *Illustrious*. At last, Andrew was on his way home.

Crowds filled the quayside at Portsmouth. The skies were full of helicopters and light aircraft, and the Solent was packed with pleasure craft, large and small. Through them ploughed the royal barge carrying the Queen, Prince Philip and Princess Anne. Prince Charles was not on board.

The barge moored alongside the *Invincible* and met Andrew for an emotional reunion in one of the warships' state cabins. The family must have spotted a difference in the man who had left five months earlier.

"It will be very interesting going back to reality in the UK," he said. "It's been one hell of an experience."

He was not altogether happy to be back in Blighty though.

"I suppose I'm not looking forward to going back to being a prince," he said. "I would gladly keep going, particularly with this ship's company and with the men I served with down in the Falklands. I am obviously looking forward to going home, but who knows what awaits me when I get home. I am sure I have changed somewhat since the Falklands. I guess I had to after seeing what I have seen and feeling what I have felt.

"I think my life has gone round the corner since I left Portsmouth in April. I have to pick up where I left off. It may not be easy. I have learnt things about myself that I never would have learnt anywhere else."

There had been a time when he thought he would not come through.

"During those moments when there was fear, I overcame it with the simple maxim that I must think positively. I told myself, 'I am going to survive this.' I was going to add 'come hell or high water' but I won't."

Within hours of being back in sight of Britain, Prince Andrew's life was already going back to normal in one way. Two private detectives were among the first to come aboard while *Invincible* was still several miles out at sea. His valet was close behind them to attend to the Prince's belongings. But being home again was going to take a little while to sink in.

"I daren't start thinking about plans for at least a week," he said. "I will wind down and acclimatise to life again in the UK, to the sweet smell of grass and the silence, after the air conditioning in the ship and the noise of the Sea Harriers and Sea Kings."

When asked what he was most looking forward to now he was back on British soil, he said, "A pint of milk – fresh milk." For months, he had only been able to drink the powdered variety.

Before that he had to face the cheering crowds on the quayside at Portsmouth. His parents walked down the gangplank of the *Invincible* first to warm applause from thousands decked out in Union Jacks. Andrew bounded down the gangplank after them to wild cheers. Someone handed him a single red rose which he clenched in his teeth in a broad grin.

Andrew had returned a war hero both in the eyes of his mother and the general public. He had seen action, while Charles had merely commanded an aged minesweeper. Despite reports of his heroism, Andrew was only awarded the South Atlantic Medal, like everyone else on the campaign, but no other decorations. Nevertheless, he accompanied the Queen when she summoned a meeting of the editors of national newspapers to Buckingham Palace to celebrate the victory.

Charles could only look on in envy. Later, when Prince William's military career was curtailed, keeping him out of active service for the same reasons, Charles sounded a note of resignation, saying: "It was very difficult for William not to go. But I did say to him, 'You know, look, when I was in the Navy… I had the same problem. They wouldn't send me anywhere!'"

CHAPTER THIRTEEN
CIVVY STREET

Charles had not exactly shone during his time in the Navy. However, having been in command of no-matter-how-humble a vessel, he had gained in confidence – though not the sort of confidence Andrew would later exhibit swaggering down the gangplank of HMS *Invincible*. Now, at the age of thirty, Charles wanted to find a purpose in life.

"Perhaps I'm wrong or have an over-inflated sense of my own importance," he wrote when he decided to leave the Navy, "but I feel I could be more useful at home than miles away."

Now in Civvy Street, what was he to do? In a speech at Cambridge University, he said: "My great problem in life is that I do not know what my role in life is. At the moment, I do not have one. But, somehow, I must find one."

It was thought, perhaps, he should have a "proper job". One option was that he should become governor general of Australia. The problem was that he did not have a wife who could act as hostess at formal occasions and would protect him from the hordes of young Aussie women who dreamt of marrying into the House of Windsor. Besides, the post was too political. Similarly, his appointment as ambassador to France would make him the voice of Margaret Thatcher in what was then the European Economic Community.

The Queen expressed her opinion that Charles needed to do something outside the "royal round", otherwise the public would get the impression that he spent his time hunting, shooting and skiing. Nigel Dempster, gossip columnist of the *Daily Mail*, wrote him a spoof wanted ad: "Situation sought: Prince, 29, degree, ex-Army, Navy, RAF, seeks employment. Will go anywhere, try anything once."

Briefly, Charles was dispatched to the National Economic Development Office to learn a little about government, but he showed no enthusiasm for the job. He should have had enough to do anyway with the Duchy of Cornwall and the portfolio of roles he accrued in the Prince's Trust, the Prince of Wales Environmental Committee for Wales, the United World Colleges and the Joint Jubilee Trusts. He was chancellor of the University of Wales, commander-in-chief of five regiments and patron of the British Sub Aqua Club and the Royal Anthropological Institute.

While Randy Andy knew that everyone loved a bad boy, Charles courted public approval by being a good boy. He began with a bit of God-bothering and launched himself on a voyage of self-discovery, rejecting scientific materialism in favour of mysticism. Rather than being "Defender of the Faith" when he became king – a title inherited from English and Scottish monarchs since the sixteenth century – he would become "Defender of Faith", he said, though that was dropped when he finally succeeded.

In this time, he fell under the spell of South African writer, explorer and mystic Laurens van der Post, author of *The Lost World of the Kalahari*. Van der Post wanted Charles to accompany him when he retraced his journey into the Kalahari Desert for the benefit of the BBC. With the war of liberation in Zimbabwe, then Southern Rhodesia, at its height, the Foreign Office vetoed the plan.

Instead, Charles put the Jungian ideas he had imbibed from Van der Post into his children's book *The Old Man of Lochnagar*, transposing revelations in the Kalahari to a mountain overlooking Balmoral. He also dabbled in Hinduism and Buddhism. All this seemed rather at odds with his love of fox hunting.

Charles eventually decided to concentrate his efforts on the Prince's Trust, which he had established in 1976 to support young people. An act of pure altruism, he had begun it with £7,471, his pay-off from the Royal Navy. But his charitable work soon began consuming enormous amounts of money and fundraising became a major concern.

By 1996, besides the Prince's Trust, Charles had created charities for education, the environment, architecture, complementary medicine, animals, the sick, the poor and rural communities. But he was careless about their governance. The trustees were supposed to have a free hand, as Charles was barred by law from having any role in their management. But they depended on him for fundraising and the Charities Commission complained that he played an unauthorised part in their running.

Charles spread himself thinly between the various charities. There was a great deal of duplication with different organisations working in the same field, while Charles would hit on the same donors for different organisations. His personal staff also interfered.

"They were always negative that he should not do things," complained one charity executive, "but they hadn't seen the real world, and got it wrong."

Charles would come up with ideas off the cuff, leaving others to sort out the details. Sycophancy prevented others questioning him.

And given Charles was sensitive to confrontation, contradiction would be met with a stony silence. If someone told him "no", he would find someone else who would say "yes". This led to deadly rivalries within the various organisations.

Then there was the excessive amounts spent on administration. By 2019 the Prince's Trust employed 1,241 people. The annual wage bill was £38 million, the organisation's largest single expenditure. It sought a global reach with the Prince's Trust International, the Prince's Trust Australia, the Prince's Trust Canada, the Prince's Trust New Zealand, the Prince's Trust America and Prince's Trust Trading.

Not content with that, Charles launched two more charities to help disadvantaged youth – Inner City Aid and the Prince's Youth Business Trust. In October 1985, his main helper, Rod Hackney, a pioneer of community architecture, told the *Manchester Evening News* that Charles was "prepared to force his way through parliamentary red tape to ensure that his country is not split into factions of haves and have-nots". The piece was headlined: "Prince Charles: My Fears for the Future".

Prime Minister Margaret Thatcher was incensed, saying Charles was dabbling in politics. She demanded an explanation. None was forthcoming and Hackney discreetly disappeared from the court of Prince Charles. But Charles was chastened by the backlash.

"They want to destroy me, or get rid of me," he told a friend.

In pique, he went on Radio 4's *Today* programme and said: "There is no need for me to do all this, you know. If they'd rather I did nothing, I'll go off somewhere else." A spokesman simply said that Charles had been "misunderstood".

Being the point man for a large group of charities was not enough for Prince Charles. He wanted to challenge what he saw as vested interests in medicine, education and architecture. When he was elected president of the British Medical Association, he criticised the medical establishment's rejection of complementary or alternative medicine.

His grandmother had introduced him to traditional cures, while Laurens van der Post advocated homeopathy. Charles also embraced acupuncture, osteopathy, chiropractic therapy and naturopathy. God acting through the Divine Spirit could cure a patient through their "inner awareness", putting them in a holistic relation with the cosmos. His speech to the BMA received polite applause on the night and derision from ITV's satirical programme *Spitting Image*.

"Perhaps, we just have to accept it is God's will that the unorthodox individual is doomed to years of frustration, ridicule and failure in order to act out his role in the scheme of things, until his day arrives and mankind is ready to receive his message," he told the doctors. A prophet is never recognised in his own land.

No doubt these highly qualified medical men appreciated being lectured on their field of expertise by someone who had a modest degree in history. So, out for deference, Sir James Watt, the president of the Royal Society of Medicine, laid on eight seminars and a BMA working party to look into complementary medicine. Charles attended some seminars, but was short with those who tried to oppose him.

"Science has tried to assume a monopoly – or rather, a tyranny – over our understanding of the world around us," he said. "Religion and science have become separated, and science has attempted to separate the natural world from God… We are only now beginning to understand the disastrous results of this outlook."

In an article in the *Guardian*, he went on to blame "the increase in soft furnishings" for an epidemic of allergies. The *Sunday Telegraph* snapped back: "One wonders what bad experiences the sensitive prince has had with unsympathetic sofas or aggressive pouffes. But his latest intervention merely confirms our view that alternative medicine should remain the luxury of the well-to-do hypochondriac."

The BMA then issued a report saying that alternative medicine was useless. Undeterred, Charles supported an "alternative" drug-free cancer clinic in Bristol and the first department dedicated to the study of complementary medicine set up at Exeter University under Edzard Ernst, Britain's first professor of complementary medicine. He also encouraged the establishment of the Foundation for Integrated Health under herbal practitioner Simon Mills. And he set up his own foundation under Michael Fox, the CEO. But when Fox disagreed with Charles about the effectiveness of some alternative remedies, he was told that the Prince was "not used to opposition".

After five years of study, Professor Ernst found that alternative medicine was not only ineffective, it could be positively harmful if patients relied on it rather than seeking conventional treatment. The makers of homeopathic medicines and other practitioners were simply conning the public, he said. Ernst lost his job and his department was closed down. He blamed his royal mentor. Prince Charles was, he said, "unwilling or unable to distinguish between real health care and blatant quackery, between medicine and snake oil, or between the truth and some half-baked obsessions of his own".

He also attacked Charles's foundation saying: "The information the foundation puts out is dangerous and misleading. It's an attempt to brainwash GPs and patients."

In response, Clarence House said: "The Prince of Wales believes in… treating the whole person rather than just the symptoms of disease and taking into account the effects on health of factors such as lifestyle, the environment and emotional well-being. His Royal Highness is patron of over thirty healthcare organisations."

Even when hearings of the House of Lords Science and Technology Committee gave complementary medicine a mauling, Charles put pressure on the Department of Health to give £18.5 million to the Royal Homeopathic Hospital and the NHS was urged to give patients access to the "new sciences" and the integrated medicine promoted by Charles's own foundation.

While Professor Ernst has dismissed the BSc in alternative medicine awarded by Exeter University as "a course in claptrap taught by uncritical believers to brainwash youngsters with mystical nonsense", Charles encouraged the university to introduce a postgraduate course in the subject.

When his attempt to champion complementary medicine did not attract the plaudits he had hoped, Charles looked around for another cause. He converted the Duchy of Cornwall's farm to produce exclusively organic foods and showed interest in a book about aliens recommended by Charlie Palmer-Tomkinson.

At the Bath Festival in 2018, Charles told BBC music controller John Drummond that the Bartók and Schoenberg played sounded "like scraping a nail over a blackboard".

After a pause, Drummond said: "Your taste in music is as execrable as your taste in art and architecture."

As the two men continued to argue, the Lord Lieutenant of Somerset, who had accompanied the Prince to the concert, became anxious.

"You must stop this," he urged one of Charles's courtiers. "Interpose your body between them."

The Prince laughed and said: "I'm enjoying this. I like John. No one's honest with me like that."

It has been said that Prince Charles was at war with the Enlightenment. When it came to architecture he was opposed to anything that did not belong stylistically in the eighteenth century. In 1984, he got the construction of a new wing of the National Gallery in a modernist style cancelled after saying that what was proposed was "like a monstrous carbuncle on the face of a much-loved and elegant friend". He delivered this damning judgement at the 150th anniversary celebration of the Royal Institute of British Architects whose members were largely dedicated modernists.

Also at RIBA's 150th anniversary bash was property developer Peter Palumbo, who planned a nineteen-storey block at No 1 Poultry, adjacent to the neoclassical Bank of England and Mansion House. Charles said: "It would be a tragedy if the character and skyline of our capital were to be further ruined and St Paul's dwarfed by yet another giant glass stump better suited to downtown Chicago than the City of London."

There was consternation. Peter Ahrends, designer of the new wing of the National Gallery, said: "'The prince's remarks were offensive, reactionary and ill-considered. He seems to be looking backwards rather than forwards."

Others simply found the Prince rude for using the occasion to attack their profession.

"Why did you say that?" Palumbo asked Charles at the dinner afterwards.

"I just thought I'd stir things up a bit," replied Charles, clearly pleased with himself and unconcerned by the effects on Ahrends and Palumbo, whose plan for No 1 Poultry was abandoned. He dismissed Charles as a fogey.

This began a long-running argument with architect Richard Rogers who was responsible for the Lloyd's Building, a glass tower with the pipework on the outside, and the white fibreglass Millennium Dome. They had also come to blows over a proposed postmodern development in Paternoster Square next to St Paul's Cathedral, with

Charles saying: "You have to give this much to the Luftwaffe: when it knocked down our buildings, it didn't replace them with anything more offensive than rubble." Rogers's plan was quickly dropped.

In Charles's eyes, Birmingham Central Library built in 1974 looked like "a place where books are incinerated, not kept". It has since been demolished. The British Library (where I am writing this) was "more like the assembly hall of an academy for secret police", while the National Theatre on London's South Bank was "a clever way of building a nuclear power station in the middle of London without anyone objecting".

Much to the chagrin of architects, Prince Charles's outbursts did find appreciative audience around the country and his tweedy image found a particular resonance when the "young fogey" was very much in fashion. However, he did find opposition in unexpected quarters. When Charles asked why César Pelli's fifty-storey office block in Canary Wharf "need be quite so high", Roy Strong, the curator of the Victoria and Albert Museum, and in many ways the epitome of young fogey, replied: "With all due respect, sir, if that argument had pertained in the Middle Ages, we would not have got the spire of Salisbury Cathedral." No more was said.

Strong was one of the avid gardeners summoned to Highgrove, the Prince's Gloucestershire country retreat. His role was to advise on the cultivation of hedges. At the end of the work, he presented Charles an invoice for £1,000. He was never thanked or asked to return.

"He's shocked by the sight of an invoice," Strong noted. "So he likes people who don't charge for their services."

None of those who seemingly volunteered their services were thanked when Charles himself received the Victoria Medal of Honour from the Royal Horticultural Society for his services to gardening at the 2009 Chelsea Flower Show. It was presented by his mum, the Queen.

CHAPTER FOURTEEN

DIVINE SOURCES
AND BLACK SPIDERS

To take up arms against modernism, Charles organised a summer school for architects at Villa Lante, a sixteenth-century palazzo just outside Viterbo owned by the Italian government. The following year, The Prince of Wales Institute of Architecture was set up in Crown Estate property at 14 and 15 Gloucester Gate in Regent's Park. In a prospectus for sponsors, he emphasised the principles of "the architecture of the Heart".

"There was a Divine Source which is the Ultimate Truth as passed down by our predecessors," he said. "That Truth can be expressed by means of numbers – i.e. through geometrical principles and that, if followed correctly, these principles can be expressed with infinite variety to produce Beauty. Beauty, in turn, issues from the fact that its manifestation is a reflection of the order of the Cosmos."

"Man is," he continued, "a microcosm of this macro-cosmos and that, in order to reflect the inherent harmony of the Universe in this Earthly Dimension, we need to follow the basic Geometrical principles in this building process."

Clearly, Charles was getting closer to God, but this was hardly a blueprint for an educational institution. Charles told his secretary in architecture: "I want the Institute to teach its students reverence – reverence for the landscape and the soil; for the human spirit which is a reflection in some small measure of the Divine."

The aim was to allow "the correspondence of the natural world with the idea of God; the expression of God within the human spirit; and the potential for architecture to give physical form to those sublime relationships". It sounded like he was starting a cult.

With funds from the ruling family of Saudi Arabia, other Arab sheikhs and the Sultan of Brunei, the institute had a generous budget. Each student cost over £40,000 to educate, with free trips to New York and Italy for short architectural courses thrown in. This was six times what educating an undergraduate in the state sector cost. But its courses had not been endorsed by RIBA and fewer than thirty people enrolled each year.

"The students were being used as Charles's cannon fodder to promote traditional architecture," said noted architect Professor Adrian Gale. "They didn't like that. They just wanted a career. It was a token folly."

While two of his charities for young people had foundered due to poor management, losing £14 million, Charles was accused of using his royal status to set up the institute without paying sufficient attention to how it would work. Jules Lubbock, an architect who tried to rescue the failing institute, travelled by train to Highgrove to ask for his salary. When he patiently explained that he relied on his income to live, Charles grew irritated and left the room. A private secretary then came in to tell Lubbock that the interview was over and he should leave. No car was provided to give Lubbock a lift back to the railway station and he had to walk.

As the turnover of staff continued, the institute found it had run up a £2.5 million annual deficit. PR man Mark Bolland, brought in to rescue Charles's image, wrote it off as "a basket case". But Charles was determined to rescue it.

"I must subsidise it," said Charles. "I'll sell my paintings to support it."

Bolland was too much of a diplomat to mention that Charles was lucky to get £15,000 for his watercolours. They were not highly regarded. He once asked Lucian Freud whether he would swap one for one of his oils.

"I don't want one of your rotten paintings," Freud replied.

Instead, Charles must cut back. First to go was *Perspectives*, a magazine he had created in 1994 to restore the "spiritual sense... to the evolution of a new architecture". But Charles's wordy contributions did not spell out a clear agenda. The editor, Giles Worsley, complained of being "compromised and ultimately silenced" by Charles. The magazine was deeply in debt and closed in 1998.

Rather than slim down the institute, Charles broadened its remit. It would become the Prince's Foundation for Architecture and the Urban Environment. Its headquarters moved from their Palladian buildings in Regent's Park to an abandoned warehouse in Shoreditch, a district of east London due for renovation. Over lunch at Highgrove, Charles agreed to find a donor to buy the building and restore it. Some £4.6 million would be needed. The Prince then hosted fundraising dinners for the wealthy to raise the cash.

Charles was also irritated by abstract art, so he also opened the Royal Drawing School in Shoreditch. It was to teach figurative art and life drawing. Again, wealthy donors, including the Saudi government, were invited to cough up. One of them was the Turk Cem Uzan, who was later sentenced *in absentia* to jail terms in the UK, USA and Turkey for fraud-related offences.

Modernist Adrian Porter was brought in "to make Charles less fogeyish and more modern", but he found "a lot of manoeuvring around Charles. Everyone was jockeying for position. It wasn't double- but triple-speak. ... No one would talk straight. His officials were buttering Charles up and telling him what he wanted to hear."

Sycophancy abounded.

"It was tremendously unclear what Charles wanted," said Porter. "He had a very short attention span and was surrounded by people who assured him that he was doing the right thing. And then Charles suddenly went quiet."

In 2009, Charles opposed Rogers's modernist design for hundreds of homes on the site of Chelsea Barracks and wrote to Sheikh Hamad bin Abdullah Al Thani, the Emir of Qatar who owned the land, complaining the plans were "unsuitable", thereby jeopardising the £81 million fee of the brothers Nick and Christian Candy who were organising the deal. The Qataris sacked Rogers and replaced him with other more traditional firms that would follow guidance from the Prince's Foundation for Building Community.

Outraged, Rogers said: "I don't believe that the Prince of Wales understands architecture. He thinks it is fixed at one point in the past (for him, classicism – an odd choice as it is not a style with deep roots in England), rather than an evolving language of technology and materials."

Rogers challenged him to a public debate over Britain's built environment, citing other developments where Charles had used undue influence to have architects changed.

"It hardly matters whether his opinions are right or wrong," said Rogers. "He occupies a privileged position, and he should not use that to damage the livelihoods of people he disagrees with."

The debate did not happen.

"Developers do not seek approval from The Prince of Wales for the architects and designers that they might wish to use either directly or indirectly," said a spokesman for the Prince. "The Prince's Foundation for Building Community, an independent charity established by The Prince, is however often approached for advice and works with local authorities to encourage sustainable development built around people."

The *Guardian* piped up: "When Charles blasts modern architecture, he is essentially blasting the historical processes set in motion by the industrial revolution, and lamenting the diminution of his royal power in the world that it brought about. His dreams of traditionally designed cities are dreams of a world where people forever know their place and the 'divine order' would be resurrected."

In an attempt "to roll back some of the more ludicrous frontiers of the 1960s", Charles commissioned Poundbury, a new town of 2,500 houses on land owned by the Duchy of Cornwall near Dorchester in Dorset. It was intended to showcase all the traditional designs and values espoused by Charles.

Modern civilisation, he maintained, was dependent on unsustainable technology, consumerism, economic growth and globalisation. It had disrupted nature and the "organic order". The brutalist tower blocks built by modernist architects were a threat to the ancient mysticism that binds mankind.

"The prerequisite of the health of each of the Earth's vital support systems," he said, was "an interconnected, harmonic system which could be geometrically measured". For centuries, the ancient system protected the world and the natural, divine order of life. Modernist architecture disturbed "spiritual harmony" and led to human misery.

Again, the *Guardian* rose to the challenge: "To visit Poundbury is to be delivered to the furniture floor of a provincial department store in 1954, translated into architecture. It is fake, heartless, authoritarian and grimly cute. What can be said about a presiding intelligence that demands central heating flues be disguised by cast concrete gargoyles?"

Driving to Dorset in his Bentley, Charles was introduced to the owners of a new two-bedroom house.

"I have always stuck to the principle," he told the couple, "that I would not let anyone build a house here that I could not personally live in." As the resident of six palaces and grand country houses – all of which had many more than two bedrooms – Charles did not see the irony.

To spell out his wisdom, in 2010 Charles published the book *Harmony: A New Way of Looking at Our World*. The blurb says Charles "examines how areas such as architecture, farming and medicine have each abandoned the balance with nature that existed in pre-industrial times... he explores the way in which mankind must work to restore the delicate balance with nature that we've lost in the centuries since the industrial revolution began." Naturally, this involved an absolute monarch ruling over a pastoral society, using spiritualism as practised in medieval times. There were three hundred pages of it.

It would be easy to argue that Charles was out of touch. Three years after he was married to Camilla, he came home from the theatre to find his supper wrapped in clear plastic and shrieked.

"What's this?" he demanded.

"It's cling film, darling," she said to his evident puzzlement.

He also once told a friend he'd been on the Tube, only for his companion to reply, "Yes, but only to open a line."

When the Labour government allowed the introduction of genetically modified crops, Charles saw another bandwagon he could jump on. Mark Bolland approached the *Daily Mail* to carry an article from the Prince condemning "tampering with Nature when we can't be sure that we know enough about all the consequences".

"Are we going to allow the industrialisation of Life itself, redesigning the natural world for the sake of convenience and embarking on an Orwellian future? And, if we do, will there eventually be a price to pay?" he asked.

Charles had penned the article after meeting Dr Arpad Pusztai who alleged that rats fed GM potatoes suffered damage to their immune systems. However, Dr Pusztai's results were condemned in an independent report compiled by fellow scientists at the Royal Society and was later forced to abandon his work at the Rowett Research Institute in Aberdeen.

Supported by the *Mail*, Charles was presented as the voice of reason, while Prime Minister Tony Blair fumed, particularly because he had promised £100 million to the Prince's Trust and was forced to attend a reception hosted by Charles at St James's Palace. A few days later Charles boycotted a reception hosted by the visiting Chinese president in honour of the Queen, to protest the occupation of Tibet.

"He did this as a deliberate snub to the Chinese because he did not approve of the Chinese regime and is a great supporter of the Dalai Lama whom he views as being oppressed by the Chinese," said Mark Bolland. "The Prince of Wales was delighted at the coverage."

Fox hunting was the next issue he took up. The Labour government were out to ban it, while Charles saw it as the God-given right of everyday country folk. In defiance, he took seventeen-year-old William out with the Beaufort Hunt. The government accused him of playing politics. It was the government that had made fox hunting political, Charles retorted.

Nevertheless, he reluctantly agreed to stand down as patron of the Countryside Alliance when its members took to the streets. In support of fellow fox hunters, he told Blair: "If we as a group were black or gay, we would not be victimised or picked upon." He also accused the government of "destroying the countryside". If fox hunting was banned, he threatened to spend the rest of his life skiing.

Charles insisted that his opinions needed to be taken into account. "Why can't they understand this all means a lot to me," he lamented.

He wrote a long letter to Blair saying he could not stay silent about GM crops and outlining the benefits to the environment of hunting. At the time, Blair was trying to rally support for the war in Iraq, so he put his weight behind that ban, which then passed.

Before his meeting with Tony Blair at St James's Palace, the letter was leaked. Charles also condemned the government's abolition of the right of hereditary peers to sit in the House of Lords. Charles, of course, believed in the hereditary principle. The question was asked at the time: once you abolished the rights of hereditary peers, would abolition of the rights of hereditary monarchs naturally follow?

Blair cooled towards the monarchy and expressed little enthusiasm about his weekly audiences with the Queen. But he needed her to attend the millennium celebrations at the controversial Dome. When Charles refused to attend, Blair's press secretary Alastair Campbell dismissed him as "an over-privileged twit".

Andrew had fought in the Falklands War but, seventeen years later, it fell to Charles to go to Buenos Aires to shake the hand of the new democratically elected President Carlos Menem. Charles was criticised for meddling again by drawing attention in his speech to "another modern, if rather smaller, democracy just a few hundred miles off your coast".

Menem did not react and his daughter Zulemita danced the tango with Charles. He followed this with the Don Juan Tango with thirty-three-year-old professional dancer Adriana Vasile.

"He is a good dancer, light on his feet," she said.

However, it drew fire from Vice-President Carlos Ruckauf who said: "The [Falkland] islanders have no right to self-determination. This is a typically British trick."

The *Guardian* said: "At best, the prince's ham-fisted reference to the sovereignty of the Falkland Islands was a misjudgement. At worst, it was extraordinary incompetence." After a game of polo, Charles flew to the Falklands to commemorate the Battle of Goose Green where eighteen British troops had died, along with some fifty Argentines.

Invited to make one of the BBC's annual Reith Lectures, Charles used it as a platform to condemn GM crops. "If literally nothing is held sacred any more," he said, "what is there to prevent us treating our entire world as some 'great laboratory of life', with potentially disastrous long-term consequences?"

Charles, of course, had an answer. It was to renew the "sacred trust between mankind and our Creator, under which we accept a duty of stewardship for the earth. ... It is only recently that this guiding principle has become smothered by almost impenetrable layers of scientific rationalism."

As the self-appointed spokesman for rural England, Charles wrote a six-page letter to Blair after the outbreak of foot-and-mouth disease in 2001. He blamed the EU whose regulations had closed down smaller abattoirs, meaning that animals had to be transported further, spreading the disease. As a self-confessed "interfering busy-body", he also chastised the government for its lack of understanding of country matters, voicing his concerns again at an anniversary party for BBC Radio 4's long-running countryside soap *The Archers*.

Further crossing the line, he criticised Blair's support for Britain becoming an ever closer part of the EU and cautioned against the creation of a European superstate. Despite being warned again about meddling in politics, he gave £500,000 to farmers who were suffering financially due to the cull.

"It's amazing he can lead the news with small change given their wealth and we can get fuck all for spending billions," complained Alastair Campbell.

Charles's next idea was that Britain should be transformed into an "organic oasis". When it was pointed out that this was unrealistic as the country already imported half its food, he grew angry. Losing patience, Tony Blair complained to the Queen about Charles's interference.

But Charles continued to interfere, firing off letters to government in secret on such diverse subjects as farming, genetic modification, global warming, social deprivation, planning, architecture, the military, education, deradicalisation and foreign policy. These were known as the "black spider memos", after his distinctive handwriting, and earned him the sobriquet "The Meddling Prince".

"I don't call it meddling," he said. "I call it mobilising."

The letters were sent, ostensibly, as a private citizen, but also on behalf of his various charities, foundations and campaign groups. When they were published after a five-year legal battle, Mark Bolland, who by then had moved on, said the Prince routinely meddled in political issues and wrote sometimes in extreme terms to ministers, MPs and others in positions of political power and influence.

The first letter that saw the light of day railed against American-style compensation culture and a decision by Norwich Council to cut down chestnut trees in case people were injured by falling conkers.

In a ten-page statement, Bolland said: "The prince used all the means of communication at his disposal, including meetings with ministers and others, speeches and correspondence with leaders in all walks of life and politicians. He was never party-political, but to argue that he was not political was difficult... These letters were not merely routine and non-controversial... but written at times in extreme terms... containing his views on political matters and individual politicians at home and abroad and on international issues.

"He often referred to himself as a 'dissident' working against the prevailing political consensus. ... I remember on many occasions seeing in these day files letters which, for example, denounced the elected leaders of other countries in extreme terms, and other such highly politically sensitive correspondence."

This did not bode well for the future. The Prince's friend and biographer, Jonathan Dimbleby, said that royal aides had informally started to consider redefining the role of the monarch to allow a future King Charles "to speak out on matters of national and international importance in ways that at the moment would be unthinkable".

For the moment, though, he was ignored. But as the future king, he knew he would have the royal touch that could cure all ills and would not be stopped.

"I have come to realise that my entire life so far has been motivated by a desire to heal," he explained, "to heal the dismembered landscape and the poisoned soil; the cruelly shattered townscape, where harmony has been replaced by cacophony; to heal the divisions between intuitive and rational thought, between mind and body and soul so the temples of our humanity can once again be lit by a sacred flame."

CHAPTER FIFTEEN

IT MUST BE LOVE...?

But Charles has not always been so high-minded. After losing his virginity to Lucia Santa Cruz, daughter of the Chilean ambassador, the plucky prince scaled the walls of the all-female Newnham College to sample the delights of Sibylla Dorman, daughter of the governor general of Malta. Soon after, he was photographed escorting Audrey Buxton to the May Ball at Trinity College.

While Andrew dated actresses and models, perfect tabloid fodder, Charles's aristocratic escorts managed to keep themselves out of the papers. There was Lady Jane Wellesley, daughter of the 8th Duke of Wellington; the daughters of the Duke of Northumberland, Lady Caroline and Lady Victoria Percy; the Duke of Westminster's daughters Leonora and Jane, who became the Duchess of Roxburghe; the Duke of Rutland's daughter Lady Charlotte Manners and her cousin Elizabeth; the Marquis of Lothian's daughter Lady Cecil Kerr; the Duke of Grafton's daughter Lady Henrietta Fitzroy; Lord Astor's daughter Angela; Lord Rupert Nevill's daughter Angela; Sir John Russell's daughter Georgiana and so on through *Burke's Peerage*. He kept these amours quiet by entertaining the young ladies concerned at Broadlands, the country estate of his Uncle Dickie.

However, some slipped under the wire. There was a good deal of fevered press speculation about Prince Charlie's relationship with Lady "Kanga" Tryon and some snobbish tut-tutting about his drinks with Sabrina Guinness, daughter of the famous brewing family.

When he took up with the rich and stylish Davina Sheffield, her jilted lover James Beard spilt the beans about their cosy cohabitation in the Sunday papers. And when Prince Charles started seeing Lord Manton's daughter Fiona Watson, the papers had a field day. The curvaceous Fiona had once stripped off for the soft porn magazine *Penthouse*, so here was a royal scandal complete with juicy pictures.

Then in 1972, Charles met the love of his life, Camilla Shand. He was introduced to her at the upmarket Mayfair disco Annabel's by Andrew Parker Bowles, the Guards officer whom he would later cuckold.

Camilla made no secret of her scandalous intent. She introduced herself to the Prince as the great-granddaughter of Alice Keppel – the last mistress of Edward VII. Alice famously remarked that her job was to "curtsy first and then hop into bed". They had a brief romance but then, the following year, he left Camilla on the dockside and shoved off on HMS *Minerva*. Given it had already been made clear to Camilla that she was not the material queens were made of, four weeks after she had kissed her sailor prince goodbye, she accepted the proposal of Andrew Parker Bowles. Within months, they were married and, the very next year, Prince Charles became godfather to the couple's first child.

Prince Charles consoled himself with other women. After dining at his flat in Buckingham Palace, many women would stay the night. The prince's valet would often find items of ladies' underwear concealed around the house. These would be laundered and returned in an Asprey's box, if the owner was known. Otherwise, they would be given to members of the Palace staff.

The Palace managed to keep the details of these affairs out of the press. At the time, Prince Andrew told a girlfriend that Charles was trying to compete with Warren Beatty who, it is said, had laid every starlet in Hollywood. That was surely more Andrew territory. The *Daily Mail* even reported that Charles had a slush fund to buy the silence of women who objected to being used once, then cast aside.

During this promiscuous period, Charles was seeing Sarah Spencer, Diana's older sister, who was deemed unsuitable as a wife as she was a heavy smoker. Meanwhile, his young brother Prince Andrew was having a brief dalliance with Di herself.

Charles was now thirty and the pressure was on for him to do what the heir to the throne is supposed to do – produce more heirs. The race was on to find him a suitable wife. Foreign princesses, including Marie-Astrid of Luxembourg, were vetted. But all those of a suitable age and disposition were Catholics. Under the Act of Settlement (1701), it was deemed unlawful for the heir to the throne to marry a Catholic.

So the Royal Family looked closer to home and their eyes soon alighted on Diana. She was everything they could have wished for: English, upper class, naïve and – by her own admission – none too bright. More importantly, she was a virgin. At least this was the firm assertion of her uncle Lord Fermoy, though no one asked how he was in a position to know.

Her virginity, again, was important under English constitutional law. Catherine Howard had been executed for treason, not just because she had fooled around after her marriage to Henry VIII but also because she had had her cherry popped before it.

Randy Andy, apparently, had got nowhere with Diana, though he was not averse to trying his hand again. When she was brought to Balmoral for royal approval, Andrew and Edward competed to sit next to her at picnics.

Apparently neither had author and socialite George Plumptre whom she had been going out with for more than a year. Or, at least, he was not saying. The public swallowed this, particularly because she looked the part. With her blushing good looks and her innocently averted gaze, she could have been tailor-made for the role. She was everyone's idea of the fresh, unsullied maiden who gets to marry Prince Charming.

But Charles was not Prince Charming. In fact, his coolness towards his mouth-watering young bride was palpable. In their first face-to-face interview with the press, he was asked whether he was in love with her. He replied, awkwardly: "Yes, whatever that may mean."

"I think an awful lot of people have got the wrong idea about love," he said in an interview four years previously. "It is rather more than just falling madly in love. It's basically a very strong friendship. I think you are very lucky if you find the right person attractive in both the physical sense and the mental sense. If I am deciding whom I want to live with for fifty years, that's the last decision on which I would want my head to be ruled by my heart."

He could have been talking about Camilla.

The problem was not just that Diana was not Camilla. She was not of royal blood, nurtured in regal seclusion. She had not been brought up to play the aristocratic game, to turn a blind eye to her husband's misdemeanours and conduct her own affairs, if she felt the need to have any, discreetly. She was a modern young woman who expected more. She wanted to be loved and she was not going to put up with her fiancé fooling around.

And fooling around he was. While they were courting, Charles was seeing Davina Sheffield and Anna Wallace, who, in turn, was seeing other men. He was also maintaining an interest in Camilla Parker Bowles. Just weeks before the royal wedding, Diana found a bracelet in Charles's desk drawer. At first, she thought this expensive gift was for her. But on closer examination, she spotted the initials "F" and "G" engraved on it. In intimate conversation, Charles and Camilla adopted the *Goon Show* nomenclature "Fred" and "Gladys".

Diana was heartbroken; Charles nonplussed. He could not see what Diana had to complain about. It seemed perfectly normal for him to carry on an active love life with other women, even though he was getting married. After all, his father, the Duke of Edinburgh, had reportedly been doing that very thing for all the long years of his marriage to the Queen. That is what royals did.

Besides, the wedding plans were almost complete. Heads of state from around the world were on their way. The TV networks had cleared their schedules. The world was waiting. It was too late to back out now. The fairy-tale wedding had to go ahead. And in the eyes of the world, Charles had snatched the prize (and, not to forget, snatched it from under the nose of brother, Andrew).

The nightmare situation she had walked innocently into must have been apparent to Diana from the very first night, which the young couple spent at Broadlands. Instead of extending that first night of bliss with his bride long into the following day, Charles had slept off the exertions of their long and tiring wedding day, then leapt from his marriage bed bright and early the next morning to go fishing with Uncle Dickie.

Their honeymoon on the royal yacht *Britannia* was more successful. Apparently, they went to bed early and rose late. Rumours spread that they had taken candid pictures of each other. Some said that these pictures fell into the hands of the press, but no newspaper dared publish them.

However, instead of having intimate dinners à deux, evening meals were formal affairs, surrounded by staff. Even when they were alone, Charles would propound his great thoughts on such weighty topics as world affairs, ecology, architecture, alternative medicine and mysticism. He was old beyond his years and to him, she was just a normal twenty-year-old airhead whose interests did not extend beyond clothes, make-up, pop music and babies. Not only was she bored by him as well, she was hurt. During the cruise, pictures of Camilla fell out of his diary. She also realised the significance of the entwined CCs on the cufflinks he wore. Fortunately, as a balm for his boorish behaviour, there were plenty of handsome young sailors and many others to flirt with.

Back on dry land, Diana flirted openly with the President of Portugal, the dashing Mario Soares. But the story circulated in the press that this was just the high spirits of a sexy young woman and the marriage was solid. That was far from the case.

Within a year of his marriage, Charles made it clear to Diana that he had no intention of giving up his friendship with Mrs Parker Bowles. When Diana confronted him about Camilla, he replied: "Do you seriously expect me to be the first Prince of Wales in history not to have a mistress?"

As heir to the throne, having a *maîtresse en titre* was not only right and fitting, it was practically his duty. Diana did her duty too and, in 1982, produced Prince William.

Soon after giving birth, Diana overheard Charles on the phone saying: "Whatever happens I will go on loving you."

These are the words every young mum would love to hear from her husband, but not when he is saying them to his mistress.

With the birth of a second son, Prince Harry, securing the succession, Diana's duty was now done. Publicly she was seen as a loving mum and she loyally turned up at Charles's side at state occasions. Outside of this, her life was her own. Soon the press got wind of the fact that, like his mother and father, they slept in separate bedrooms.

While Charles was away, Diana went to all-night parties. On one occasion, she spent the weekend with Philip Dunne. Then she was seen at a David Bowie concert with Major David Waterhouse.

The gossip columns were soon reporting that Diana had an unusual number of close male "friends". Names were bandied around. These included Roy Scott, a friend of hers from the days before she was married, and Nicholas Haslam, hi-fi dealer to the aristocracy. Once the affair with Haslam was over, it was reported later, she became a phone pest.

The name that provoked the most heated rumours was Captain James Hewitt. He had taught Prince William to ride and eased Diana back into the saddle, getting her riding again. Hewitt's long-term girlfriend stormed out of the relationship, claiming that he was besotted with the Princess. During the Gulf War, Hewitt was posted to the Middle East and he and Diana exchanged torrid love letters.

Next, there was the upper-class car dealer and scion of the gin family James Gilbey. They had been friends in her single days and, trying to put the best possible construction on the Princess's increasingly reckless social life, it was generally assumed that she was using him merely as a shoulder to cry on.

But Diana was now being tailed by journalists. One evening in 1989, at 8pm in the evening, they saw Diana's bodyguard, Sergeant David Sharp, drop her off at Gilbey's flat. They waited. No one left or entered the flat for the next five hours.

At 1am, she emerged, slightly dishevelled. Sergeant Sharp drove up. Furtively, Diana got in the car and they sped away. When journalists asked what the two of them had been doing for five long hours, Gilbey said gallantly that they had been playing bridge. You need four people to play bridge.

By now the press was feverishly speculating that there was something wrong with the royal marriage. Buckingham Palace managed to keep a lid on it. But then Andrew Morton's sensational book *Diana: Her True Story* blew the whole thing out of the water.

Although everybody – including Morton – stoutly denied it at the time, it was plain that the book had been produced with Diana's active co-operation. After her death, it became clear that she had actively colluded with Morton on the book. It was her mouthpiece. The book exposed the marriage as a sham from the very beginning. The Royal Family had employed her simply as a baby machine. In the book, Morton claimed they had isolated and excluded her to the point she fell prey to the eating disorder bulimia nervosa. And Charles's cold and unfeeling behaviour had driven her to attempt suicide.

The book was quickly followed by *Fall of the House of Windsor* by Nigel Blundell and Susan Blackhall. It maintained that it was Diana's petulant tantrums that had alienated the Royal Family. Charles, it said, had been driven into the arms of another woman by his young wife's unreasonable behaviour. It also mentioned the existence of the notorious "Squidgygate tapes".

On New Year's Eve 1989 and 4 January 1990, secretarial agency manager Jane Norgrove and retired bank manager Cyril Reenan had recorded mobile phone conversations between two people who were obviously physically intimate with each other. One purported to be James Gilbey, the other the Princess of Wales.

They had been touted around Fleet Street for two years. In 1992, they surfaced in the US. It was only then that the British press ran them. At first derided as fakes, they pretty soon proved to be the real McCoy. In them, Diana cursed "the f***ing family". Now the Royal Family had a full-scale scandal on its hands.

The tapes were known as Squidgygate tapes because throughout, Gilbey refers to Diana as "Squidgy". They went like this:

Gilbey: You know, all I want to do is to get in my car and drive around the country talking to you.

Diana: Thanks [*Laughs*].

Gilbey: That's all I want to do, darling. I just want to see you and be with you. That's what's going to be such bliss, being back in London.

Diana: I know.

Gilbey: Kiss me, darling [*Blows kisses down the phone*].

Diana: [*Blows kisses back and laughs*]

Gilbey: Squidgy, laugh some more. I love it when I hear you laughing. It makes me really happy when you laugh. Do you know I am happy when you are happy?

Diana: I know you are.

Gilbey: And I cry when you cry.

Diana: I know. So sweet. The rate we are going, we won't need any dinner on Tuesday.

Gilbey: No. I won't need any dinner actually. Just seeing you will be all I need...

[*Pause*]

Diana: Did you get my hint about Tuesday night? I think you missed it. Think what I said.

Gilbey: No.

Diana: I think you have missed it.

Gilbey: No, you said: "At this rate, we won't want anything to eat."

Diana: Yes.

Gilbey: Yes, I know. I got there, Tuesday night. Don't worry, I got there. I can tell you the feeling's entirely mutual.

Then the topic turned to making babies.

Diana: You didn't say anything about babies, did you?

Gilbey: No.

Diana: No.

Gilbey: Why, darling?

Diana: [*Laughs*] I thought you did.

Gilbey: Did you?

Diana: Yes.

Gilbey: Did you, darling? You have got them on the brain.

Diana: Well yeah, maybe I...

[*Pause*]

Diana: I don't want to get pregnant.

Gilbey: Darling, it's not going to happen.

Diana: [*Sighs*]

Gilbey: All right?

Diana: Yeah.

Gilbey: Don't worry about that. It's not going to happen, darling. You won't get pregnant.

The conversation continued in the same vein.

Gilbey: Oh, Squidgy, I love you, love you, love you.

Diana: You are the nicest person in the whole wide world.

Gilbey: Pardon?

Diana: You're just the nicest person in the whole wide world.

Gilbey: Well, darling, you are to me too.

Diana: You don't mind it, darling, when I want to talk to you so much?

Gilbey: No. I love it. Never had it before. Darling, it's so nice being able to help you.

Diana: You do. You'll never know how much.

Gilbey: Oh, I will, darling. I just feel so close to you, so wrapped up in you. I'm wrapping you up, protecting.

Diana: Yes, please. Yes, please.

Gilbey: Oh, Squidgy.

Diana: Mmm.

Gilbey: Kiss me please [*Blows more kisses*]. Do you know what I'm going to be imagining I am doing tonight at about twelve o'clock? Just holding you so close to me. It'll have to be delayed action for forty-eight hours.

Diana: [*Titters*]

Gilbey: Fast forward.

Diana: Fast forward.

Plainly these were two people in the first flush of love who could not wait to get it on. But subterfuge was called for.

Diana: I shall tell people I'm going for acupuncture and my back being done.

Gilbey: [*Giggles*] Squidge, cover them footsteps.

Diana: I jolly well do.

If all that was not damning enough, there was a portion of the transcript that was so raunchy that the newspapers did not dare publish it. Of course, journalists and other insiders knew what was said and this helped fuel the scandal. The missing section was a very indelicate discourse on masturbation.

Gilbey: Squidgy, kiss me.

[*Sounds of kisses being exchanged*]

Gilbey: Oh God, it's wonderful, isn't it? This sort of feeling. Don't you like it?

Diana: I love it.

Gilbey: Umm.

Diana: I love it.

Gilbey: Isn't it absolutely wonderful? I haven't had it for years. I feel about twenty-one again.

Diana: Well, you're not. You're thirty-three.

Gilbey: Darling, mmmm. Tell me some more. It's just like sort of mmmm.

Diana: Playing with yourself.

Gilbey: What?

Diana: Nothing.

Gilbey: No, I'm not actually.

Diana: I said it's just like, just like…

Gilbey: Playing with yourself.

Diana: Yes.

Gilbey: Not quite as nice. Not quite as nice. No, I haven't played with myself, actually. Not for a full forty-eight hours. [*They both laugh*] Not for a full forty-eight hours.

CHAPTER SIXTEEN

TIT FOR TAT

Although no one could doubt their authenticity, there was still a mystery that surrounded the tapes. From the tapes it is plain that James Gilbey was talking on the mobile phone in his car. As he drove, the phone would automatically be passed from one mast to the next on the cellular network. As such, an amateur radio enthusiast tuning into the call would only catch part of the conversation as the phone jumped frequency between stations. It was quickly concluded that the recording was made using a bug in the landline at Diana's end, then rebroadcast on a fixed frequency in the hope that someone would pick it up.

But who could have done such a thing? Suspicion fell on the security forces – MI5, Special Branch, the Royal Security Squad or the government listening station in Cheltenham, GCHQ. Plainly, orders to tap the phone of possibly the future Queen of England would have to come from the highest authority. Diana's supporters suspected Charles. They said that he used the security forces to gather evidence he could use in a divorce, but had leaked the information to get his own back for Diana's collusion in *Diana: Her True Story*.

With the press on his tail, James Gilbey went into hiding. But Diana pressed home her advantage. She demanded an immediate divorce, a sizeable financial settlement, unfettered access to her sons, the retention of her royal titles and a court of her own.

The Palace fought back. They leaked stories that Charles and Diana had had a romantic reconciliation at the annual Ghillies' Ball at Balmoral. ITN aired an hour-long documentary assuring the world that divorce was off the agenda.

But Charles's faction could not sit still. They said that the Prince loathed Diana. Co-operating in *Diana: Her True Story*, he considered, had been an act of betrayal. He called her "Diana the Martyr" and said the Squidgygate tapes had given her a dose of her own medicine.

The Palace insisted that the couple made one last attempt to bluff it out. Together they made a state visit to South Korea. It was a glittering occasion with plenty of photo opportunities for the world's press. But it was plain from their body language that the royal couple detested each other.

With the two parties still clearly at each other's throats, something had to be done. It fell to the luckless Prime Minister John Major to make a statement to the House of Commons.

"It is announced from Buckingham Palace that, with regret, the Prince and Princess of Wales have decided to separate," he told the packed chamber. "Their Royal Highnesses have no plans to divorce and their constitutional positions are unaffected. Their decision has been reached amicably, and they will both continue to participate fully in the upbringing of their children. Their Royal Highnesses will continue to carry out full and separate programmes of public engagements and will, from time to time, attend family occasions and national events together. The Queen and the Duke of Edinburgh, though saddened, understand and sympathise with the difficulties that have led to this decision. Her Majesty and His Royal Highness particularly hope that the intrusion into the privacy of the Prince and

Princess may now cease. They believe that a degree of privacy and understanding is essential if their Royal Highnesses are to provide a happy and secure upbringing for their children, while continuing to give wholehearted commitment to their public duties."

It would prove to be an optimistic, if misguided, hope.

Mr Major added that the succession was unaffected and that when he became king, Charles would still become head of the Church of England. Some doubted that. Even senior churchmen shook their heads at Charles running around with a married woman and made it clear that, if he attempted to marry Camilla, they would press for the Church to be disestablished.

The *Sun* proclaimed that John Major's announcement was a "Victory for Di". But she felt that she had been outmanoeuvred by the Palace, who were seeking to sideline her. The game was far from over though.

That there should be one tape could be considered a misfortune, but that there were two smacked of carelessness. Yet two there were.

The second came to light in Australia. It purported to be a telephone conversation between Prince Charles and Camilla recorded on the night of 18 December 1989 – two weeks before the notorious Squidgygate tapes. Its authenticity has never been questioned because its content was so sensational.

A man, claiming to be a radio ham, sold them to at least one national newspaper, but they were thought to be too tawdry to publish. However, in January 1993, an Australian magazine called *New Ideas* got hold of a copy of the transcript and broke the story Down Under. Within minutes of publication, copies were being faxed around the world. Now there was no reason for Fleet Street to hold back.

The conversation is said to have taken place between Camilla, who was at her family home in Wiltshire, while Charles was lying on his bed with a mobile phone in the Cheshire country home of the Duke of Westminster, where he was a guest. The recording begins when the conversation is already in progress.

Charles: ... he was a bit anxious actually.

Camilla: Was he?

Charles: He thought he might have gone a bit far.

Camilla: Ah well.

Charles: Anyway you know, that's the sort of thing one has to be aware of and sort of feel one's way along with, if you know what I mean.

Camilla: Mmm. You're awfully good at feeling your way along.

Charles: Oh stop! I want to feel my way along you, all over you and up and down you and in and out...

Camilla: Oh.

Charles: Particularly in and out.

Camilla: Oh, that's just what I need at the moment.

Charles: Is it?

Camilla: I know it would revive me. I can't bear a Sunday night without you.

Charles: Oh God.

Camilla: It's like that programme *Start the Week*. I can't start the week without you.

Charles: I fill up your tank.

Camilla: Yes, you do.

Charles: Then you can cope.

Camilla: Then I'm all right.

Charles: What about me? The trouble is I need you several times a week.

Camilla: Mmmm, so do I. I need you all the week. All the time.

Charles: Oh, God. I'll just live inside your trousers, or something. It would be much easier!

Camilla: [*Laughing*] What are you going to turn into, a pair of *knickers*? [*Both laugh*] Oh, You're you're going to come back as a pair of knickers!

Charles: Or, God forbid, a Tampax. Just my luck. [*He laughs*]

Camilla: You're a complete idiot. [*She laughs*] Oh, what a wonderful idea.

Charles: My luck to be chucked down a lavatory and go on and on forever swirling around the top, never going down…

Camilla: Oh, darling.

Charles: … until the next one comes through.

Camilla: Oh, perhaps you could come back as a box.

Charles: What sort of box?

Camilla: A box of Tampax so you could just keep going.

Charles: That's true.

Camilla: Repeating yourself. [*She laughs*] Oh, darling. Oh, I just want you now.

Charles: Do you?

Camilla: Mmm.

Charles: So do I.

Camilla: Desperately, desperately, desperately. I thought of you so much at Yaraby.

Charles: Did you?

Camilla: Simply mean that we couldn't be there together.

Charles: Desperate. If you could be here – I long to ask Nancy sometimes.

Camilla: Why don't you?

Charles: I daren't.

Camilla: Because I think she's so in love with you.

Charles: Mmm.

And on it goes with Charles's usual reticence – even at moments of passion. He tells her that he loves her twice; she tells him eleven times.

He calls her "darling" seven times; she calls him "darling" eighteen times. Her husband is referred to simply as "A" or him. At one point, she says: "He won't be here Thursday, pray God."

The assignation arranged, she begs him to get some sleep and to call her in the morning. Then they say goodnight to each other no fewer than nineteen times. The final flurry goes like this:

Camilla: … night, night.

Charles: Night, darling, God bless.

Camilla: I do love you and I am so proud of you.

Charles: Oh, I am so proud of you.

Camilla: Don't be silly, I've never achieved anything.

Charles: Yes, you have.

Camilla: No, I haven't.

Charles: Your great achievement is to love me.

Camilla: Oh, darling. Easier than falling off a chair.

Charles: You suffer all these indignities and tortures and calumnies.

Camilla: Oh, darling, don't be so silly. I'd suffer anything for you. That's love. It's the strength of love. Night, night.

Charles: Night, darling. Sounds as though you're dragging an enormous piece of string behind you, with hundreds of tin pots and cans attached to it. I think it must be your telephone. Night, night, before the battery goes. [*He blows a kiss*] Night.

Camilla: Love you.

Charles: Don't want to say goodbye.

Camilla: Neither do I, but you must get some sleep. Bye.

Charles: Bye, darling.

Camilla: Love you.

Charles: Bye.

Camilla: Hopefully talk to you in the morning.

Charles: Please.

Camilla: Bye. I do love you.

Charles: Night.

Camilla: Night.

Charles: Night.

Camilla: Love you forever.

Charles: Night.

Camilla: Goodbye. Bye, my darling.

Charles: Night.

Camilla: Night, night.

Charles: Night.

Camilla: Bye, bye.

Charles: Going.

Camilla: Bye.

Charles: Going.

Camilla: Gone.

Charles: Night.

Camilla: Bye. Press the button.

Charles: Going to press the tit.

Camilla: All right, darling. I wish you were pressing mine.

Charles: God, I wish I was. Harder and harder.

Camilla: Oh, darling.

Charles: Night.

Charles: Love you [*She yawns*]

Camilla: Love you. Press the tit.

Charles: Adore you. Night.

Camilla: Night.

Camilla: Night [*She blows a kiss*]

Charles: Night.

Camilla: Goodnight, my darling. Love you…

Finally Charles hung up – no doubt, to the great relief of the reader.

Not only were people shocked by the "Tampax exchange", they realised that they could not figure out Prince Charles at all. Here was a man who was married to one of the most beautiful women in the world, but who was obviously besotted by a woman who was a trifle more homely. She was a little older than Charles and a good thirteen years older than his glamorous young wife.

If Charles had been cut in the mould of his great-great-grandfather Bertie, the public would have forgiven him for fooling around. If he had been seen out on the town with a supermodel on each arm, he would have got away with it. He could even have been a Randy Andy. But the public could not understand how he could cast aside a great beauty like Diana for the, frankly, homely Camilla.

The sad truth was that Charles was no playboy prince, no dashing ladies' man with a heart of gold. He was, like his mother, deeply middle class. He was a one-woman man. And, unfortunately, that one woman was not Diana.

Again there were concerns about where the Tampax tape had come from. The author and former MI6 officer James Rusbridger pointed the finger at GCHQ. A year later he was found hanged in bizarre circumstances in his West Country home, but it would be best not to stray too far into the territory of conspiracy theorists.

Next out of the woodwork was James Hewitt. In 1994, a "novelised" version of the torrid love affair between Hewitt and Diana called *Princess in Love* was published by Anna Pasternak, a distant relative of the author of *Dr Zhivago* and former girlfriend of Hewitt.

Open warfare between Charles and Di continued on TV when, in an interview with Jonathan Dimbleby, Charles admitted to having an affair with Camilla Parker Bowles. This was after his marriage had already irretrievably broken down. His response to

Diana: Her True Story was an authorised biography, also provided by Jonathan Dimbleby.

Diana then appeared on *Panorama*, where she admitted to committing adultery with James Hewitt and confirmed the accuracy of the Squidgygate tapes with James Gilbey. Her justification was that there were "three in our marriage, so it was a bit crowded" – referring to Camilla Parker Bowles. Nevertheless, she begged to be the country's "Queen of Hearts". She said she wanted to be a British goodwill ambassador to the world – despite the fact that, as consort to the heir to the throne, by admitting adultery, she was also technically admitting treason under the Treason Act of 1351. No one from Scotland Yard was sent to investigate.

In what was seen as a low blow, she questioned whether Charles would ever succeed as king.

"I would think that the top job, as I call it, would bring enormous limitations to him and I don't know whether he could adapt to that," she said.

"Would it be your wish that when Prince William comes of age that he were to succeed the Queen rather than the current Prince of Wales?" she was asked.

"My wish is that my husband finds peace of mind, and from that follows other things… yes," she replied.

The battle of the documentaries was a draw, or perhaps a Pyrrhic victory to Diana. Both parties limped from the battlefield, licking their self-inflicted wounds.

Diana then threw herself into a charm offensive. She was seen very publicly doing good works. There were plenty of photo opportunities showing her with sick children. And, in front of the world's TV cameras, she began a campaign against landmines. This blew Charles off the front pages completely.

Diana then won a £15 million divorce settlement, but was forced to drop the title "HRH" in the process. Even a much-publicised affair with England rugby captain Will Carling, which lost him his wife, failed to dent her popularity.

Then she shot herself in the foot. She began a serious affair with Dodi Fayed, son of Harrods' boss Mohamed Fayed. This was a dangerous move. Mohamed Fayed's business methods had long been a source of criticism and he had been refused a British passport. Although Dodi Fayed himself listed his profession as "movie producer", he was better known for his activities on the casting couch than those behind the lens. The newspapers referred to him as a "millionaire playboy".

Dodi wooed Diana on his yacht on the Côte d'Azur. Their love blossomed in front of the telephoto lenses of the paparazzi, for the delectation of tabloid readers worldwide. Meanwhile, Charles seized the opportunity to walk out the freshly divorced Camilla, laying on her fiftieth birthday bash. It seemed the scandal would never end. But end it did, and tragically.

Mohamed Fayed revelled in the publicity his son's royal affair afforded him. He had bought the house in Paris where the last British royals to be ousted by scandal, Edward and Mrs Simpson, had spent their exile. It was rumoured that this was where his son and the exiled Princess of Wales would set up home too.

But it was not to be. On the night of 30 August 1997, Dodi and Diana enjoyed a romantic dinner at the Ritz Hotel in Paris where he proposed – though a Hollywood starlet was quick to say that Dodi was already engaged to her and produced a rock to prove it. The couple left the Ritz late that evening apparently on their way to view their putative matrimonial home. On the way, the car they were being driven in crashed into a pillar in an underpass, killing them both.

Criticism of Diana ended that moment. Fears that the mother of the heir to the throne – and hence a future head of the Church of England – might marry a Muslim were put aside. No further mention was made of the fact that Di's marriage to Dodi Fayed could have been opposed by the establishment simply because of the colour of his skin. But the idea that the powers that be were so against the match that they had the happy couple bumped off has spawned a lively new playground for ever-active conspiracy theorists.

The press, perhaps feeling guilty over their own role in the hounding of Di, now shot the line that the fairy-tale princess had died in the arms of her handsome young "sheikh". When the Royal Family maintained their usual regal decorum, they were pilloried for being cold, old-fashioned and out of touch. This was nothing the cold, old-fashioned and out-of-touch Charles could do anything about. Step in fresh young modernising Prime Minister Tony Blair, dubbing her "the People's Princess".

The tabloid-reading public blamed the paparazzi for hounding Di to her death. Echoing public sentiment, the press were vilified from the pulpit by Diana's brother, the adulterous Earl Spencer, whose own messy divorce was already attracting the newspapers' scrutiny.

Slowly, Prince Charles turned the situation to his advantage. With Diana dead, Charles now had no rival on the global stage. He was now keeper of the flame – and the royal children. Even when Camilla emerged as stepmother in waiting, no one said a thing. Everything was going swimmingly.

But then, in an ill-judged move, biographer and journalist Polly Toynbee did an Andrew Morton and published *The Prince's Story*. The book told the story of the royal marriage from the Prince's side, seemingly with the collusion of, if not Charles himself, certainly those in his camp. When it came to the key issue – adultery – his defence was simply "she did it first". It was tit for tat. Suddenly, the longest running royal scandal of the twentieth century showed that, even though its central, most glittering character had been written out, the show could still go on.

CHAPTER SEVENTEEN
TOPS TO TOES

After service in the Falklands War, Randy Andy continued hitting the headlines with his scandalous sex life. At twenty-three he had a brief fling with topless model Vicki Hodge when his ship, HMS *Invincible*, docked in Barbados where she had a holiday home. She tried to put reporters off the scent by having him pose with her friend Tracy Lamb. In the end, she took £40,000 from the *News of the World* for explicit details of their romps on a beach holiday they had enjoyed, including details of making "love among the scented flowers". The story was accompanied by a photograph of Andrew standing naked in the surf, waving his swimming trunks over his head.

Vicki said she had discovered why his previous affairs had been so brief. He finished far too quickly. She took him in hand to slow things down, telling him to distract himself by counting – later complaining that he put her off by counting aloud. Nevertheless, she claimed to have converted Randy Andy from a sprinter to a marathon runner.

His affair with Katie Rabett, a dancer with the group Hot Gossip, hit the front pages in 1984; she caught Andrew's eye when they bumped into each other leaving a London gallery. During their fling, she hosted his twenty-fourth birthday party and was reportedly introduced to the Queen, who indicated her approval. The relationship foundered when nude pictures of her appeared in the tabloids. She went on to become a Bond girl in *The Living Daylights*.

But the real headline-grabber was his relationship with American soft porn starlet, now photographer, Koo Stark. They had met at Tramp before the Falklands War. Andrew and his boisterous friends had been making a racket on the dance floor when she came over and asked them to turn the volume down.

"Stop being so boring," said Andrew. "We're having a great time; come and join us."

She did. They fell into conversation, danced and Andrew bought a bottle of champagne. It was the beginning of what was thought to have been his first real love affair, with him visiting her regularly in her basement flat in Chester Square.

Before he went to the Falklands, they managed to keep their relationship secret, agreeing not even to tell their parents. When Koo's father, Hollywood producer Wilbur Stark, flew over to London while Andrew was away, she told him: "Daddy, I'm going out with a really nice guy. He's very special to me." But she did not tell him his name.

Andrew wrote to her while he was in the South Atlantic. She sent pictures – one in a black T-shirt with the words "Weird Fantasy" on the front. Another in a skintight outfit. He was also writing to Carolyn Seaward at the time.

Naturally, when they found out, the newspapers made a great play of Koo's film career, which began in 1976 with *The Awaking of Emily* where she masturbates on camera.

"I felt very vulnerable," she said. "The masturbation scene was very difficult because in my personal experience it has never done anything for me. Emily was supposed to be seventeen, had not made love to any man before and what she was doing was just giving herself innocent pleasure. It was not the sort of masturbation where she was imagining a man making love."

Then there was the lesbian shower scene with actress Ina Skriver.

"We were not given any direction at all," said Koo. "But by the time we came to shoot, it was running very late and people were arriving on the set at Shepperton for the end of picture party. I looked around and suddenly thought: 'Hell, I'm naked and in front of all these people too.' I got them cleared off immediately. These people were staring and making me feel terrible. By this time, tension was really high. Ina got into the shower and gave me a really hard back massage. When I was kissing her body, I had to close my eyes because of the water and I could only tell where I was by touching her breast or around her waist. It was only afterwards that the strain hit me mentally. I felt so drained I could hardly stand."

Next came *Cruel Passions*, based on the stories of the Marquis de Sade. In it, Koo played Justine, who wants to remain innocent and virginal. But when she refuses to pleasure some nuns she is thrown out of her orphanage and falls into a life of debauchery, torture, whipping, sadism and slavery. Sodomised by Lord Carlisle, she is savaged by dogs and raped by two grave robbers.

She also appeared on late-night TV in *The Blue Film*, which also featured explicit scenes.

"I was with an actor who had what I would call a physical reaction to my body," she said. "He and I were chatting for about fifteen minutes lying a couple of feet apart in bed waiting for all the lighting men to get things together to shoot the scene. As soon as our bodies touched I thought, 'Oh dear,' and got out of bed right away. The director gave him a couple of minutes to cool off. He was very embarrassed."

Her career as an actress was seen to taint her relationship with Andrew, but in the 1970s there was a glut of soft porn films. Performing in them was seen as a break in the acting profession.

"I never wanted to do an erotic film," she said, "but it's all about what's being produced."

She did not feel comfortable in the studio.

"I hate jokes about nudity on set," she said. "Some technicians try it on and make cracks, attempting to be ultra-casual. That I can't stand, nor that sort of man either. In fact, I hate men who are crude about sex. It is a subject which should be treated with sensitivity and love."

Nor did she think she was right for those kinds of parts.

"I feel very insecure at times," she said. "I hate my bottom. It looks so fat and I have a thing about it."

It was not known whether Andrew saw any of these films. While she began her career playing a seventeen-year-old sex kitten, Koo Stark was two years older than Andrew and infinitely more sophisticated. Their affair brought headlines and approbation. It says much for both his loyalty and the intensity of their relationship that he did not quietly drop her.

In 1982, Andrew invited Koo to Balmoral where she appeared in an extremely short gold rah-rah skirt. According to royal biographer Lady Colin Campbell, the Queen was "much taken with the elegant, intelligent and discreet Koo".

She was also invited to Sandringham and gained the approval of the Queen Mother who was impressed by her demure behaviour and obvious affection for Andrew. She gave him the companionship he craved and soothed the sensitive side of his nature.

Princess Margaret lent them her holiday home, Les Jolies Eaux, on the Caribbean island of Mustique. Prince Philip advised him against the trip, as it would only bring him bad press. His fatherly advice was ignored.

Before the holiday, they went to see *The Pirates of Penzance* in Drury Lane with a handful of friends to provide a distraction. This led some in the press to think that he was dating Kim Deas again.

Andrew and Koo checked in for the flight to Antigua as Mr and Mrs Cambridge. By chance, *Daily Express* photographer Steve Wood was also on the flight. He was having a Caribbean holiday with his girlfriend Katie Hobbs. Andrew's bodyguard approached Wood and told him not to take any pictures. Wood had no idea that Andrew was on board and assumed that the royal passenger was Princess Margaret. Andrew then disappeared on to the flight deck while Koo hid under an airline blanket. However, Katie had spotted them together when they disembarked.

While Andrew was sunning himself on Mustique with Koo, the story broke around the world. A reporter tracked down Koo's Spanish-born cleaning lady in London.

"I saw the *principe* leave two or three times at about nine in the morning," she said. "He always looked rather tired." She must have been keeping him up late.

The paparazzi soon arrived in force. They hired boats to get out to the island, but its wealthy inhabitants, who were used to having celebrities such as Mick Jagger and Raquel Welch to stay, closed ranks. However, local girls told reporters: "We're all jealous of Koo… He's a lot better looking than Prince Charles." And the local steel band composed the Randy Andy Mambo in his honour.

To thwart the media, the phone lines to the outside world were cut and the island's three taxis were banned from carrying journalists. So the paparazzi had to pursue Andrew and Koo on foot while they rode around in a Land Rover.

Two photographers were caught in the grounds of Princess Margaret's villa and were locked up in the island's only cell. It was a bare room next to the local church where they were entertained by a temperance sect singing gospel songs and served lobster provided by generous colleagues. Leaving the island, the Prince then evaded the press by commandeering a plane hired by a photographer from the *Daily Star*, while Koo took an early morning flight to St Lucia, then flew to Miami where she went into hiding.

Despite the intense interest of the media, Andrew and Koo managed to spend a weekend together at Floors Castle in Scotland. She also visited his rooms in Buckingham Palace. But rumours that she would spend New Year's Eve with him at Sandringham proved baseless. Instead, she went skiing in St Moritz.

Though her background was far from royal, Koo was popular with the public. While shopping for the skiing trip, she was approached by a young housewife who said: "Marry Andrew and to hell with the consequences." Koo replied that she was in love with Andrew and Andrew loved her. But the marriage was not to be. Courtiers at the Palace deemed the relationship inappropriate and they broke up in 1983. She was reportedly offered £1 million to tell all about her romance with Andrew, but turned it down.

Things began to go seriously south for Andrew in the following years. He dropped in on his ex, Sandi Jones, while on an official visit to California, during which he sprayed a group of journalists with paint during a press stop in Los Angeles and compounded the offence by refusing to apologise. His behaviour was judged so bad that he was dubbed the Duke of Yob by the British media. The American press called it "the most unpleasant royal visit since they burned the White House in 1812". In one fell swoop, he showed his disregard for public opinion as well as a dismissive attitude to those who tried to advise him. The incident also invoked fury from his parents.

"Andrew's romantic escapades, together with some much-publicised midshipman japes (he has a penchant for practical jokes), earned him the reputation of Royal Lout-About-Town, a label that saddened his mother and annoyed his father," reported journalist Sue Arnold in *Vanity Fair*.

However, it was also said that secretly Prince Philip admired Andrew's macho action-man image. Apparently, it reminded Philip of his younger self.

The Palace were more sanguine with Sarah Ferguson – aka Fergie – the former live-in lover of racing driver Paddy McNally and daughter of Prince Charles's polo manager Major Ron Ferguson. She and Andrew had known each other as children. However, they met again in 1985 at a party held at Windsor Castle, during Royal Ascot week, a race meeting held nearby. He was then twenty-five; she was twenty-six. Within a week, they had become romantically attached. It seems that Princess Diana had played matchmaker.

Andrew invited Sarah to Sandringham, the first girlfriend he had taken there since he had broken up with Koo Stark. Like Charles and Camilla, his relationship with Fergie was once again hampered by his duties in the Royal Navy. But in February 1986, he was on shore leave and they were staying at Floors Castle in Scotland when he dropped to his knees and said: "Miss Ferguson, will you marry me?"

"Certainly, sir, I will," she replied, adding: "If you wake up and change your mind in the morning, I'll quite understand."

Princess Diana helped Fergie create a wardrobe for her new role as royal fiancée. They also tried to gatecrash Andrew's stag night at Aubrey House in Holland Park with comedienne Pamela Stephenson dressed as policewomen, but were foiled by the pressmen waiting outside. Inside Elton John sang, Billy Connolly told jokes and four young ladies provided "bachelor entertainment".

The couple married in Westminster Abbey on 23 July 1986. It was not St Paul's and Fergie was not Diana – now acknowledged as one of the most beautiful women in the world. It seemed that Andrew had come second in the marriage stakes. Or perhaps not. Diana confided to biographer Andrew Morton that Charles had told her: "Why can't you be more like Fergie?"

Their marriage was passionate at first and their very public displays of affection sometimes embarrassed friends. On one occasion, the Prince even interrupted a naval exercise so that he could spend two hours with her in a cabin on a support ship. This was not a privilege extended to other seamen. The excuse – seasickness.

Fergie exacerbated the juvenile side of his nature. This was amply demonstrated at *It's A Royal Knockout*, a TV charity event organised by Prince Edward in 1987. It followed the format of *It's a Knockout* (the British version of *Jeux sans frontières*), a slapstick TV game show and featured as its contestants the stars of showbiz and members of the Royal Family. Charles and Diana stayed well away.

The tone was set at the dinner the night before filming. Food was thrown around and Andrew ended up with the contents of a bowl of sugar in his hair – courtesy of his wife. During the filming Andrew and Fergie threw fruit at each other, hardly a spectacle to burnish the dignity of the Crown.

Things turned sour when Andrew tried to push the singer Meat Loaf in a moat after Fergie had taken a shine to him.

"Fergie wasn't exactly flirting with me, but she was paying attention to me, and I think Andrew got a little – I could be wrong, I'm just reading into this – I think he got a little jealous," Meat Loaf said. "Anyway, he tried to push me in the water. He tried to push me in the moat. So I turned around and I grabbed him and he goes, 'You can't touch me. I'm royal.' I said, 'Well, you try to push me in the moat, Jack, I don't give a shit who you are; you're goin' in the moat.'"

The *Sun* branded the programme "excruciating", saying it was the "lowest day" in the history of the Royal Family.

Fergie had always deferred to Andrew in domestic and official decisions, but when they decided to leave Princess Beatrice behind when they toured Australia, she took the blame. She did so again when they allowed *Hello!* magazine to print pages of their tawdry family photographs, though he had made the decision.

Their holiday to Mauritius was spoiled as he doggedly refused to leave their guest bungalow because photographers were outside. Instead, they spent their time behind closed curtains watching videos. He insisted on drinking mineral water during an official wine-tasting tour to Bordeaux and beamed with pride when he discovered a technical error in the Nikon camera manual.

In their early days, Sarah would tease him mercilessly when he became too wrapped up in Navy jargon at dinner parties. There were complaints that he took the best efforts of Fergie's friends too much for granted. One recalled: "After all, he is a Prince and one is understandably nervous and apprehensive when they come to stay. One does one's best to make sure everything is perfect. But he never seemed to notice."

Nor was he a great socialiser. At a party hosted by Fergie's mother, he sat sulking at his table because there was no one in the company he knew and guests kept talking across him.

"He clearly felt ignored," one friend recalled. "Then Fergie came up, kissed him loudly on the ear, ran her hands over his dress shirt and said: 'Cheer up, Andrew,' and took him for a dance."

Though some women found him charming, he had already developed that callous disregard for the sensitivities of others that he would display later. On one of his first official duties – a 1988 visit to Lockerbie, where eleven people had died on the ground when Pan Am Flight 103 crashed on the town – he told the grieving locals that the disaster had been "much worse" for the Americans who'd been on the plane and said that it had "only been a matter of time" before an aircraft fell out of the sky.

He was no better with his staff. Royal bodyguard Ken Wharfe said he was once moved from a window seat on a plane from Balmoral because he was obstructing Andrew's view. "His manners," Wharfe said, "are just awful."

An aide said: "I've seen him treat his staff in a shocking, appalling way. He's been incredibly rude to his personal protection officers, literally throwing things on the ground and demanding they 'fucking pick them up'. No social graces at all. Sure, if you're a lady with blonde hair and big boobs, then I bet he is utterly charming."

During their marriage, the old disco-dancing Randy Andy was forgotten and he became a carpet slippers and cocoa man. Stolid, dependable, but uninspiring. He was a man with little ambition or drive but prickly about his status. As a royal he required careful and diplomatic handling. While he craved a cosy domestic life, he was always more comfortable around things than people. His photographs are empty of people and his passion in life was for golf, a hobby he put before all else.

He preferred a round of golf to a day with his children, a spot of putting practice on the drawing room carpet at their home, Sunninghill Park, to a conversation with his wife. They began their married life with him wedded to the Navy. It ended with Fergie a golf widow.

Fergie rapidly grew tired of Andrew. In the Navy, he was always away on duty. In 1990, she complained that they had only spent forty-two nights together during their four years of marriage. Meanwhile, she put on weight, causing the press to dub her the Duchess of Pork. She later capitalised on this by becoming the US spokesman for WeightWatchers International. The *Daily Mail* commented: "She gives the impression of a council estate girl in the typing pool who's married the boss's son and is exploiting it for all she can get."

Bored, Fergie began gallivanting round London clubs with the newly liberated Princess Di and jetting off on endless holidays at the taxpayers' expense. She also shredded all Prince Andrew's love letters on the pretext that they might be stolen. She was criticised for having too many holidays and accepting too many free gifts, earning her the nickname "Freeloading Fergie". In response, she complained that her allowance was too paltry to cover first-class air travel. She demanded payment for interviews and asked designers to give her frocks for free. Furthermore, she only made 108 official engagements in 1991, compared to Princess Anne's 768.

In the meantime, Fergie's dad Major Ron had found himself the subject of some embarrassing photographs taken at the Wigmore Club, a London massage parlour where sexual services were also provided. These snapshots heralded a veritable deluge of incriminating pictures, which were to haunt the Royal Family throughout the coming year.

In January 1992, 120 photographs were found by a cleaner in the London flat of Texan playboy Steve Wyatt. They showed the American and Fergie on holiday together, sunning themselves by the pool. She had also introduced him to the Iraqi oil minister at a Buckingham Palace reception, furthering his business interests.

Although the pictures seemed innocent enough, there was something in the complex relationship between Andrew, Fergie and Wyatt that led the Prince to ask for a divorce and to turn for succour to his former lover Koo Stark. Another old flame, thirty-eight-year-old divorcée Jane Roxburghe also provided a shoulder for him to cry on.

The Queen ordered Fergie to stop seeing Wyatt, but the newspapers reported that she secretly visited his flat on at least two more occasions. The announcement that the Yorks had separated was made on 19 March 1992.

To escape from the growing scandal, Fergie headed to Florida where she stayed with a notorious womaniser, sixty-six-year-old Robert Forman, who prided himself on his boast of going out with girls young enough to be his granddaughters.

Then she went for a holiday in the Far East with her financial adviser Johnny Bryan, who was later dispatched back to Britain to find out what sort of divorce settlement the duchess could expect. Unless a satisfactory figure could be arrived at, there was always the threat that the Duchess of York might publish her memoirs, which, at a conservative estimate, could be worth £4 million.

It was at this sensitive juncture that details of Major Ron's affair with a glamorous thirty-three-year-old horsewoman, Lesley Player, were serialised in the Sunday papers. To put the icing on the cake, Fergie was photographed topless in the south of France, with her children and two male bodyguards looking on. And who should be with her, kissing, cuddling, tucking her hair behind her ears, rubbing suntan lotion into her naked back and sucking her toes, but the same financial adviser who was negotiating her settlement, Johnny Bryan. The divorce was finalised in 1996.

Both Charles's and Andrew's marriages had ended in failure. But there was one key difference. When Charles split from Diana, he was seen as the villain. When Andrew and Fergie divorced, she was to blame and Andrew survived unscathed. How things would change.

CHAPTER EIGHTEEN
PALACE COUP

While Charles had quit the Navy after five years, Andrew stuck it out for twenty-two. His career was undistinguished, though he rose steadily through the ranks, making Commander in 1999.

Andrew ended his naval career in 2001 with a spell working in the Ministry of Defence as a staff officer in the Directorate of Naval Operations. He was not a bundle of interfering energy like his brother, but he told the MoD's in-house journal *Focus* that the work there had proved a strain.

"It got a little bit wearing at times," he said. "It became very evident in the summer of last year that I was doing too much. I was feeling tired. No, no, no, it was just doing little things, you're not always on peak performance. But that's the way the cookie crumbles and you just get on with it."

Then he came off the active list, but still managed to get promoted. Three years later Commander York was made an honorary captain. On his fiftieth birthday in 2010, he was promoted to rear admiral and made a vice admiral five years later. But still, he needed a job.

Honours kept coming in too. To mark the death of the Queen Mother in 2002, it was suggested that Prince Philip be elevated to become a knight of the Royal Victorian Order. Philip rejected the offer saying it was "an order for servants". However, in 2003, Prince Andrew was made a Knight Commander of the Royal Victorian Order. Then, in a private ceremony at Buckingham Palace in 2011, the Queen invested Andrew as a Knight of the Grand Cross of the Royal Victorian Order, the highest rank of the order, to add to his glittering array of honours and medals, before the two of them settled down for tea.

He has since been stripped of his honours and military titles, though the Palace confirmed that he retains the service rank of vice admiral which, given the circumstances of his fall from grace, is not altogether inappropriate. But at the time, he had higher accolades in his sights.

Andrew also retained his wings. Charles gave up flying following his crash in the Hebrides in 1994 where a Queen's Flight passenger jet was damaged to the tune of £1 million. The Prince was at the controls of the BAe 146 when it landed awkwardly and too fast in high winds on the Isle of Islay, causing a tyre to burst and another to deflate. The plane slewed off the runway at Port Ellen and came to a halt with its nose buried in mud. Six crew and five passengers were on board but no one was injured.

Prince Charles was not blamed because, despite holding the rank of group captain, he was regarded as a passenger who was invited to fly the aircraft. The RAF board of inquiry can only pass judgement on the crew and the aircraft's captain was found to have been negligent by allowing Charles to take the controls.

The following Christmas, Prince Charles was also diving in the public opinion polls because of his continuing association with Camilla Parker Bowles and he began to suspect that Diana and Fergie were plotting against him, aided and abetted by Andrew and Edward. After the *Panorama* interview where Diana said that she did not think Charles would be king, he convinced himself that they had plans to replace him as heir and to announce that, on the Queen's death or abdication, Prince Andrew would be regent until William came of age.

"Andrew wanted to be me," Charles told his private secretary Mark Bolland. "I should have let him work with me. Now he's unhelpful."

The idea of a regency had first been posited two years earlier by Anthony Holden, two-time biographer of Prince Charles. In *The Tarnished Crown*, he predicted that the heir to the throne would never be king; that a constitutional arrangement would be made to remove him.

"Charles would earn warm public respect for assenting to the Privy Council decision that his brother Andrew (not, as rumoured, his sister Anne) will serve as Regent," he wrote in 1993.

Besides, William was arguably more fitted to be king.

"Diana brought to the Windsor line the only royal blood it lacked, that of the Stuarts," said Holden. "Her son, Prince William, is thus the first potential monarch in British history to be descended from every British king and queen who had issue."

Charles had ruled himself out, Holden said: "The would-be Defender of the Faith has broken at least two of the Ten Commandments," and might normally be expelled from the military for violating Rule D, "adultery with a spouse of a serving member of the armed forces".

Holden pointed out that Camilla was a Catholic, so if Charles married her he would be precluded from the throne by the Act of Settlement. That was conveniently ignored when they married in 2005. The law has since been amended.

William was eleven in 1993 and, Holden said, "could become king on his eighteenth birthday. The Queen is unlikely to go under a bus before then – I'm not sure she knows what a bus is – but if she did, Andrew would be Regent until William took over."

As the monarchy plunged deeper into the mire, this scenario became popular in the newspapers. In his book *Fergie: Her Secret Life*, Dr Allan Starkie, a business partner of her ex-lover John Bryan, said Fergie delayed her divorce in the hope that Prince Charles would be barred from taking the throne – making Prince Andrew a ruling regent supervising Prince William. She fancied herself quasi-queen, if only for a year or two.

In *Shadows of a Princess*, written by Diana's former private secretary, Patrick Jephson, revealed Diana's "belief that her husband would not succeed to the throne – either through death or disinclination – and that his place would be taken by the Duke of York as Regent". This plainly held some attraction for Andrew's sister-in-law: "She seldom lost an opportunity to extol the Duke's kingly qualities – and, it has to be said, the fine figure he cut, especially in tropical uniform. 'In those white shorts, he's really rather dishy…'"

The publication of the book caused a sensation when Jephson told journalists that he had not included Diana's descriptions of Charles's unusual sexual life. It attracted lurid headlines nonetheless.

At the inquest into Diana's death in 2008, the court was told that, at a secret meeting with Lord Mishcon and members of his legal firm at Kensington Palace in 1996, Diana had said Charles should move aside in favour of William, with Andrew acting as regent. Divorce lawyer Maggie Rae, a former partner at Mishcon de Reya, told the hearing that Diana had said this "several times".

Rae had also arranged a secret meeting for Diana with Tony Blair, then Leader of the Opposition. Over dinner at Rae's house, Diana again said that Charles should not be king.

The firm's head of family law, Sandra Davis, who was also present at the Kensington Palace meeting, told the court that Diana was convinced her prediction that Charles would be forced to stand aside would come true. In that event, she said, the Duke of York would act as regent until Prince William was old enough to take the throne. She too recalled Diana saying this "on a number of occasions".

Lord Mishcon had died since the meeting twelve years before the inquest, but he had recorded details of the conversation in the so-called Mishcon Note, which was later handed to police.

The note, which was read in court, said: "HRH [Diana] said in her view the happiest outcome for the future of the monarchy was for the Prince of Wales to abdicate in favour of Prince William and that without any malice whatsoever she wished to put that view forward in the interests of the Royal Family and everyone."

There were other dangers. In the run-up to the signing of the 2011 Perth Agreement, which ended the preference of men over women in the succession and the discrimination against Catholics, *The Times* sounded the alarm bell: "As things stand, should Princes William and Harry die childless, King Charles III would be succeeded by King Andrew. The Duke of York has lately had to stand down as special representative for trade and investment in unhappy circumstances and may not be everybody's first choice for King."

There was even a brief scare by an ITV documentary in 2020, that the rest of the Royal Family would be decimated by Covid, leaving Andrew to be regent or king. No matter what, he was always in the picture.

Confirmation that there had been a plot to remove Charles and make Andrew regent came in Angela Levin's book *Camilla*. In it, she quoted a "senior insider" saying that Andrew tried to persuade the Queen to block Charles marrying Camilla "by being quite poisonous, mean, unhelpful and very nasty about Camilla".

She was not aristocratic enough. Nor could she be trusted.

"The same individual went on to say that 'when Diana was alive, through her friendship with Andrew's wife Sarah, she plotted with Andrew to try to push Prince Charles aside so Prince Andrew could become Regent to Prince William, who was then a teenager.'"

According to the insider, these "were dark and strange times, where paranoia became reality, and this was a worry. Andrew lobbied very hard with the hope that Charles would not become king when his mother died... His behaviour was very, very negative and extremely unpleasant to the Queen, who disagreed. I was told it was one of the rare occasions he didn't get his way. Nonetheless, he was apparently very angry he couldn't rule the country in some way."

Though he had failed in his bid to become regent, Andrew remained so hostile to Camilla that it was thought he would never be forgiven.

In an attempt to keep the peace in the family, the Queen had set up the Way Ahead Group – comprising herself, Prince Philip, Prince Charles, Prince Andrew, Prince Edward, Princess Anne, The Lord Chamberlain, and the Private Secretaries of The Queen, Prince Philip and Prince Charles – to plan the future of the monarchy. Charles used this as a forum to advocate a slimmed down monarchy which would exclude those he considered "minor royals". Andrew saw this as an attack on him.

But while Charles tried to pull rank, this cut no ice with his mother and father, who always favoured Andrew. Instead, he would have to proceed by stealth. To strike back, Charles tried to remove Andrew's daughters Beatrice and Eugenie from the royal payroll. But Andrew made efforts to keep his daughters close to the Queen to ensure their future as fully paid-up members of the family. He also wanted Beatrice and Eugenie to retain the rank of working royals and to have round-the-clock security.

Andrew complained to senior personnel how he and other minor members of the Royal Family were being pushed aside. He thought it was an insult that his daughters were discouraged from carrying out royal duties even though they were the only two "blood princesses" of their generation.

In May 2011, he was again outraged when Scotland Yard had informed him that his two daughters, Princesses Beatrice and Eugenie, the fifth and sixth in line to the throne at the time, were to be stripped of their twenty-four-hour police protection. Andrew had fought ferociously to keep his girls' security detail, despite the huge cost to the taxpayer. His rationale was that with the HRH title before their names they should be treated accordingly.

A Scotland Yard cost review looking to prune the £50 million annual security bill for the Royal Family found no clear reason why the government should pay £250,000 a year apiece for two full-time bodyguards to protect twenty-one-year-old Eugenie in her first year at Newcastle University, or for her twenty-three-year-old sister Beatrice, who was studying in London. The Queen had already made it clear that her two granddaughters, whom she was very fond of, should expect to get jobs after they left university rather than be supported as working royals.

Andrew lobbied to reverse that decision. He wanted Beatrice and Eugenie to be designated as working royals to shore up his position. At a dinner in June after the annual Hillsborough Castle garden party in Northern Ireland, Andrew had a private drink with Tory MP Hugo Swire and asked him to have a word with Prime Minister David Cameron about the decision. He said he was concerned that, in the age of Twitter, Facebook and instant messaging, an antagonistic force could be mobilised against his daughters in a matter of minutes.

The problem was those same internet platforms often showed the two sociable young princesses tottering out of expensive London nightclubs in the early hours with protection officers in tow. An official SUV would be waiting outside to ferry them back home, not so much to forestall an attack, but as a glorified taxi service.

The following year, Andrew had further reason to feel snubbed. In the Diamond Jubilee river pageant, he had been assigned to number two barge. Shortly before he boarded, he learned that he and his daughters were to be cut out of the official photo on the balcony of Buckingham Palace. Nor were they on the list for the lunch for seven hundred dignitaries at Westminster Hall. This was clearly a demotion.

It was doubly galling for Andrew, who not only heard this news from staff just before the event, but also would have had to continue with them knowing that the arrangements would have been run by his mother, who was usually on his side. Another guest on the follow-up barge that heard him whingeing noisily about it was Sophie Wessex, whose invitation to the lunch also got lost in the post.

Buckingham Palace balcony shots were started by Queen Victoria in 1851, when she waved to the public during celebrations for the opening of the Great Exhibition just up the road in Hyde Park. They gradually became a fixture and the pictures became a staple in the national photo album. Annually, the balcony shot took place after the Trooping the Colour, which celebrated the Queen's official birthday in June, a practice dating back to George II. The extended Royal Family turned out to be seen with their necks craned skyward to watch the fly-past of the Royal Air Force.

Not that year though. After twenty years of petition, the Way Ahead Group finally caved in to Charles's plan to slim down the monarchy. In George VI's day, he argued, only "us four" appeared on the balcony – the King, Queen and their two daughters. Since then, the numbers had swelled. Charles was now more eager than ever to reduce numbers, a move that removed Andrew and his brood.

So, in the 2012 Jubilee photo, there was the Queen, Charles, Camilla, William, Kate and a pre-Meghan Harry. Prince Philip was, at the time, in hospital. Then when Andrew got himself embroiled in the Jeffrey Epstein scandal it was easy to exclude him from the Platinum Jubilee events in 2022. Charles and William were in the ascendancy and it was all downhill for Andrew.

CHAPTER NINETEEN
A PLEA OF POVERTY

Andrew's divorce from Fergie had been relatively amicable. Indeed, they still lived together on and off. Otherwise, he was having a high old time, again running around with models including, in 1999, Lady Victoria Hervey, an "It Girl" who became one of his staunchest advocates in his subsequent troubles. Meanwhile Charles was having to deal with the fallout of his acrimonious split from Diana and her subsequent death.

Her personal butler, Paul Burrell, had private letters, intimate photographs and some of the Princess's clothes in his possession. Burrell's house was full of memorabilia, though the tape was nowhere to be found. He insisted that Diana had given her personal possessions to him. Nevertheless, he was charged with theft. The Palace feared that if he was prosecuted, details of the tape would come out. What's more, Burrell had been a confidant of Diana's and had smuggled her lovers in and out of Kensington Palace. He knew her most intimate secrets. The last thing Charles needed were those coals to be raked over again. Burrell even had a letter from Diana saying that her husband was planning to kill her in a car accident. Nevertheless, the Crown Prosecution Service went ahead.

Things came to a head when, on 14 October 2002, Burrell stood in the dock of the Old Bailey charged with stealing 310 items worth £4.5 million. Two weeks later, the Queen suddenly recalled that she had had a meeting with Paul Burrell soon after Princess Diana's death and agreed that he should take care of the Princess's papers. Clearly, she could not be called to testify. The Crown can hardly appear in the Crown's own court and the prosecution was dropped.

Despite hostile public opinion, Charles was determined to keep Camilla in his life. She fulfilled a role similar to the one Fergie did for Andrew in their early days and jollied Charles along when things went badly, while he paid off her overdraft, stabled her horses and provided a car. Given she was clearly there to stay, PR guru Mark Bolland was set the task of brushing up her image. This was no easy task. The home wrecker in the Diana saga, she was now on the way to becoming the wicked stepmother to William and Harry – no easy sell to the British public.

"She has never worked in her life and is terrified of being on public display," said Bolland. "A member of her family described her to me as 'the laziest woman to have been born in England in the twentieth century'."

Charles took her on a family holiday, a Mediterranean cruise of the Aegean on the *Alexander*, the world's third largest private yacht. They were the guests of Yiannis Latsis, a foul-mouthed Greek shipping billionaire whose fortune, it was rumoured, was based on black marketeering, collaboration with the Nazis and bribing Arab states for a stake in the oil trade. Andrew was not the only one with a fondness for dodgy businessmen. Latsis had given Charles £1 million for his Youth Business Trust.

Camilla and her two children had been flown out to Greece on a private jet, at Charles's expense. The cruise was marred somewhat by reports in the *News of the World* that her twenty-four-year-old son Tom had been caught offering friends cocaine. There were concerns that he might be an influence on Prince Harry who, in a confrontation with his father, also admitted taking drugs.

The Queen was not happy seeing pictures of Charles and his mistress at play. Nor did she like Charles using her home, Buckingham Palace, as the venue for fundraisers for his various charities, often raking in millions from some less than savoury characters. She disapproved of his lavish entertaining and did not want Camilla in Buckingham Palace.

There was no love lost between mother and son. When the Queen arrived punctually for the ceremony of the Order of the Bath at Westminster Abbey, Charles was late – bad weather had prevented his helicopter landing, he said. She was irritated, but once he had arrived, they treated each other with courtesy, though as usual barely demonstrated any open affection towards each other.

In May 2000, at the Queen's request, Charles had become the Lord High Commissioner of the Church of Scotland. Another step closer to God. Rather than copy the pattern of his mother's unpretentious engagements and modest dinner parties for a maximum of twelve, he arranged a week of high-profile events culminating in a dinner for two hundred with guests being entertained by jugglers and fire-eaters. The idea was to promote Camilla.

Things got worse when the *Daily Mail* published photographs of the Prince, during an official visit to New York, at a "hookers and pimps" party with some seedy characters. He had arrived with Ghislaine Maxwell (the daughter of the disgraced newspaper magnate Robert Maxwell) who had been seen near a known prostitute. Soon after, Andrew was photographed on a yacht in Thailand with topless girls.

These revelations came as no surprise to Charles. He had long feared that his brother's antics would besmirch the monarchy. Relations between them were already frosty. Earlier that year, Charles refused an invitation to Andrew's fortieth birthday party sent by Fergie.

Charles had still not forgiven her for being photographed topless while her "financial adviser" Johnny Bryan sucked her toes eight years earlier. He felt that such vulgarity had no place in royal circles. She made matters worse by, at a later meeting in Highgrove, chasing him around with a Bible, begging to be allowed to swear her innocence on it.

At the next meeting of the Way Ahead Group, the plan to make Andrew Britain's roving trade ambassador after he left the Navy was discussed. Charles seized the opportunity and renewed his attempt to strip the privileges enjoyed by Andrew's daughters and other minor royals, but again Andrew rallied support from the Queen and Prince Philip. It was reported that the thwarted Charles stomped out of the room.

Things came to a head when Sophie Wessex got caught in a *News of the World* sting by Mazher Mahmood, aka "the Fake Sheikh", flaunting her royal connections to secure a £500,000 publicity contract. In the same sting, she also spilled the beans on senior royals and said that Charles and Camilla would not marry until "the old lady dies". Charles insisted that the Palace should be cleansed of such practices and that working royals should not be involved in private business.

This did not go down well with his siblings. While Charles was raking in over £10 million a year from the Duchy of Cornwall, Andrew, Anne and Edward had to get by on Mummy's handouts. Philip was also annoyed that, while he and the Queen attempted a frugal lifestyle, Charles sucked up to trashy American billionaires to fund his pet projects. And why was he continuing his affair with

Camilla, the former wife of a brother officer? In Philip's day, such things were not done.

Charles regarded this as blatant hypocrisy. Throughout Philip's marriage, there had been rumours of affairs with aristocrats, actresses, even a waitress at Fortnum & Mason. Never close, the two of them now communicated formally by letter.

To make matters worse, on the eve of his eightieth birthday, Philip told *Daily Telegraph* journalist Graham Turner that Prince Charles was "precious, extravagant, and lacking in dedication and discipline that he will need to make a good king". When this appeared in print, Philip offered his son an apology.

While Charles squabbled with his parents, they were more tolerant with others. Edward, whom Charles saw as Andrew's ally in the attempted Palace coup, planned a TV documentary about Charles and Camilla. When this failed to get off the ground, Edward began a documentary about Prince William, who had enrolled as a student at St Andrews University. This was in direct violation of the agreement the Palace had sought with the media to leave William and Harry alone until they had completed their education. Charles was so angry that he refused even to take calls from Edward.

And Prince Philip had his own bones to pick. He erupted when he heard that Andrew had spent a week playing golf and had run up a bill of £500,000 on private jets that year.

"You're selfish and lazy," Philip fulminated, accusing Andrew of "just lounging around".

But what else were the princes supposed to do? Andrew had no profession to fall back on and Edward's career in TV production had foundered since *It's a Royal Knockout*.

Meanwhile, Charles continued to do his own thing. While Andrew and other members of the Royal Family opposed Charles marrying Camilla, Bolland continued to promote her presence at charity fund-raising dinners at Buckingham Palace. Cem Uzan still made generous donations for favourable seating, until he was sentenced by the High Court to fifteen months for failing to appear at a hearing. American newspaper heiress Patty Hearst was also on the guest list. She had been convicted of bank robbery in 1976, though was later pardoned by President Clinton.

Other supporters included Blaine and Robert Trump, brother of Donald, and Eva Rausing who was later arrested after trying to enter the US embassy in London carrying wraps of cocaine and heroin. This was particularly rich as she was the UK patron of international drug abuse prevention charity Mentor and, together with her husband, she provided financial backing to Action on Addiction, a charity that helped young people with drink and drug problems. Then there was Lily Safra, a billionaire socialite who amassed considerable wealth through her four marriages. Two of her spouses died in suspicious circumstances.

And there was Joe Allbritton, CEO of Riggs Bank which was fined $31 million for laundering money for murderous Chilean dictator Augusto Pinochet, among others. Nevertheless, Charles was willing to accept a donation of £190,000 and the loan of his Gulfstream jet. Later, Allbritton was persuaded to invest some £500,000 in the failing Duchy Originals, the Prince's overpriced food brand that produced and sold organic oat biscuits, sausages and a growing number of other products through duchy shops. In exchange, in 2007, Allbritton and his wife got to ride the fourth carriage behind the Queen at Ascot.

Pick of the bunch was Armand Hammer whose vast wealth was built on illegal trading with the Soviet Union. He spent around £40 million contributing to Charles's charities and his personal expenses in an effort to rehabilitate his reputation. At a charity gala in Palm Beach he pledged $50,000 each time Diana danced with one of his friends, mostly Mafia bosses.

For a hefty donation, Charles was available at social events. At dinner at Highgrove, Charles would sit on a gilded armchair – throne, if you will – covered with crimson brocade, while billionaire donors would have to make do with silver bamboo ballroom chairs. The meals featured organic fare from Highgrove. There, dinners were lit by twenty candelabras brought from Buckingham Palace. On one occasion, Fawcett ransacked the vaults of St James's Palace and found crates of plates, candlesticks and napery given to the monarch over the centuries dating back to Catherine the Great. Visitors to Highgrove still talk of parties so lavish they could rival the most over-blown in Hollywood.

One guest at a star-studded Highgrove bash described elaborate decorations laid out in vast marquees with silk-lined starry ceilings. She said: "It is not uncommon for Charles to order souvenir marble menus with gold calligraphy and harpists dressed in Roman costume. It is not always in the best possible taste. He once decorated a dinner party with flowers from South Africa at £100 a stem. The place was filled with these rare blooms at an immense cost."

Every dish prepared for Charles or his guests was entirely organic, with most ingredients sourced from his Highgrove estate. Even when he visited Sandringham, he had produce flown up from Highgrove to maintain this all-organic diet.

These extravagant fundraising events were arranged by the ever-faithful Michael Fawcett and Robert Higdon, CEO of Charles's charitable foundation in America. They raised millions, though much of the money was paid out in salaries and administrative cost. The phrase "rent-a-royal" got attached to Fawcett, while Higdon called himself "Mr Cash Cow".

"But Charles never said 'thank you'," he recalled. Higdon was also upset when Charles called his guests "donors" instead of "friends". "Charles and I had a dysfunctional relationship," he said.

Fawcett had to resign temporarily in 1998 after being accused of bullying, but was reinstated within a week – and promoted.

"I can manage without just about anyone except for Michael," Charles said. He received so many freebies discarded by Charles that he was nicknamed "Fawcett the Fence" by the staff and turned a healthy profit by selling unwanted gifts. An investigation also revealed that Fawcett had been given valuable "benefits" by suppliers – including a Rolex watch worth £2,500, membership of Mosimann's Dining Club costing £3,000 year, a Tiffany watch, a Pasha pen and several consignments of champagne. But then the ultra-loyal Fawcett always stuck up for his boss. The investigation cleared Fawcett of any financial impropriety.

At even the most lavish fundraising events, Charles pled poverty. During an after-dinner speech at Waddesdon Manor, Lord Rothschild's Buckinghamshire home, Charles complained that his host employed more gardeners than he did – fifteen against his ten.

"His Royal Highness lives modestly," Fawcett told a donor. "He hasn't got a yacht and doesn't eat lunch." Not since the taxpayer stopped paying for the *Britannia* at least. Then there's the seven boiled eggs he got to choose between at breakfast.

In his book *On Royalty*, former *Newsnight* presenter Jeremy Paxman said that Charles was so fussy about how he likes his eggs after a morning's hunting that his staff cook seven. The prince would then test each egg, ranging from runny to rock hard, before choosing the one that met his approval. Paxman himself said the egg story as "so preposterously extravagant as to be unbelievable", but said it came from one of the Prince's friends.

Clarence House quickly dismissed the story as a storm in an egg cup.

"It is completely untrue," said a spokeswoman for the Prince, adding that the environmentally conscious royal would never be so wasteful.

However, it then emerged that Charles's finicky attitude to his eggs had previously been documented in another book, *The Housekeeper's Diary* written by Wendy Berry, a housekeeper at Highgrove for nine years.

Higdon also noted that Charles and Camilla did not like all the people who gave his charities money, but somehow managed to keep smiling through. Such glitzy fundraising particularly annoyed Prince Andrew. In his opinion, his elder brother was promoting himself with displays of phony *noblesse oblige* at other people's expense.

Of the millions that came in from the Duchy of Cornwall each year, accounts show Charles spent nearly all of it. He admitted that he lives well on the proceeds, which were over £24 million in the 2021–22 financial year. He voluntarily paid 40 per cent tax on that, after the comprehensive use of loopholes. As Prince of Wales, he also received money from the Sovereign Grant for his official expenditure. This amounted to £999,000 in 2022. Little was saved from this vast income.

Charles had paid £150,000 a year for Princess Diana's "grooming expenses", and now that Camilla was making more public appearances, her wardrobe had switched from old tweed skirts to Valentino, Versace and Oscar de la Renta. He paid for much of this and leased a Vauxhall Omega with a chauffeur for her.

"His lifestyle would seem extravagant to Louis XIV," said the *Guardian*, "a team of four valets so that one is always available to lay out and pick up his clothes; a servant to squeeze his toothpaste on to his brush, and another who once held the specimen bottle while he gave a urine sample. Step into the world of the Prince of Wales, a lifestyle so pampered that even the Queen has complained that it is grotesque."

Royal author Graham Turner told the *Sunday Express*: "I certainly think he baffles the Queen. At times she must look at him and be thinking, 'How did one produce that?' I once suggested that Prince Philip was baffled by Charles and certainly not a great fan of his. The Palace murmured discontent, but when I went on to suggest that the Queen had not been the world's greatest mother, the Palace gates clanged shut.

"But I would say that Charles is definitely more royal than all the royals put together. I have a great affection for him but also a lot of sympathy. Here is a man who has never been sure of unconditional love from either parent and who still craves affection."

The Queen was said to be so appalled by Charles's extravagance that she sent accountant Sir Michael Peat into St James's Palace to be Charles's private secretary with orders to slash his spending and build bridges between the two Palaces. It was soon noted that, instead of laying down the law, Peat was becoming servile, rushing to put on his jacket rather than be seen by Charles in his shirtsleeves, then bowing deeply.

But Peat's real job, it was thought, was to get rid of Bolland who, Buckingham Palace suspected, had aggravated the scandals involving Prince Andrew, Prince Edward and Sophie Wessex, and even William and Harry, to promote Charles and Camilla. Charles finally agreed that Bolland should leave, provided they could retain him as a consultant.

When the Queen Mother died, Charles made a television tribute to his grandmother. The Queen allowed Camilla to attend the funeral, but not as Charles's plus-one. It fooled no one. Soon the tabloids were urging the couple to marry.

A truce between mother and son was brokered during the Queen's Golden Jubilee when she visited his "healing garden" at the Chelsea Flower Show. According to Jinny Blom, who helped the Prince design the garden and used to work as a transpersonal psychologist – a New Age discipline popular in California – "every part of the garden has deep significance and meaning". At a lunch at London's Guildhall, Charles then paid a moving tribute to "Mummy".

"I am so proud and grateful for everything you have done for your country and Commonwealth over fifty wonderful years," he said. "You have embodied something vital in our lives – continuity."

Then, as what has been interpreted as a deliberate dig at Tony Blair, he made reference to the "non-politically correct second verse of the national anthem". This reads:

O Lord our God arise,
Scatter our enemies,
And make them fall!
Confound their politics,
Frustrate their knavish tricks,
On Thee our hopes we fix,
God save us all!

Although he had made some reconciliation with his mother, Charles did not share the Queen's devotion to the Commonwealth. It was observed that he frequently made visits to the "white" Dominions – Canada, Australia, New Zealand – but the black and brown countries were seldom on his itinerary. He visited the US more often than any country, not to mention Switzerland to go skiing at Klosters.

At meetings with Commonwealth representatives, he noted that the diplomats were only interested in getting their pictures taken with him for publication back home. When the Foreign Office mentioned a series of visits, Charles declined, though he was eager to go to the Middle East due to his affinity towards Islam. Those who tried to persuade him otherwise were dismissed as stupid.

In response, the Foreign Office adopted the tactic of the "add-on". If he had decided to go to the Middle East, they would organise an "add-on" trip to India where he could check out the local wheat for his Duchy Original biscuits. Charles would agree, only he would not travel on a commercial airline. The FO would have to lay on a private Airbus.

After his grandmother's death, Charles decided to move into Clarence House. The estimated cost of refurbishment soared from the original budget of £3 million towards £6 million, all paid for by the taxpayer. Charles also took over Birkhall and held in trust the Castle of Mey, the Queen Mother's fifteen-bedroom house in Caithness.

His sixth home, the Castle of Mey would be refurbished with the aid of a £1 million gift from Julia Kauffman, a Canadian-born heiress living in Kansas City. Charles's extravagance passed unnoticed by the public, and it was grudgingly tolerated by civil servants.

Charles's profligacy came to public attention thanks to Paul Burrell who, after charges against him were dropped, was able to speak out. In 2003, he released a memoir, *A Royal Duty*, about a palace servant's life "below stairs". It then became open season on British royals – not least because Charles's lavish lifestyle was in stark contrast to the life most Britons led. Nevertheless, Michael Peat pled poverty on the Prince's behalf.

"Charles does not enjoy a champagne and caviar lifestyle," he said. He also claimed that Charles had only one car and did not own his own home. In fact, he had six cars at his disposal – a Bentley, an Audi, a Range Rover, a Land Rover and two Aston Martins, at least one of which had been adapted to run on plonk and cheddar. His various homes – Clarence House, Highgrove, Birkhall, the Castle of Mey, Balmoral and Sandringham – were owned variously by the Crown, the Royal Family, the Duchy of Cornwall or by a trust.

In 2003, Michael Fawcett quit after Sir Michael Peat had led an inquiry into the sale of royal gifts and financial mismanagement in the Prince's household. Nevertheless, he continued to work for Charles on a freelance basis as a fixer and party planner. Despite his "resignation" Fawcett still played a significant role in Charles's life.

CHAPTER TWENTY

SEPARATE WAYS

Although divorced, Andrew and Fergie continued to live in Sunninghill Park, adjoining Windsor Great Park. The original 1770 house on the site was to have been the first home of the Queen, then Princess Elizabeth, and the Duke of Edinburgh, but burnt down in 1947. The land was given to the Yorks by the Queen as a wedding present.

They built a two-storey fifty-room red brick mock Tudor mansion there with a staff of eleven. It was mocked as "Southyork" after "Southfork", the Texan oil tycoon's estate in the 1980s soap opera *Dallas*. It has also been compared to an out-of-town Tesco and very large Pizza Hut. Charles would not have approved of the design, though other aspects might have got his royal approval. For example, it was furnished by equipment suppliers who were expected to kit out the kitchen and bathroom free of charge. One of the most notable features was a giant marble bathtub that the builders dubbed HMS *Fergie*. A spiral staircase from the balcony led to the swimming pool and tennis court. The couple's initials "A & S" were embossed on towels and loo rolls, while the musical toilet roll holder played "God Save the Queen".

"It looks like a tart's bedroom," said Prince Philip.

Andrew lived there until 2004 when he moved into the Royal Lodge in Windsor which had been vacated following the death of the Queen Mother. Fergie moved out in 2006. She rented Dolphin House, just next door to the Royal Lodge. The following year, there was a fire at Dolphin House after Fergie left a scented candle alight in the lavatory when she went out for a business meeting. She then moved into Royal Lodge with her former husband.

After five years on the market, Sunninghill Park was sold in 2007 for £15 million – £3 million over the asking price – to an offshore trust in the British Virgin Islands. It later transpired that the owner was Kazakh billionaire Timur Kulibayev, a friend of Andrew's. Kulibayev was the son-in-law of the president of Kazakhstan Nursultan Nazarbayev whom Andrew had met as UK trade envoy. The house was then allowed to fall into disrepair and, in 2015, it was knocked down.

"There is no question of the Duke of York having benefited from his position as special representative in his sale of the property," the Prince's spokesman said. "Any suggestion that he has abused his public position is completely untrue. The sale was a straight commercial transaction."

The sale was brokered by Kazakh oligarch Kenges Rakishev. Andrew was in touch with Rakishev again in April 2011, when he was still UK trade envoy, on behalf of Greek water company EYDAP and its Swiss financiers Aras Capital who wanted to build water and sewage networks in two of Kazakhstan's largest cities. Andrew was to get one per cent on the £383 million deal.

In the event, the deal fell through when Kazakh police opened fire on a group of striking oil workers in the city of Zhanaozen, killing fourteen. Fearing that they would be caught up in political turmoil, EYDAP pulled out and Andrew stood down as trade envoy, amid criticism of his involvement.

"Prince Andrew's continuing close relationship with questionable figures in Kazakhstan brings the Royal Family into disrepute," said former Liberal Democrat MP Norman Baker who published a damning book about royal finances. "There are also serious questions about a conflict of interest in his former role as trade envoy, which on the face of it seems to be more about enriching himself than helping the UK."

Andrew's reputation for egotism had not mellowed over the years. On his fortieth birthday, the Yorks pulled up at the Millennium Wheel in their official Jag and jumped the queue, forcing others to wait in the cold for an extra hour.

"I can't believe they have made us all wait this long just so Andy and Fergie could get a free ride," said Derek Brown who had brought his family up from Reading. "We were all ready to go up at twelve but then, after we made some enquiries, we were told we could be almost an hour late."

Another would-be rider was more forthright, shouting: "You lot are nothing but freeloaders."

Despite the boos, Andrew and Fergie smiled and waved at the crowd.

In one incident that was typical of his selfish behaviour, Andrew was overheard in an early morning exchange in his £13 million ski chalet in Verbier, bought with the help of the Bank of Mum. A young guest was making his breakfast tea when Andrew suddenly appeared.

"Andrew, would you like a cup?" asked the guest.

"I'm Prince Andrew to you," Andrew snapped at the host, and walked off.

And he was no more deferential to a British rear admiral.

"You can call me 'Andy'," Andrew said.

"And you can call me 'sir'," the admiral replied.

Five of Andrew's former girlfriends turned out for the birthday party Fergie put on for him. Former *Playboy* model Caprice could not make it that day, so Andrew later prevailed on the staff at St James's Palace to let him have a suite of state apartments for the night and to lay on a lavish dinner for the absent guests. The table was decked with elaborate candlesticks, flowers, silver cutlery and china carrying the royal crest, and the meal was served by liveried footmen.

Around this time, his name was linked to that of twenty-three-year-old French professional golfer Audrey Raimbault, whom he sneaked into Buckingham Palace for a tour of his private quarters. She also stayed at Windsor on at least two occasions. Next came blonde Australian PR girl Emma Gibbs, who was thirty-three – "she laughs at his awful jokes," a friend said. Then in July 2001, his name was linked with that of twenty-four-year-old PR girl Caroline Stanbury.

And all the while, Ghislaine Maxwell was never far away. The couple were spotted dining together at Nello on Madison Avenue in New York in April 2000, causing some newspapers to speculate they were dating.

There was also continued talk that Andrew and Fergie would remarry. In an interview in *Tatler* magazine in June 2000, he said: "I don't rule remarriage out and I certainly don't rule it in. If ever the opportunity arose, I do not know what I would do, as it is not in the plan." Fergie added: "I simply say, if it should happen, great. It is not in, nor is it ruled out."

The couple had recently been on a holiday with daughters Beatrice and Eugenie in the Bahamas. He would repeat the trip, but this time with supermodel Elle Macpherson.

However, before the *Tatler* interview could even be published, Andrew was seen out at London's trendy Met Bar with supermodel

Christy Turlington. Then there was Cadbury's Flake model Catrina Skepper, society beauty Caroline 'Cazzy' Neville, auburn-haired PR executive Aurelia Cecil, golf star Sally Prosser, raven-haired BBC researcher and Koo Stark lookalike Henriette Peace, South African former burger bar waitress turned model Heather Mann (who was invited to the Queen Mother's hundredth birthday party at Windsor), former Miss USA Julie Hayek, whom he dined with à deux in Manhattan, and former *Playboy* model Denise Martell: "We kissed a lot. He kept trying to move forward in the romance but I stopped."

Even American rock star and former heroin addict Courtney Love claimed that Andrew came knocking at her door at one in the morning "to look for chicks". While at Mar-a-Lago, Donald Trump's Florida estate, he was seen with Christine Drangsholt, a former model whose company sold Testosterol, a hormone substitute which, according to company literature, increases the length and girth of the penis and makes the maturing male "feel like a horny teenager all over again". The firm uses advertising slogans such as "Get more bang for your buck!", "Get hard as a rock" and "Show your partner that there really is a superman". A far cry from organic oat biscuits.

Actor George Hamilton introduced Andrew to his former daughter-in-law Angie Everhart who had appeared in several *Sports Illustrated* swimsuit issues and posed nude for *Playboy*. Since breaking up with his son Ashley, she had dated a string of famous men including Prince Albert of Monaco, Kevin Costner, Sylvester Stallone, Howard Stern and Joe Pesci, whom she was briefly engaged to. Angie recalled that her former father-in-law George Hamilton had called her one day and asked her if she'd like to go to a dinner with a prince. The attraction, apparently, was that she was a ginger top like Fergie.

"George told me, 'He likes redheads and he has a wish list of girls he'd like to meet while he's in town – and you're on it'," she said.

Angie took the possibility of becoming the next Duchess of York seriously.

"I'd have been a bit more popular than the last American, that Duchess of Windsor. But I was already divorced when we met," she later told the *Mail on Sunday*. "Maybe things would be different now that everyone has accepted Charles's divorce. But when I first met Andrew I don't think it would have been acceptable."

She later had a run-in with Harvey Weinstein who, she claimed, masturbated in front of her. Convicted for rape and other sexual offences, Weinstein was sentenced to twenty-three years in jail in New York, and another sixteen years in California.

Andrew's name was later linked with that of billionaire Kazakh socialite Goga Ashkenazi, who was photographed with Andrew in 2007 having lunch in Ascot just three days after the birth of her son to Timur Kulibayev. She also had an affair with Italian tycoon Flavio Briatore. Goga said: "It is every girl's dream to have a prince on one arm and a billionaire on the other."

The list goes on.

Royal watcher Margaret Holder said: "The playboy image is not one Prince Andrew discourages. He's been seen many times on these party yachts and he thinks it enhances his reputation. Attracting luscious young ladies makes him feel young." By 2010, she reckoned he had been through about fifteen more serious girlfriends since his divorce in 1996.

However, as former BBC royal correspondent, Jennie Bond was more sceptical.

"It is rather difficult to know whether the girls he's seen with are serious consorts or not," she said. "There is definitely a huge advantage in being seen with the Prince. And there's no getting away from the fact that Prince Andrew is a great catch, except of course he still lives with his ex-wife in Windsor Great Park."

It was even suggested that Fergie was a matchmaker, introducing Andrew to some non-threatening girls. In 1998, when Andrew's relationship with Aurelia Cecil was getting serious, it was Fergie who intervened by introducing him to Heather Mann and the relationship with Cecil soon petered out.

The only real threat was businesswoman Amanda Staveley, who spent weekends at Buckingham Palace. Prince Philip thought she was the ideal choice to be the next Duchess of York. He had always vehemently opposed Andrew's remarriage to Fergie. In 2004, Andrew proposed, but Staveley turned him down.

"If I married him all my independence would have disappeared," she said.

Despite these conquests, Andrew did not think his millionaire playboy lifestyle made him out of touch. He told *Tatler*: "I am a good deal more down to earth than people would expect of a member of the Royal Family. The ivory tower is not a syndrome from which I suffer."

He also insisted to *Focus*: "My life is a great deal more ordinary than perhaps is portrayed in the media. And that's about it, really. There's a great deal more normality in my life than people first imagine."

A former *Playboy* model who partied with him during an official visit to Los Angeles in 2000 told a tabloid: "He is a real prince charming." However, a woman who met him at a party in St Tropez complained: "He doesn't have much conversation other than himself."

"He's everything people tell you," another said. "Boorish, interrupts you and laughs at his own jokes."

Something had to be done about him.

After Prince Philip's tongue-lashing, a job was found for Andrew as the UK's Special Representative for International Trade and Investment. The position was unpaid, but offered plenty of opportunities for lucrative sidelines. Otherwise, he would have had to live on the £249,000 a year his mother gave him and the £20,000 a year pension he got from the Navy.

But this was clearly not enough. He ran up millions of pounds in expensive jet-setting around the world at the taxpayers' expense. Meanwhile he set up companies in tax havens under false names and rubbed shoulders with unsavoury characters.

Holidaying in January 2001, he was photographed on board a luxury yacht off the Thai island of Phuket surrounded by a bevy of topless beauties. The yacht belonged to Swedish millionaire Johan Eliasch. Andrew made no excuses for his presence on board the yacht. He barely glanced at the bare breasts, he said: "I was just reading my book. I wasn't really aware of what everyone else was doing." The photographs tell another tale.

Monaco-based tycoon Eliasch was also said to have paid for Andrew's stay at the luxurious Amanpuri Hotel in Thailand, where villas cost up to £25,000 a night.

It was later alleged that, in 2002, the Prince set up the company Naples Gold with Eliasch using the pseudonym Andrew Inverness. One of Andrew's lesser-known titles is Earl of Inverness. His job title was "professional consultant" and the date of birth on the company's records was as 19 February 1960, the same as the Prince's. A creditor of the luxury ski company Descent International was one "Andrew Inverness, care of Buckingham Palace". When the company collapsed in 2009, a spokesperson for the liquidator told the reporters at the time: "We understand that to be Prince Andrew."

In Thailand, Andrew had toured the red light district of Patong with a police bodyguard in tow. In one go-go bar – bearing the motto "good food, cold drinks, hot girls" – he danced with half-naked young women. A regular said: "You certainly wouldn't get a member of the Thai royal family in a place like this. The area is very raunchy and many of the girls are prostitutes." There was a bar above, under the same management, that promised: "Topless girls upstairs."

Aides at the Palace were said to have been furious, given his appointment as Britain's roving trade envoy.

"Prince Andrew is keen to bang the drum for British exports," a Palace spokesman had said when the appointment was announced.

"Heaven help Britain's exporters," was the response of an editorial in *The Sunday Times*.

Some doubts were even expressed in the Palace. One courtier said: "If he goes off to America to promote business, people will worry about what he is doing in his time off. Will he be going off with Ghislaine Maxwell to a nightclub? The trouble with Andrew is that his private life will, willy-nilly, intrude into his public role."

Within months of his appointment, Andrew was besieged with complaints. Too often, the Foreign Office's protocol department said, he refused to stick to the agreed itinerary and "left a trail of glass in his wake".

"Andrew's relations around the world are dicey," commented one official at the weekly heads of department meeting, "He's showing bad judgement about people. He's rude, lashes out to lay down the law, and it's so difficult to sell him."

It was then decreed that complaints from British embassies about Andrew were not to be made in writing. Diplomats had been warned by the Foreign Office not to include adverse comments in their dispatches. Anything unfavourable was to be conveyed by telephone.

Pampered with private jets and five-star hotels, he remained rude and arrogant. Initially, the FO relied on Andrew's private secretary to ask him to behave better. She failed. Following complaints from embassies in the Middle East and Latin America, senior officials met to discuss "the Andrew problem". The Queen needed to be told. She prevaricated and suggested that Prince Philip be consulted. He was annoyed and advised that Andrew be officially told to "sharpen up his act or lose his job". An official met Andrew and issued an appropriate warning. It fell on deaf ears.

CHAPTER TWENTY-ONE

AIR MILES

The press dubbed Prince Andrew "Air Miles Andy" after the government published a list of his travels at the taxpayers' expense. These were not official tours or trade missions but flights to golf tournaments, football matches and social visits to beautiful girlfriends across the globe. Like his brother, he refused to fly on commercial airlines. In 2003, it was reported that Andrew spent £325,000 on flights. This included £2,939 on a helicopter he used to make a 120-mile round trip to Oxford, and RAF planes to fly him to St Andrews for two golfing jaunts. He would never take a car when a helicopter would do.

Most of his trips were to places that had golf courses. He took a trip to the US that took in the Masters golf tournament. In 2004, he was criticised for taking an RAF jet to Northern Ireland, where he played a round of golf which made him late for the royal garden party he was there to attend. There were other sporting events that year. A trip to Bahrain coincided with the Grand Prix. The *Mail on Sunday* said: "If Prince Andrew does not swiftly learn the limits of public patience, he will endanger not just his own position, but that of the monarchy as a whole."

MP Ian Davidson, a member of the Public Accounts Select Committee, complained: "There is a question mark over what are genuine royal duties which the public should pay for. I'm not entirely clear what benefit the public get from him being the captain of one of the most exclusive clubs in the world. Second, there is a question about whether there is due economy when travel plans are being made. There is also a wider issue – what do the junior royals do, and are they carrying out worthy public duties?"

Andrew took no notice and, the following year, his travel expenses soared by 74 per cent. This time the National Audit Office was on the case. It investigated forty-one of his journeys, including a £3,000 bill for a helicopter to a business lunch in Oxford, when the train would have cost £97, and three trips to golfing events as part of his captaincy of the Royal and Ancient Golf Club of St Andrews at a cost of some £12,000. On another occasion it cost £4,645 for him to take an RAF jet to the course in Fife so he could finish eighteen holes.

"The idea that because train journeys were unreliable, he therefore got a helicopter is outrageous," said Davidson. "This option is not open to many of us and this junior member of the Royal Family appears to regard the public purse as a bottomless pit to be drawn on as and when he wishes."

The NAO report said that the Prince's flights, most of them paid for by the taxpayer, had cost £565,000. *The Times* noted that Andrew greeted the furore with insouciance.

"In terms of the return on investment to the UK," he said, "I would suggest that £500,000 is cheap at the price."

While the NAO managed to audit his expenses, no one had come up with any figure of how much money he had made for the country in his travels – if, indeed, he had made any at all. However, the Treasury could not even give him a rap on the knuckles because, apparently, no rules on royal travel had been broken. And Andrew, himself, was unapologetic, saying later: "I could have worse tags than Air Miles Andy, although I don't know what they are."

The *Guardian* thoughtfully listed them for him: "Playboy Prince, Randy Andy, Prince of Freebies, Air Miles Andy, Junket of York, the Duke of Yob."

Of course, he wasn't actually clocking up any air miles because he didn't travel on commercial airlines and the criticism washed over him. On top of the £250,000 stipend he was given by the Queen and his Navy pension, *The Sunday Times* reported in July 2008 that for "the Duke of York's public role... he last year received £436,000 to cover his expenses."

That year, he travelled to the US in a private jet that cost a whopping £100,000. A trip to China and the Far East cost taxpayers £30,000 for transport and accommodation. In January 2009, a visit to Switzerland cost £21,700 in hotel, travel and other overheads. The following year he was severely chastised for using the Queen's helicopter on a 146-mile trip hopping around official engagements that were in the same area. The same year, he flew from Windsor to Kent for a party at a golf course where he was patron.

"The helicopter is very often the most efficient way of packing in as many engagements as we can," the Prince explained. "It enables us to see more people all over the country, do more things and get better value for time and money out of my role as Special Representative." However, he conceded that: "He couldn't expect the British people to accept his explanation because he also used the helicopter and other means of travel looking for the finest golf courses."

Perhaps in an effort to save money, Andrew hired contractors to build a nine-hole golf course in the landscaped grounds of Windsor Lodge. Certainly, it would save the taxpayer thousands if he could cut out the helicopter and walk out of his back door to play a round.

But the expense continued. On 8 March 2011, the *Daily Telegraph* reported: "In 2010, the Prince spent £620,000 as a trade envoy, including £154,000 on hotels, food and hospitality and £465,000 on travel."

Abroad, he travelled with a team of six, including equerries, private secretaries, protection officers and a valet with a six-foot ironing board so that he could always have perfect creases in his trousers. The deputy head of the mission in Bahrain Simon Wilson said: "His arrival, not just in the Gulf but elsewhere as well, is now part of the folklore of the diplomatic service because of the reams of instructions about his likes and dislikes – ranging from demands that the drinking water should be served at room temperature to detailed food preferences."

His behaviour was "cocky" and "rude", and he regarded himself as an expert on every matter. There he took after his father. Prince Philip once told a group of industrialists: "I've never been noticeably reticent about talking on subjects about which I know nothing."

Wilson said: "Unfortunately, HRH the Duke of York is more commonly known among the British diplomatic community in the Gulf as HBH: His Buffoon Highness. This nickname stemmed from his childish obsession with doing exactly the opposite of what had been agreed in pre-visit meetings with his staff. He frequently refused to follow his brief – we wondered if he had actually read it…"

Despite copious meetings in advance of any visit, including briefings by senior officials from the Foreign Office and the Trade and Industry Department, the Prince usually ignored all advice and plunged straight in.

"Colleagues put this behaviour down to an inferiority complex about being mentally challenged," said Wilson. "This may be a trifle unfair, but his attitude certainly drew attention to the fact that he was usually out of his depth at meetings."

According to Wilson, on a 2005 visit to the Gulf, instead of promoting Britain's trade, Andrew was hawking his house, Sunninghill Park, around during meetings of Gulf royals.

Sir Ivor Richards, ambassador to Italy, who hosted Andrew's visit there, said: "His kind of diplomacy is not mine, in the sense that it has not always led to improved relations with the people he is supposed to be schmoozing." He described Andrew as "brusque to the point of rudeness". At a party, Andrew dismissed the head of a well-known fashion house with the words: "Never heard of you."

"I had to send my deputy the next week to smooth ruffled feathers," said Sir Ivor. "I would never have thought of him as the natural choice to be trade envoy in the first place. If the net result is negative, you wonder whether he should be in that position."

In a cable published by WikiLeaks, Tatiana Gfoeller, Washington's ambassador to Kyrgyzstan, recorded how Andrew called the UK's Serious Fraud Office "idiots" for investigating bribery claims around an arms deal between BAE Systems and Saudi Arabia, and accused *Guardian* journalists of "poking their noses everywhere" for investigating it.

She said Prince Andrew told her that the UK, Western Europe and the US were now "back in the thick of playing the Great Game" – the nineteenth-century rivalry between the British and Russia Empires over influence in Asia.

"More animated than ever," she wrote, "he stated cockily 'and this time we aim to win'."

"The problem with Andrew," a senior Buckingham Palace official said in 2001, "is that his mouth engages before his brain does."

His jaunts around the world allowed him to collect a wide circle of dubious friends, just as Charles did. These included one-time Libya dictator Colonel Gaddafi and his son Saif al-Islam who is wanted by the International Criminal Court for crimes against humanity. Then there's Sakher el-Materi, the son-in-law of the deposed Tunisian president Zine al-Abidine Ben Ali, whom Andrew entertained at Buckingham Palace three months before the regime collapsed. He fled into exile in the Seychelles. Tried *in absentia* for corruption, he was sentenced to sixteen years.

A trip to visit President Ilham Aliyev of Azerbaijan led to the headline "The Duke and the Despot". Amnesty International was asking for Aliyev to stop torturing political opponents. A skiing trip with convicted Libyan gun-runner Tarek Kaituni led to "Prince Takes Holiday with Gun Smuggler" headline. Andrew was also said to have accepted a £20,000 gold necklace from Kaituni for his daughter Beatrice.

During the Libyan Civil War in February 2011, Andrew's questionable connections there led UK Shadow Justice Minister Chris Bryant to ask in the House of Commons: "Isn't it about time we dispensed with the services of the Duke of York?" The Speaker then intervened, accusing Bryant of breaking rules that ban MPs from criticising royals in the House. Bryant retorted that the ban only applied to the monarch.

Andrew went goose shooting with Nursultan Nazarbayev, the president of Kazakhstan and then one of the longest serving non-royal leaders in the world, in office from 1990 to 2019. No election was judged free and fair since the country had gained its independence from the Soviet Union, and Nazarbayev has been accused of human rights abuses.

In April 2015, Nazarbayev was re-elected with almost 98 per cent of the vote, as he ran virtually unopposed. In 2019, he handed the presidency to a close ally and has remained a good friend of Vladimir Putin. It was through Nazarbayev that Andrew met Timur Kulibayev who bought his house, Sunninghill Park.

Andrew has even been known to blatantly scorn national and international laws. In 2002 he told a police officer who pulled him over for speeding that he was in a hurry – to get to a golf tournament as it turned out – and drove off before he could be given a ticket. Three years later there was a stand-off at Melbourne airport in Australia when he refused to subject himself to routine security screening before boarding a flight to New Zealand. "Who does he think he is?" one member of the airport security team said. "What a pompous prick."

And like his brother, he could not resist meddling. He nearly caused a diplomatic incident when he publicly criticised George W. Bush's White House for failing to listen more to the advice of the British government over the post-war strategy for Iraq. "It is frankly embarrassing," said the *Guardian*, "that Britain should be represented in any capacity by such a halfwit."

Damned as "useless" across Whitehall, he would undertake so-called "official trips" in the Far East and America, where many felt he was simply chasing women, with protection officers and the rest of his retinue in tow, at a cost of between £140,000 and £250,000 per trip, including private jets. Back in Britain, he drew criticism for inviting John McEnroe and Bjorn Borg to use the tennis court at Buckingham Palace for a charity match sponsored by bankers.

In the last year of his trade role, Andrew clocked up 77,000 air miles. The year after, 2012, it was 93,500. The next year, taxpayers funded a trip to New York for a series of official engagements that coincided with his daughter Princess Eugenie moving to the city. The timing, the Palace insisted, was coincidental.

Throughout his time of rubbing shoulders with the rich, famous and, in some cases, corrupt, Andrew got to know Jeffrey Epstein, who was invited to Balmoral, Windsor and Sandringham. Although in 2008 Epstein had already been convicted of sex offences involving underage girls and spent thirteen months in jail in Florida, Andrew asked Epstein to help out with ex-wife Fergie's multi-million-pound debts.

The two of them were photographed strolling together in Central Park. When the picture was published in the *News of the World* in August 2011, Andrew was summoned to Buckingham Palace by officials to discuss with the Queen whether he should continue as a trade ambassador for Britain. Warned in advance, Andrew asked a public relations consultant to discuss how to improve his position. As the visitor was escorted down the Palace corridor to the Prince's office, he could hear Andrew screaming down the telephone at a minion.

"It was appalling behaviour," the consultant said. "He was demanding respect for his entitlement."

There was no choice. Andrew had to step down as trade envoy, but not before he had resumed his playboy career. In 2010, he had been photographed on a 154-foot yacht off the coast of Sardinia with a twenty-five-year-old bikini-clad beauty rubbing suntan oil on him. She was half-Spanish, half-Filipino model Alexandra Escat, who was half his age.

She later recounted how Andrew had asked her to fetch some sunscreen and was then taken aback when he asked her to apply it for him. She was not comfortable with this.

"This is somebody I have barely met and he's royal. I mean, that's just weird, right?" she said.

Royal sources initially claimed that the pair were just friends and that Escat was married to another guest on the yacht. In fact, she was single. He was photographed kissing her hand and they were later seen jetting off to Malaga together.

She protested her innocence, telling the *Mail on Sunday*: "I can see what a juicy bit of gossip it must have seemed – one day, I'm putting oil on Andrew's back; the next, we're getting on a private jet together. It all looks so romantic, doesn't it? But I know what happened – and what did not."

Just a week after the photo of Andrew and Epstein appeared in the papers, Andrew's press secretary, Ed Perkins, got a phone call from Sian James, an assistant editor at the *Mail on Sunday*, who told him that they had obtained an interview with Virginia Roberts. She claimed that Epstein had turned her into an underage prostitute and had taken her to London, at the age of seventeen, to have sex with Prince Andrew.

The paper also had the picture of Andrew with his arm round her bare midriff. With them in the picture was Ghislaine Maxwell whom Roberts accused of recruiting her as Epstein's sex slave. Andrew denied everything. He was embroiled in another scandal at the time. The cash-strapped Fergie had been caught offering access to Andrew for £500,000 by an undercover reporter for the *News of the World* posing as a businessman. The meeting was secretly filmed.

"If you want to meet him in your business, look after me, and he'll look after you. You'll get it back tenfold," Fergie could be heard saying on the video. "That opens up everything you would ever wish for. And I can open any door you want. And I will for you."

She walked away from the meeting with a briefcase carrying a large cash down payment. She was forced to return the money and temporarily moved out of the Royal Lodge. In her apology, Fergie denied that Andrew had any knowledge of the bribe and said he "was not aware or involved in any of the discussions that occurred".

However, in the tape she told her would-be benefactor that Prince Andrew "knows that he's had to underwrite me up to now because I've got no money".

She was thought to be anywhere from £2 million to £5 million in debt, owing at least £200,000 to a firm of London solicitors in unpaid legal fees. She was being propped up by Andrew's friend and financial adviser, property tycoon David Rowland, who had resigned as Tory party treasurer after doubts about his aggressive business tactics and who was a tax exile on Guernsey. In exchange, Andrew had plugged the Rowlands' Luxembourg-based Banque Havilland for the super-rich when on trade envoy missions overseas. Leaked emails obtained by the *Mail on Sunday* indicate that the Prince and his advisers had also provided Rowland private government documents, including a Foreign Office diplomatic cable and a Treasury memo.

Meanwhile, Rowland let Andrew use his luxurious Bombardier Global Express private jet to fly around the world rather than use planes from the RAF's Queen's Flight which drew censure from government auditors.

Andrew also held a 40 per cent share of a business Rowland had registered in a Caribbean tax haven. The prince's wealthy royal contacts were then lured into investing in a tax-free offshore fund. As trade envoy, there was a clear conflict of interest. Called Inverness Asset Management, the company was registered in the British Virgin Islands. Its business prospectus says it had a long and successful relationship between "DR [David Rowland] and HRH Prince Andrew".

One email exchange revealed that, when Andrew was facing the sack from his envoy role because of the Jeffrey Epstein scandal, Rowland's son and business lieutenant, Jonathan, suggested their commercial activities could continue "under the radar". Andrew responded: "I like your thinking."

Chris Bryant demanded a parliamentary inquiry into the Prince's business behaviour.

"It all just stinks," said Bryant. "I don't think he has ever been able to draw a distinction between his own personal interest and the national interest. It's morally offensive. He clearly was never fit to hold that office. Either the Foreign Affairs Committee or the Public Accounts Committee should launch an inquiry into this."

He told the *Daily Mirror*: "It should look at the evident conflict of interest when he was travelling at great expense to the taxpayer as a trade envoy but actively pursuing his own financial interests and those of his mates."

Norman Baker told the *Daily Mail*: "This is outrageous behaviour by Prince Andrew. Any Minister who behaved in this way would be summarily sacked. Even an MP who behaved in this way would face questions from the Commons Standards Committee. We have all had enough of Prince Andrew. He should have his HRH designation removed. As far as I am concerned, he should be persona non grata and not be seen in any way to represent this country."

Although Andrew was not Britain's trade envoy any more, other public duties continued. In 2013, he was elected a royal fellow of the Royal Society, but Britain's pre-eminent scientific institution faced unprecedented dissent from members over the move, with one professor describing the duke as an "unsavoury character". Besides, he had no background in science.

In December 2017, Andrew took out a £1.5 million personal loan with Banque Havilland which was extended on the grounds it could open up "further business potential with the Royal Family". The loan was paid off by Albany Reserves Ltd, which Rowland was a director of.

A spokesperson for the Duke of York said in a statement: "We don't intend to comment on the veracity or otherwise of the string of assertions you have put to us, other than to state that the duke is entitled to a degree of privacy in conducting his entirely legitimate personal financial affairs, on which all appropriate accounting measures are undertaken and all taxes duly paid."

CHAPTER TWENTY-TWO

HEIR MILES

While Andrew was clocking up the air miles, Charles spent his time shuffling around his six homes in the UK, accompanied by a butler, two valets, a chef, a private secretary, a typist, royal protection officers and a truck carrying suitcases and other chattels.

In his book *Rebel King: The Making of a Monarch*, Tom Bower outlined the complex arrangements that would have to be made. Before a visit to a friend, Charles sent his staff ahead a day early with a truck carrying furniture to replace the perfectly adequate contents of the guest rooms. The truck contained Charles and Camilla's complete bedrooms, including the Prince's orthopaedic bed and his own bed linen. Next came a delivery of organic food. This makes Andrew's over-sized ironing board and request for room temperature water seem positively modest.

Royal biographer Gyles Brandreth quotes the Queen saying: "The amount of kit and stuff he takes about – it's obscene."

Her cousin Margaret Rhodes said: "The Queen finds Charles very difficult. He is extravagant and she doesn't like that."

His staff had also made sure to pack a small radio, a bottle of Laphroaig whisky and bottled water for Charles and Camilla's separate bedrooms, plus two landscapes of the Scottish Highlands. Charles had his own private lavatory seat with rolls of Kleenex Premium Comfort lavatory paper.

It was redoubtable Michael Fawcett who laid all these things on. He was also in charge of ensuring that Charles's childhood teddy bear would travel in a plastic bag everywhere the Prince went. When it was in need of a fix, Charles's former nanny Mabel Anderson would patch up the old toy.

Not to be outdone, Andrew had a large collection of teddy bears from all over the world, some dressed up like sailors. A maid was given a day's training in exactly how he wanted them arranged. She said that the smaller bears would usually be stacked in an unused fire-place, while some of his more beloved stuffed toys, such as two hippos and a black panther named "Daddy", "Ducks" and "Prince", were placed on his bed or around the room. But Andrew's two favourite teddy bears were always placed in mahogany thrones by his bedside.

"It was so odd," she said. "After all, he was a grown man who had served in the Falklands. But he absolutely loved the teddies and was very clear about how he wanted them arranged."

Fawcett began his royal service in 1981 as a footman to the Queen, moving up to the post of sergeant footman. He then became Charles's assistant valet at Kensington Palace, laying out his £2,000 bespoke suits and £200 handmade Turnbull & Asser shirts in the morning and pick them up in the evening when they were strewn on the floor. He would pack Charles's highly polished shoes, while hand-kerchiefs and ties for overnight engagements lay protected between folds of tissue paper. As discussed earlier, when the Prince broke his arm playing polo in 1990, the devoted aide would squeeze out the toothpaste from its crested silver container on to his toothbrush and held the urine bottle when a specimen was required.

"Wherever he is in the world, Charles demands that at least one of the senior valets or two of the assistants are available around the clock to prepare his wardrobe," a Palace source said.

An assistant was on call in his office until Charles went to bed and would suffer regular tirades.

"Even my office is not the right temperature," Charles would complain. "Why do I have to put up with this? It makes my life so unbearable."

On another occasion, he rued: "Nobody knows what utter hell it is to be Prince of Wales."

While the Queen was happy to eat what she was served, Charles always stipulated his menu preferences up front or an aide would deliver a bag containing the Prince's own food – organic, of course. And he would attend dinners with a pre-mixed Martini, which was carried by his protection officer. This would be given to the butler to be served in Charles's own glass.

The Queen abhorred his extravagance. Charles took a trip on the royal train from Highgrove to Penrith to visit a pub as part of his "Pub in the Hub" scheme to revitalise villages. The journey cost £18,916. And he spent £20,980 for a day trip by plane from Scotland to Lincolnshire to watch William receive his RAF wings. Meanwhile, the Queen was perfectly happy travelling to Sandringham at Christmas on First Capital Connect for £50, instead of spending £15,000 to roll out the royal train.

When he first turned up at Sandringham with Diana, the Queen was shocked to find that he demanded to have eight rooms. She also lamented the way he demanded his senior staff drive three hours from London to Highgrove for the briefest of meetings only to be left hanging around for most of the day.

"Charles is absolutely desperate for his mother's approval and knows he'll never really get it," a Highgrove regular said. "He's the wrong sort of person for her – too needy, too vulnerable, too emotional, too complicated, too self-centred, the sort of person she can't bear. Arts, charitable causes that aren't wrapped in a rigid sense of duty – it's all anathema to her."

Like Air Miles Andy, Charles was devoted to private planes. He had learnt his lesson. Flying to Hong Kong for its handover to Beijing – or "The Great Chinese Takeaway" as he called it – the Prince complained in his journal that he was seated in Club Class in a chartered British Airways plane: "It took me some time to realise… that this was not first class (!) although it puzzled me as to why the seat seemed so uncomfortable. I then discovered that others like [ex-prime minister] Edward Heath, [ex-Home Secretary] Douglas Hurd, the new foreign secretary, Robin Cook, several former governors of Hong Kong such as Lord MacLehose and Lord Wilson, and the leader of the Liberal Democrats, Paddy Ashdown, were comfortably ensconced in first class immediately below us. 'Such is the end of Empire,' I sighed to myself."

In April 2000 he was persuaded again to take a commercial flight to Europe on a British Airways plane instead of by private jet. He returned vowing never to repeat the experience. His regular flights between London and Scotland on a private jet cost him £20,000.

"He wanted the convenience and not to mix with hoi polloi," observed one onlooker.

However, when he flew to New York to collect the Global Environmental Citizen award from Harvard Medical School, which was presented by Al Gore, the Foreign Office persuaded him to fly on BA, as turning up on a private jet might not strike the right note – just as when he had his Bentley driven to Prague when the British Embassy there had recently acquired a new Jaguar. But Camilla baulked and only conceded when the couple were allowed to take fourteen staff – a butler, a dresser, press officers, a doctor, five police protection officers and her hairdresser. Even so, Charles complained about BA's "incredibly uncomfortable first-class seats".

Buckingham Palace also complained about him accepting free holidays from questionable hosts, so shortly after this wrist-slapping, Charles chartered a private yacht for an eleven-day Caribbean cruise, at a cost of some £210,000. Camilla later grumbled that the boat was smaller than Yiannis Latsis's.

While Fawcett and his travelling entourage may have known where he was going, often his hosts did not. Once a family was asked to put Charles up in their house on the Welsh borders. The hosts invited friends over, ordered food, hired staff and filled the place with cut flowers.

On the Friday afternoon when he was expected to arrive, they got a call saying that Charles was unavoidably delayed by pressure of work, but would be there the following morning. St James's Palace phoned again the next day, saying Charles would miss lunch, but would be there for dinner. That afternoon, the whole visit was called off due to an "unforeseen circumstance". According to Bower, "Charles later revealed to his stricken hostess the reason for his cancellation. He had felt unable to abandon the beauty of his sunlit garden at Highgrove, he said."

Otherwise, he would do the rounds of aristocratic friends – the Earl and Countess of Halifax at Garrowby, at their 20,600-acre estate in Yorkshire, or Sir Chips and Lady Sarah Keswick in remote Invermark, Scotland, where he liked to fish.

As a single man, he had been the guest of the Earl of Powis at Powis Castle in Welshpool, but he could hardly stay there with Camilla as there was only one bathroom.

"However close the Prince and Mrs Parker Bowles are, they do not share bathwater," said a friend of Charles.

Cost was another consideration. After each stay at Powis, Charles always wrote a cheque to the Welsh National Trust for a five-figure sum to cover the upheaval of coping with his entourage and loss of revenue from castle visitors. Meanwhile Fawcett, Charles's assistant, the butler, chef, private secretary, typist and police bodyguards were dispatched to find more suitable accommodation from among Charles's Welsh friends. When together, Charles and Camilla stayed at Vaynor Park, the 4,000-acre estate of his old friends William and Kate Corbett-Winder.

Three times a year they were visitors at Chatsworth, the 175-room home of the Duke and Duchess of Devonshire, aka Debo Mitford. She put aside a whole wing for them for up to three weeks.

During the shooting season, Charles would stay with Gerald Grosvenor, the Duke of Westminster, at either Eaton Hall, near Chester, or at Abbeystead, the Duke's shooting lodge in the Forest of Bowland in Lancashire. Grosvenor and his wife Tally were among Charles's oldest friends.

In August, Charles was sometimes to be found for a few days shooting at Mossdale, the Yorkshire grouse moor of his old friends, investment banker Hugh van Cutsem and his wife Emilie. Hugh was a founding member of the Countryside Movement and in 1994 he won a Country Landowners' Association award for his restoration of an old barn on his Hilborough estate in Norfolk. Charles presented the award.

Another favourite was Newby Hall, near Ripon, the handsome eighteenth-century stately home of Robin and Janey Compton. Robin was formerly chairman and chief executive of the publishing company Time Life International, and the couple had created one of the finest gardens in the country.

When the Prince was performing duties in the Duchy of Cornwall or in South Wales, he liked to stay at Glyn Celyn House, near Brecon, which was the home of merchant banker Nic Paravicini and his wife Sukie. It was there in 1996 that Charles and Camilla made their first tentative steps to go public when they were photographed together in the grounds.

Arriving by chauffeur-driven Bentley or helicopter, they also stayed at the Hotel Tresanton in St Mawes, Cornwall. It was owned by friends, writer William Shawcross and his wife Olga Polizzi, daughter of hotelier Lord Forte. The hotel was closed to other guests during their stay.

These were truly a very different crowd from the sort of people that Andrew hung out with.

Charles frequently went on a monastic retreat on Mount Athos in Greece for a week of solitary meditation. In the year 2000, monks helped unload no fewer than thirty items from the Prince's Land Rover when he arrived there. These included suitcases, briefcases, camera bags, holdalls and rucksacks, all with bright red "HRH Prince of Wales" luggage tags. One large white case contained a state-of-the-art satellite telephone system so he could stay in touch with friends all over the world, particularly Camilla Parker Bowles who could not accompany him to the retreat as women were excluded. Wherever he went without Camilla, he took a high-tech scrambler phone to prevent a repeat of "Tampongate".

After the death of the Queen Mother in March 2002, he returned to Mount Athos with a butler, two valets, chef, private secretary, typist, bodyguards and forty-three pieces of luggage. He also had a lumbar support cushion, which he kept with him at all times to ease his backache. There were also three cool boxes that contained provisions for the Prince, as he does not enjoy Greek food, which he finds too oily.

Charles also brought along his watercolours, together with two umbrellas with the trademark Prince of Wales feathers glinting in the sunshine and boxes full of religious books to read. Some retreat.

Two years later, Charles and his party arrived at Mount Athos on Yiannis Latsis' multi-million-pound yacht. While boasting that he did not own a yacht himself, like Andrew, Charles was happy accepting hospitality on other people's. Andrew has yet to be drawn to Mount Athos or, indeed, any monastic retreat.

While Andrew had a staff that numbered in the tens, Charles employed over 120, including twenty-eight personal servants. Among them were four valets, so that two would always be available to help change his clothes, which he did up to five times every day. Visitors to St James's Palace were escorted to Charles's office by no fewer than three footmen, each responsible for a short segment of corridor.

"Why anybody in this day and age needs that number of servants is completely beyond me," said Labour MP Paul Flynn. "Even the President of the United States makes his own breakfast."

Charles had one private secretary for each of his interests – his charities, architecture, complementary medicine and the environment. There were ten gardeners at Highgrove, costing £2 million a year. They had a particularly hard time. As Charles refused to use pesticides, herbicides or any chemicals, four of them would have to lie face down on the trailer as it was pulled slowly across the lawn, plucking out weeds. In addition, retired Indian servicemen would prowl through the undergrowth at night with torches and hand-pick slugs from the leaves of plants.

CHAPTER TWENTY-THREE

THE UNRAVELLING

Despite his enormous income from the Duchy of Cornwall, Charles was always worried about money. In an effort to enhance his reputation as a do-gooder, he had set up some twenty charities and was patron of 350 organisations. "I was better at starting organisations than running them," he admitted.

He was studiously ignorant of money matters. When an accountant working for the Duchy told him a project was unaffordable, he said: "Why is it unaffordable?"

"Because you haven't got the money," was the reply. Charles left, saying he never wanted to see that man again.

With his reputation in tatters after the Burrell revelations, donors were fleeing in droves. To help him put his charity empire back on a sound financial footing, he solicited help from people such as Fred Goodwin, CEO of the Royal Bank of Scotland, which made a loss of £24.1 billion in 2008, the largest annual loss in British corporate history.

Although Michael Fawcett had resigned a second time in 2003, he was still on hand. He had been cleared of any financial impropriety for the numerous gifts he had received in the course of his royal service. While he had been paid off with a £500,000 golden handshake and allowed to keep his grace-and-favour home in Richmond, he was retained as a freelance fixer. He laid on events, including one where Irish dancer Michael Flatley performed with a troupe of female dancers who whipped off their traditional robes to reveal skimpy bikinis with violin music apparently coming from speakers concealed in their bikini bottoms.

"Jaws dropped. These were high-end donors, some of whom had paid tens of thousands of pounds to be there, maybe more. It was inappropriate," said one guest.

At one point the Prince's Trust was failing, even though it was shored up by £50 million from the government. Both the Prince's Drawing School and the Prince's Teaching Institute, dedicated to "real" teaching and the understanding of literature through weekend schools, were on the verge of insolvency. The answer was a star-studded Shakespearean gala and a show called "Fashion Rocks" at the Royal Albert Hall.

Donors were called in again. Some clearly thought that giving generously might earn them a knighthood. The government got worried that it might appear that Buckingham Palace was for sale. Sir Michael Peat was issued new rules of engagement. In future, favourable seating at the Prince's fundraising dinners would not go to the highest bidder. Instead, donors would buy a table for £20,000 on the understanding that they would make a hefty donation on top.

Warned some reorganisation was required, Charles simply brushed it aside. When he was told that he should reduce the number of charities he had, he simply created new ones.

There were calls for more transparency after there appeared to be some jiggery-pokery over the non-payment of inheritance tax on the Queen Mother's estate, which included a Monet valued at over

£50 million. Then it was revealed that Prince Andrew had spent £3,000 on a single flight from London to Oxford and that £750,000 had been spent on eighteen journeys on the royal train. This prompted the National Audit Office to take an interest in all the royals' accounts, including those of the Duchy of Cornwall.

Summoned to Westminster to be questioned by MPs, Peat presented a document showing that in 2003 Charles had undertaken 517 engagements, met ten thousand people, received nine thousand guests, sent two thousand letters, visited eighteen regiments and raised £109 million for charity – though half that amount had come from the government. On the other side of the ledger, Charles had received £4.1 million from the government to perform his official duties and another £11.9 million from the Duchy of Cornwall.

With the payment of taxes being entirely voluntary, the net worth of the Duchy had increased from £110 million in 1996 to £463 million in 2003. While Charles took an income from the Duchy he was not allowed to sell off any of the assets. Even so, there were other ways to benefit. The Duchy had bought Highgrove and rented it back to Charles at £336,000 a year, which, as income, went straight back into his pocket, tax free. Camilla's upkeep – including her hair, clothes and jewellery – were also on the accounts as she had to make public appearances at official engagements. She was also provided with a chauffeur-driven car and flew only on private jets at Charles's insistence. In due course, the taxpayer would have to fork out £1.8 million on security at her home, Ray Mill House in Wiltshire, just fifteen miles from Highgrove, and £200,000 a year on travel.

Peat argued that the Duchy of Cornwall was not a public body, but a private estate which was not accountable to outside bodies. The MPs on the Public Accounts Committee concluded that it was a giant tax fiddle. But what they thought was immaterial to Charles. The Duchy of Cornwall made a record profit of £14 million the following year. By 2007, he was taking home £16.3 million and increased his staff to 146.

In 2007, Charles decided to buy Dumfries House, a Palladian mansion that had been boarded up and abandoned in the coalfields of Ayrshire. The valuation was £25 million. Charles bought it for £43 million with its collection of Chippendale furniture. And to pay for it, a new charity would be set up to borrow £40 million.

The loan was to be paid off when the East Ayrshire Council redesignated the surrounding agricultural land for housing. But the value of the land plummeted in the 2008 financial crash and Charles targeted rich donors who were flown in for lunch or dinner with the Prince. Fundraising meals would be held at other people's homes and the host was instructed to buy the foodstuffs from the Duchy's organic suppliers. The richest guest would be seated next to Charles who, after examining the donors' pledges, would add an extra zero.

Ever the eco-warrior, at the beginning of 2009 Charles chartered a jet for a ten-day environmental tour of Chile, Brazil and Ecuador. This cost £700,000. Two months later he flew in a chartered Airbus A319 to Italy and Germany to promote the British government's climate change policies. This cost £80,000, instead of the £15,000 he and his entourage would have paid for scheduled flights. His justification was the inordinate amount of luggage he needed. His accoutrements, as usual, included organic foods that were to be cooked in British embassies where he was staying. On his return he used the royal train for a five-day green tour to encourage young people to "tread more lightly on our planet". That journey cost £90,000.

Soon after, he and Camilla travelled on the royal train to a conference at the Museum of Science and Industry in Manchester. In keeping with his Edwardian image, it was to be pulled by a steam engine that produced ninety times more carbon dioxide than a family car.

Meanwhile the Prince's financials were going down the toilet again. The mismanagement of Duchy Originals resulted in a £3.3 million loss in 2009, so Joe Allbritton was asked to ante up once more. When the Foreign Office refused to pay for a private plane to take Charles to visit President Obama in Washington as he had spent nearly £2 million on flights the previous year, Allbritton lent him his Gulfstream. This had to fly across the Atlantic empty to pick up the Prince, fly back with the Prince on board, fly him across the Atlantic again to return him, then fly back to America empty. The Allbrittons were then given prime seats in Westminster Abbey for William and Kate's wedding. Duchy Originals were eventually saved from insolvency by selling the rights to Waitrose.

While banging on about the loss of agricultural land, Charles had sought to pay for Dumfries House by building on nearby fields. He also allowed the Duchy of Cornwall to pave over fifty-five acres of prime farming land in the Tregurra Valley, east of Truro to build a Waitrose supermarket and a housing development. Ian Hibberd of the Save Truro campaign told the *Western Morning News*: "Prince Charles must have the skin of a rhinoceros not to recognise the hypocrisy of it."

"Never mind the 'spirituality' of the countryside," the campaign's website said, "these are business factors which Prince Charles has created by choosing to tarmac and concrete over this land."

While the income from the Duchy itself continued to grow, his charities continued to find themselves in trouble. By 2011, the Prince's Foundation School for Traditional Arts was losing £2 million a year. The Prince's Foundation for the Built Environment had serious debts, but still dispatched full-time officials to the Galápagos Islands, Mumbai and Sierra Leone. The Prince's Charities Foundation had a £4 million deficit without any reserves. The income of the flagship

Prince's Trust was declining, and relied on an annual £15.8 million handout from government. To cover the annual deficit of £2.6 million, the Duchy lent the trust some £9 million.

By 2016 Charles had no alternative but to cut the grants to his charities – some by half – and, to save money, finally begin to merge his twenty-one organisations into a single entity. This made sense as many of them duplicated the same function. Previously, every time Charles alighted on a new issue, he set up a new charity, even when it fell within the purview of an existing organisation.

Dumfries House was still sucking in money to repay the original £43 million purchase price and the millions spent on its renovation. On top of that, the bill for annual maintenance was £600,000. It was let out for conferences, weddings, hotel accommodation and fundraising events for Charles. It was administered by Charles's trusty aide Michael Fawcett, who ran a catering company called Premier Mode on the side that made over £250,000 a year.

Charles was also busy seeking donors. Among those targeted were the Indian businessmen Lakshmi Mittal and the Hinduja brothers. Others included Hans Kristian Rausing (wife of Eva), the Tetra Pak billionaire and former drug addict, who gave £10 million, and Cyrus Vandrevala, another Indian businessman, who contributed £200,000 for an adventure playground and paid £500,000 for Charles's sixty-fifth birthday party at Buckingham Palace. The hedge fund operator Michael Hintze gave £5 million; soon after, he was appointed chairman of the Prince's Foundation for the Built Environment.

More money was raised for Dumfries House from rich Sunni Muslims, especially Saudis and Qataris, including Dr Mahfouz Marei Mubarak bin Mahfouz, a forty-five-year-old Saudi businessman, and Sheikh Hamad bin Abdullah Al Thani, who had sacked Richard Rogers from the Chelsea Barracks development at Charles's request. Like other donors, both Dr Mahfouz and Sheikh Hamad were promised that a bench, garden or fountain in the grounds would be named in their honour although they were unlikely ever to visit the property.

Within four years, Fawcett had helped Charles raise about £19 million to repay the loan from his charitable foundation. In 2018, Dumfries House was taken over by the Prince's Foundation, which was now headed by Michael Fawcett with a salary of £95,000 a year.

In 2013, as Charles's income approached £20 million, he paid just £4.4 million voluntarily in income tax and VAT. When the Public Accounts Committee sought to look into this, they were accused of a "witch hunt" and Charles used the Human Rights Act to prevent them having access to his tax returns. He was now developing all the trappings of an autocrat. At Friday night screenings at Sandringham, he would show *Gosford Park* to assembled guests to show how upstairs-downstairs life should be conducted, while he and Camilla sat in throne-like chairs.

Some thought he was losing it. While out for a stroll one Saturday morning, Charles made a sudden outburst.

"People think I'm bonkers, crackers," he said in the middle of a field. "Do you think I'm mad?"

Clearly his parents had their doubts. Prince Philip said he had little confidence that Charles was really up to the job of being king. There was little love lost between them. Philip believed that his son would never forgive him for his apparent "sins" when Charles was a boy. These included ordering him to wear corduroy trousers to a birthday party. Even as a middle-aged man, Charles still felt the sting of the trivial humiliation of being the only boy in cords.

In Jonathan Dimbleby's 1994 authorised biography of Charles, the Prince blamed both his parents, though particularly Philip, for giving him an unhappy childhood and forcing him into an unsuitable marriage. Preoccupied by his own emotions, Charles showed no sympathy for Philip's own childhood as an exile from his native Greece, forced to move home constantly and robbed of a family life while his mother was confined in a Swiss clinic for eight years with paranoid schizophrenia.

Charles found Philip's criticism intolerable. To show his disdain, he would sit in silence through family meetings at Buckingham Palace, knowing that this would annoy his father. Philip's response was to deliver the odd withering put-down. In 2012, he assigned shooting rights at Sandringham to Princess Anne and her husband Tim Laurence, and the shooting at Balmoral to Edward. For Charles, an excellent shot, this felt like a stinging insult. He had to resort to renting the Invercauld Estate grouse moor near Birkhall or going to friends' estates for pheasant shoots.

His relationship with the Queen was little better. "My son resents me," she once complained, "because I taught him the alphabet."

What worried her most was his penchant for meddling. The monarchy depended on continuity and stability, she thought, and she had a profound dislike of change. All her life, she had loved ceremonial parades with pikes and axes. Charles thought they made it look as if the Palace was stuck in the Dark Ages. He also dismissed Trooping the Colour as a waste of money, while inspecting the guard was a needless chore. If in his reforming zeal Charles tarnished the dignity of the Crown, the Queen thought, his reign would lack the majesty and grandeur she and her father had brought to it.

In 2017, her private secretary Christopher Geidt summoned the entire royal staff to travel from Scotland, Norfolk, Windsor and the other royal estates to gather in the ballroom of Buckingham Palace, ostensibly to announce the retirement of Prince Philip. Geidt told them that Philip's retirement was "an opportunity to pause, reflect and refocus as a family".

Without the duke, everyone was required to step up to help the Queen and focus more on what the monarchy was there to do, not the various issues the princes had taken up on their own. It was also noted the royals should stick to ceremonies and leave issues to the professionals. The Queen at Buckingham Palace, the Prince of Wales at Clarence House and the Duke of Cambridge at Kensington Palace needed to come together as one family delivering for the state.

While the headlines were reserved for glowing tributes to Philip, Charles felt that Geidt's call for the focus to be more on what the monarchy was there to do was an implied criticism of his personal activities. The family pulling together would also benefit Andrew, whose relationship with Jeffrey Epstein and Ghislaine Maxwell was already coming under scrutiny. Charles was not having it. He wanted more of the limelight and insisted on taking over more of his mother's duties. Geidt duly fell by the wayside.

Although the Queen had little time for her eldest son, at the age of ninety-one, she could no longer undertake many official duties. Even walking up flights of stairs in the Palace of Westminster at the opening of Parliament was becoming more than she could manage. But she believed in the monarchy and had dedicated her life to it. That meant the strict rules of inheritance had to be obeyed. Charles's position as the king in waiting had to be demonstrated publicly. On Remembrance Sunday 2017, just a week before his sixty-ninth birthday, he would lay a wreath at the Cenotaph on her behalf. From then on, he would undertake all her foreign trips and, at the Commonwealth Summit, held in London in April 2018, it was agreed that Charles should succeed his mother as head of the Commonwealth.

Meanwhile, Charles was laying plans for his succession. His coronation would be followed by a whistle-stop tour of the nation. Portraits for his likeness on the coins were already being drawn up. He rejected those showing his thinning pate, demanding that he be shown with a full head of hair and looking considerably younger than he was.

Within the Palace there were still fears that, on the throne, Charles would continue his agenda on pet topics. They were worried that, as an elderly monarch in a hurry, he would spark a constitutional crisis. One possible cause was his appropriately cavalier attitude towards money. The plane he used in his 2017 spring tour of Europe, including his annual visit to his Romanian guest house, cost the taxpayer a whopping £154,000. As Prince of Wales, he had been spendthrift enough. Once he was king, who would be able to make him change his ways? Charles I, after all, fell out with Parliament over money.

CHAPTER TWENTY-FOUR

MISCALCULATION

After the death of Princess Diana, Charles had kept on seeing Camilla, despite public disapproval. Hostility within the Royal Family eased with the deaths of Princess Margaret and the Queen Mother. A skilful public relations campaign fought by Charles and his PR guru Mark Bolland won the public around when it became clear that the Prince of Wales was not going to give up his first love.

Eventually, the Queen, Andrew, William and Harry relented and, with the formal consent of the monarch, the government and the Church of England, the couple were allowed to wed. On 8 April 2005, they tied the knot in a civil ceremony at Windsor Guildhall, with a subsequent religious service of blessing in St George's Chapel, though there were questions whether it was lawful for a member of the Royal Family to marry in a civil ceremony.

While Charles settled into married life, Andrew remained single and continued his old womanising ways. With the birth of Prince Harry, he had slipped to fourth in line to the throne. So what did he have to lose? But other things were, apparently, going on behind the scenes.

The trouble for Andrew began on 6 July 2019, when his friend, billionaire businessman Jeffrey Epstein, was arrested on federal charges related to sex trafficking. Court papers relating to earlier cases in Florida were reopened and the FBI began a new investigation. Epstein died mysteriously in jail on 10 August and more women who claimed to have been abused by him as minors stepped forward. With Epstein dead, media attention turned to Andrew, as he had been photographed walking with Epstein in Central Park in February 2011, after he had completed his sentence on earlier underage sex charges.

Andrew had stayed in Epstein's homes in New York, Florida and the US Virgin Islands, where other guests said it would have been impossible not to know what was going on. One of Epstein's underage victims, Virginia Roberts, claimed that she had been trafficked in March 2001. At the age of seventeen, she said she had been flown to London by Epstein and Ghislaine Maxwell – later convicted of procuring for Epstein – to have sex with Andrew. They had been to the nightclub Tramp before going back to Maxwell's house in Belgravia where the infamous photograph of him with his arm round her bare midriff had been taken.

In an interview with the *National Enquirer*, Roberts made a series of allegations against Andrew in which she claimed: "He was groping me. He touched my breasts. He touched my ass. He was not my type, but I'd been trained not only to not show my emotions, but to do what was wanted... He wasn't rude. It wasn't like rape, but it wasn't like love, either. It was more like, 'I'm getting my business done.'"

She claimed that afterwards, Maxwell praised her for making Andrew happy and Epstein paid her $15,000 the following day.

A few weeks later she was flown from her home in Florida to New York. When she arrived at Epstein's mansion in Manhattan, she said, she was told, "Get ready, you are meeting someone in the library."

"Andrew was sitting there in a big leather armchair behind which there was a desk covered with photos of girls and young women, including one of me," she said. "I was almost nude in the picture. I don't think Andrew could have missed seeing it when he walked in... He was smiling ear to ear."

Her account suggested Andrew clearly knew what she was there for. Roberts took him upstairs to a room they called the "dungeon" where they undressed. She reportedly gave him a nude massage and they had sex.

"He couldn't have cared less about me as a young woman," she alleged. "He was being treated to sex for which someone else was paying. From the sniggering noises he was making, he was really enjoying the whole thing, but I felt like a total prostitute. He never even said, 'Did you enjoy it?' I was there for just one purpose."

Later Roberts reported to have had a miscarriage. She claimed she hadn't even known she was pregnant, nor did she know who the father was.

"The third time I had sex with Andy was in an orgy on Epstein's private island in the US Virgin Islands," claimed Roberts. "I was around eighteen at the time. Epstein, Andy, approximately eight other young girls and I had sex together. The other girls all seemed and appeared to be under the age of eighteen and didn't really speak English."

Buckingham Palace issued repeated denials. Then, against the advice of his staff, Andrew made the surprise decision to go on television for an hour-long interview with *Newsnight* presenter Emily Maitlis. This was broadcast on BBC Two on 16 November 2019.

Andrew said he had met Epstein in 1999 through Epstein's girlfriend, Ghislaine Maxwell, whom Andrew had known since she was at university in the UK. But he denied they were close friends. He also denied that he was close friends with Epstein, though they met up two or three times a year and he would stay in Epstein's houses, even when the financier wasn't there.

Although Andrew had the reputation of being the "party prince", he said he never really partied and "going to Jeffrey's was not about partying, absolutely not". The reason Andrew gave for getting to know Epstein was that he was about to become UK special representative for international trade and investment. His time in the Navy had left him cut off and he needed to know more about the world of international business and Wall Street.

Maitlis then put to him that Epstein was welcomed into the heart of the Royal Family when Andrew invited him to Windsor Castle and Sandringham as his guest in 2000.

Andrew confirmed that this was true.

Maitlis then brought up the birthday party that Andrew held for Epstein's girlfriend, Ghislaine Maxwell, at Sandringham.

Andrew denied this, saying it was a simple shooting weekend. Prince Charles had also been there.

Maitlis put to Andrew that it was now known that, at that time, Epstein had been procuring young girls for sex trafficking.

"We now know that – at the time there was no indication to me or anybody else that that was what he was doing and certainly when I saw him either in the United States," said Andrew. "When I saw him in the United States or when I was staying in his houses in the United States, there was no indication, absolutely no indication."

Andrew volunteered that, at the time, he was patron of the National Society for the Prevention of Cruelty to Children's Full Stop campaign… "so I was close up with what was going on in those times about getting rid of abuse to children so I knew what the things were to look for but I never saw them."

Maitlis then asked Andrew to confirm that, in all the times he had visited and stayed with Epstein at his homes, nothing had struck him as suspicious. "Nothing", replied Andrew.

He confirmed that he had been on Epstein's private plane and stayed at his homes in Palm Beach and New York, and on his private island in the US Virgin Islands.

In May 2006, an arrest warrant had been issued for Epstein for sexual assault of a minor. That July he had been invited to Windsor Castle to Andrew's daughter Princess Beatrice's eighteenth birthday. "Why would you do that?" he was asked. Andrew said because he was inviting Ghislaine. Coincidentally, Harvey Weinstein was at that party too.

At the time the invitation was sent, Andrew said he knew nothing about Epstein's arrest.

"I wasn't aware until the media picked up on it because he never said anything about it," he said. "You see this is the problem is that an awful lot of this was going on in the United States and I wasn't a party to it and I knew nothing about it."

Andrew said he had broken off contact with Epstein when he discovered he was under investigation in 2006. Epstein was convicted of soliciting and procuring a minor for prostitution in 2008 and jailed.

Maitlis then pointed out that after Epstein was released in July 2010, Andrew stayed with him in December at his New York mansion. She asked the prince why he was staying with a convicted sex offender.

"Right, I have always... ever since this has happened and since this has become, as it were, public knowledge that I was there," said Andrew stumbling, "I've questioned myself as to why did I go and what was I doing and was it the right thing to do? Now, I went there with the sole purpose of saying to him that because he had been convicted, it was inappropriate for us to be seen together."

He said a number of people were advising him to go and see Epstein, while others advised him not to.

"I took the judgement call that because this was serious and I felt that doing it over the telephone was the chicken's way of doing it, I had to go and see him and talk to him."

He said he was doing a number of other things in New York at the time.

"We had an opportunity to go for a walk in the park and that was the conversation coincidentally that was photographed which was when I said to him, I said, 'Look, because of what has happened, I don't think it is appropriate that we should remain in contact,' and by mutual agreement during that walk in the park we decided that we would part company and I left, I think it was the next day, and to this day I never had any contact with him from that day forward."

Epstein understood, but said he had accepted a plea bargain, served his time and was getting on with his life.

"I said, 'Yes but I'm afraid to say that that's as maybe but with all the attendant scrutiny on me then I don't think it is a wise thing to do.'"

The decision to see Epstein to break off the relationship in person was Andrew's alone to make: "Some people from my staff, some people from friends and family I was talking to and I took the decision that it was I had to show leadership and I had to go and see him and I had to tell him, 'That's it.'"

Maitlis said Epstein had thrown a party to celebrate his release and Andrew was invited as guest of honour. Andrew said he didn't go, then added: "Oh, in 2010, there certainly wasn't a party to celebrate his release in December because it was a small dinner party, there were only eight or ten of us I think at the dinner." One of the other guests was Woody Allen.

Maitlis asked why Andrew had stayed several days at the New York town house of a convicted sex offender?

"It was a convenient place to stay," Andrew replied. "I mean I've gone through this in my mind so many times. At the end of the day, with a benefit of all the hindsight that one can have, it was definitely the wrong thing to do. But at the time I felt it was the honourable and right thing to do, and I admit fully that my judgement was probably coloured by my tendency to be too honourable but that's just the way it is."

Maitlis then pointed out that, during the time he was staying at Epstein's house, witnesses say they saw many young girls coming and going and there was video footage of Epstein accompanied by young girls while Andrew was there.

"I never…," said Andrew stumbling again, "…I mean if there were, then I wasn't a party to any of that. I never saw them. I mean you have to understand that his house, I described it more as almost as a railway station, if you know what I mean, in the sense that there were people coming in and out of that house all the time. What they were doing and why they were there I had nothing to do with. So I'm afraid I can't make any comment on that because I really don't know."

Another guest in Epstein's house was literary agent John Brockman who had said he had seen Andrew getting a foot massage by a young Russian woman. Andrew said he could not remember and he did not know Mr Brockman. Then he said it was definitely not him who had been getting a foot massage.

Again casting doubt on Andrew's story, Maitlis said that Andrew had chosen a funny way to end his relationship with Epstein – "a four-day house party of sorts with a dinner. It's an odd way to break up a friendship."

Andrew agreed, though said it was a "difficult… stark way of putting it".

"But actually the truth of it is that I actually only saw him for about, what, the dinner party, the walk in the park and probably passing in the passage."

Was Epstein being photographed walking in Central Park with Andrew part of his rehabilitation? Maitlis suggested. Andrew didn't think so. Nor did he think that the photograph had been staged by Epstein to compromise him. He did regret the trip, he said, but he did not regret his friendship with Epstein.

"Now, still not, and the reason being is that the people that I met and the opportunities that I was given to learn either by him or because of him were actually very useful," Andrew said. "He himself not, as it were, as close as you might think, we weren't that close. So, therefore, I mean yes, I would go and stay in his house but that was because of his girlfriend, not because of him."

He claimed that his visit in December 2010 was the only time he had seen Epstein after his conviction, nor had he spoken to him since.

"Funny enough, 2010 was it, that was it because I went... well, first of all I wanted to make sure that if I was going to go and see him, I had to make sure that there was enough time between his release because it wasn't something that I was going into in a hurry but I had to go and see him, I had to go and see him, I had to talk."

"And stay with him, and stay in the house of a convicted sex offender?" asked Maitlis.

"I could easily have gone and stayed somewhere else but sheer convenience of being able to get a hold of the man was... I mean, he was in and out all over the place. So, getting him in one place for a period of time to actually have a long enough conversation to say look, these are the reasons why I'm not going to... and that happened on the walk."

If admitting a friendship with a known sex offender and staying in his various houses where these offences had taken place was not bad enough, things were about to get a whole lot worse.

CHAPTER TWENTY-FIVE

TRAMP

Having dealt with Andrew's relationship with Jeffrey Epstein, Maitlis moved on to the nub off the matter – his relationship with Virginia Roberts, who said she had met Andrew in 2001, had dinner with him, danced and had a drink with him at Tramp nightclub in London and had sex with him first at Ghislaine Maxwell's house in Belgravia, again in Epstein's house in New York and a third time at an orgy in the US Virgin Islands.

Andrew said he had no recollection of ever meeting Roberts. None whatsoever. Pushed, he repeated: "I've no recollection of ever meeting her, I'm almost, in fact I'm convinced, that I was never in Tramp with her. There are a number of things that are wrong with that story, one of which is that I don't know where the bar is in Tramp. I don't drink, I don't think I've ever bought a drink in Tramp whenever I was there."

Andrew had long been a regular at Tramp. It was where he had met Koo Stark in 1981. He had invited the club's co-founder Johnny Gold to his wedding to Sarah Ferguson in 1986. The dance floor is within ten metres of the bar. It's next to the DJ's booth. The gents was at the other end of the bar. So it would have been very difficult for him not to know where the bar was. However, Andrew insisted he could not have been at Tramp that night because he was at home with his children.

"On that particular day that we now understand is the date which is 10 March, I was at home, I was with the children and I'd taken Beatrice to a Pizza Express in Woking for a party at, I suppose, sort of four or five in the afternoon. And then because the duchess was away, we have a simple rule in the family that when one is away the other one is there. I was on terminal leave at the time from the Royal Navy so therefore I was at home."

Others recalled other occasions when he did leave the children – then twelve and ten – in the care of the staff when Fergie was away. But why did he remember so clearly what he was doing that day?

"Because going to Pizza Express in Woking is an unusual thing for me to do, a very unusual thing for me to do. I've never been… I've only been to Woking a couple of times and I remember it weirdly distinctly."

Woking is only twenty miles from London, so it would have been possible to have a pizza there in the afternoon and be in London in the evening – even if you went by car, and Prince Andrew had a proclivity for helicopters.

Then came the question of sweating. Maitlis said Roberts remembered him sweating profusely on the dance floor.

"There's a slight problem with the sweating because I have a peculiar medical condition which is that I don't sweat or I didn't sweat at the time," he said. "I didn't sweat at the time because I had suffered what I would describe as an overdose of adrenalin in the Falklands War when I was shot at and I simply… it was almost impossible for me to sweat."

The inability to sweat is called anhidrosis or hypohydrosis. It can be a congenital condition, or it occurs during heatstroke when the body has no fluid to sweat. Otherwise, it can be caused by skin damage such as burns, nerve damage or certain medications such as strong painkillers like morphine. Medical experts said that excess levels of adrenalin caused more sweating rather than less.

Andrew ruled out the possibility that he had met Virginia Roberts on another occasion. Nor could he explain the photograph of him with his arm round her waist with Ghislaine Maxwell in her Belgravia home. Friends of his had suggested it was fake, though experts can find no evidence of that. Epstein was said to have taken the picture.

"I've never seen Epstein with a camera in my life," said Andrew.

Roberts said that she had a small Kodak camera which she gave to Epstein to take the picture as a souvenir. But Andrew was adamant.

"Listen, I don't remember, I don't remember that photograph ever being taken. I don't remember going upstairs in the house because that photograph was taken upstairs," he said, beginning to get flustered. He did admit that it was a picture of him, but did not believe that it was taken in London.

"When I go out in London, I wear a suit and a tie," he said. "Those are my travelling clothes if I'm going to go… if I'm going overseas. There's a… I've got plenty of photographs of me dressed in those sorts of… that sort of kit but not there."

"Could it have been taken at Maxwell's house on a different occasion?" Maitlis asked. He immediately pulled rank.

"I'm terribly sorry but if I, as a member of the Royal Family, and I have a photograph taken and I take very, very few photographs, I am not one to, as it were, hug and public displays of affection are not something that I do. So that's the best explanation I can give you and I'm afraid to say that I don't believe that photograph was taken in the way that has been suggested."

Maitlis pressed him further: "There's a photo inside Ghislaine Maxwell's house, Ghislaine herself in the background. Why would people not believe that you were there with her that night?"

"They might well wish to believe it," said Andrew, "but the photograph is taken upstairs and I don't think I ever went upstairs in Ghislaine's house."

If he had never been upstairs at Ghislaine's house, how did he know that the picture had been taken upstairs? He was at a loss to explain it.

"If the original was ever produced, then perhaps we might be able to solve it but I can't."

He did not recall meeting Virginia Roberts, dining with her, dancing with her at Tramp or going on to have sex with her in a bedroom in a house in Belgravia. And he insisted that he never had any sexual contact with her, though in a court document in 2015 Roberts said that they had sex three times – the first time when she was trafficked to London, the second time in Epstein's house in New York.

"Yeah, well I think that the date we have for that shows that I was in Boston or I was in New York the previous day and I was at a dinner for the Outward Bound Trust in New York and then I flew up to Boston the following day and then on the day that she says that this occurred, they'd already left to go the island before I got back from Boston. So I don't think that could have happened at all."

The aide who controlled Andrew's diary pointed out that there were plenty of gaps in his schedule. Another of Epstein's victims, Johanna Sjoberg, said that Andrew visited the house at that time, though Andrew claimed that, on that trip, he had stayed with the British Consul General nearby.

"I may have visited but no, definitely didn't, definitely, definitely no, no, no activity."

The British Consul General Sir Thomas Harris said: "I have no recollection of him staying at the address in April 2001. "I don't have a note of the dates of all the visits... It doesn't ring any bells whatsoever."

The third occasion was, Virginia Roberts said, on Epstein's private island with seven or eight other girls. Andrew denied everything and said he did not know why she was saying these things – though he stopped short of accusing her of lying.

"If Virginia Roberts is watching this interview, what is your message to her?" Maitlis asked.

"I don't have a message for her because I have to have a thick skin," he said. "If somebody is going to make those sorts of allegations then I've got to have a thick skin and get on with it, but they never happened."

"For the record, is there any way you could have had sex with that young woman or any young woman trafficked by Jeffrey Epstein in any of his residences?" Maitlis asked.

"No, and without putting too fine a point on it, if you're a man it is a positive act to have sex with somebody. You have to take some sort of positive action and so therefore if you try to forget it's very difficult to try and forget a positive action and I do not remember anything. I can't, I've wracked my brain and thinking oh... when the first allegations, when the allegations came out originally I went 'well that's a bit strange, I don't remember this', and then I've been through it and through it and through it over and over and over again and no, nothing. It just never happened."

Maitlis then turned to a legal deposition made by Epstein's housekeeper saying that Andrew visited the Palm Beach residence around four times a year and got a daily massage. Andrew insisted that he had only visited the Palm Beach mansion four times in the entire time that he had known Epstein.

"Is there a chance that those massages might have been the services of someone who is being sexually exploited or trafficked by Epstein?"

"No, I don't think... I mean I... no, definitely not, definitely not..."

Maitlis pointed out that Virginia Roberts's legal team had said that you could not spend time around Epstein and not know what was going on.

Andrew's response was regal: "If you are somebody like me then people behave in a subtly different way. You wouldn't... first of all, I'm not looking for it, that's the thing, you see, if you're looking for it, then you might have suspected now with the benefit of a huge amount of hindsight and a huge amount of analysis, you look back and you go well was that really the way that it was or was I looking at it the very wrong way? But you don't go into these places, you don't go to stay with people looking for that."

Maitlis pressed the point. Again quoting Roberts's legal team, she said: "You could not spend time around him and not know."

But, as a royal, Andrew was above such things: "I live in an institution at Buckingham Palace which has members of staff walking around all the time, and I don't wish to appear grand, but there were a lot of people who were walking around Jeffrey Epstein's house. As far as I was aware, they were staff, they were people that were working for him, doing things, I... as it were, I interacted with them if you will to say good morning, good afternoon but I didn't, if you see what I mean, interact with them in a way that was, you know what are you doing here, why are you here, what's going on?"

Maitlis would not be thrown off track, saying: "But you'd notice if there were hundreds of underage girls in Buckingham Palace wouldn't you?"

Andrew conceded that he would notice if there were hundreds of underage girls around Epstein's house, but insisted there weren't, not when he was there.

"Now he may have changed his behaviour patterns in order for that not to be obvious to me so I don't…" he said. "You're asking me to speculate on things that I just don't know about."

Maitlis found this hard to swallow.

"You seem utterly convinced you're telling the truth," said Maitlis, who clearly had her doubts. "Would you be willing to testify or give a statement under oath if you were asked?"

Andrew's reply was guarded.

"Well, I'm like everybody else and I will have to take all the legal advice that there was before I was to do that sort of thing," he said. "But if push came to shove and the legal advice was to do so, then I would be duty-bound to do so."

Maitlis's thoughts were with the victims. There were many unanswered questions and they wanted closure which he could help provide. But Andrew was more concerned about himself.

"In the right circumstances, yes I would because I think there's just as much closure for me as there is for everybody else and undoubtedly some very strange and unpleasant activities have been going on. I'm afraid to say that I'm not the person who can shed light on it for a number of reasons, one of which is that I wasn't there long enough," he said. "If you go in for a day, two days at a time, it's quite easy I'm led to believe for those sorts of people to hide their activities for that period of time and then carry on when they're not there."

Maitlis pointed out that Virginia Roberts's lawyers had asked for a legal statement from him and the FBI were investigating. Again, Andrew hid behind his lawyers, saying that he would provide a statement if that was what they advised. As it turned out, he did not provide any statement to Roberts's lawyers, nor did he co-operate with the FBI or the US Department of Justice, despite repeated requests.

Andrew refused to speculate on the theory that Epstein had not taken his own life. Nor would he address the question of whether Ghislaine Maxwell was complicit in Epstein's offences. He insisted that his behaviour towards Epstein had been honourable when he had told him that he could not see him any more after he had been convicted. When it came to his old friend: "If there are questions that Ghislaine has to answer, that's her problem I'm afraid. I'm not in a position to be able to comment one way or the other."

He had met her earlier that year on 5 June, when she had been in London to take part in the Monaco rally, but they had not discussed Epstein, even though US investigators had announced that they were reopening their investigation into the disgraced financier two weeks earlier.

"There wasn't anything to discuss about him because he wasn't in the news," he said. "We had moved on."

Actually, Epstein was in the news as there were calls in Congress for an investigation into US Secretary of Labor Alexander Acosta over the sweetheart deal he had arranged for Epstein in 2008, getting him just thirteen months in jail, when Acosta was a US attorney in southern Florida. He had been forced to resign his cabinet post in July 2019.

Asked how he was moving on, Andrew said: "I'm carrying on with what I do. I have a number of things that I have been doing since 2011; they're pretty well organised, pretty successful and so I'm carrying on and trying to improve those things that I'm already doing."

He did not think that the Queen had been damaged by the scandal, but he had been. "It's been a constant drip, if you see what I mean, in the background that people want to know. If I was in a position to be able to answer all these questions in a way that gave sensible answers other than the ones that I have given that gave closure then I'd love it, but I'm afraid I can't. I'm just not in a position to do so because I'm just as much in the dark as many people."

His aim now was to reconnect with people by continuing to work with his entrepreneurial scheme Pitch@Palace and the Inspiring Digital Enterprise Award iDEA. His judgement call when it came to visiting Epstein after he had been convicted still troubled him.

"It's almost a mental health issue to some extent for me in the sense that it's been nagging at my mind for a great many years. I know that I made the wrong judgement and I made the wrong decision, but I made the wrong decision and the wrong judgement I believe fundamentally for the right reasons, which is to say to somebody 'I'm not going to see you again', and in fact from that day forth, I was never in contact with him."

The problem was social media. That was what was causing him difficulties. The allegations against him were "surprising, shocking and a distraction. But… there are all sorts of things that are on the internet."

Did he have a sense of guilt, regret or shame about his behaviour or his friendship with Epstein?

"As far as Mr Epstein was concerned, it was the wrong decision to go and see him in 2010," he said. "As far as my association with him was concerned, it had some seriously beneficial outcomes in areas that have nothing to do with what I would describe as what we're talking about today."

Meeting Epstein had been inevitable because of his friendship with Ghislaine Maxwell.

"Do I regret the fact that he has quite obviously conducted himself in a manner unbecoming? Yes."

Maitlis was visibly shocked.

"Unbecoming? He was a sex offender," she said.

Andrew back-pedalled.

"I'm sorry, I'm being polite," he said. "I mean in the sense that he was a sex offender. But no, was I right in having him as a friend? At the time, bearing in mind this was some years before he was accused of being a sex offender. I don't [think] there was anything wrong then."

But after Epstein had been convicted, Andrew had stayed with him.

"I kick myself for that on a daily basis," he said. "It was not something that was becoming of a member of the Royal Family, and we try and uphold the highest standards and practices and I let the side down, simple as that."

Drawing the interview to a close, Maitlis asked if there was anything he felt had been left unsaid that he would like to say now.

"No, I don't think so," he said. "I think you've probably dragged out most of what is required and I'm truly grateful for the opportunity that you've given me to be able to discuss this with you."

He did not take this opportunity to express his sympathy for Epstein's victims.

The establishing shot of Andrew walking through the Palace with Maitlis were filmed after the interview. Maitlis said that Andrew was pleased with himself, confident that by facing the cameras he had drawn a line under the affair. He could not have been more wrong.

"Astonished nation watches prince squirm," was the *Mail on Sunday*'s front-page headline. "Many viewers shocked by 'total lack of empathy.'" The newspaper also criticised the Prince for uttering "not one word of remorse". The *Sunday Mirror* said: "No sweat… and no regret."

The Agence France-Presse carried the headline: "Britain's Prince Andrew lambasted after 'catastrophic' interview on Epstein links."

The *New York Times* said: "Prince Andrew gets candid, and Britain is appalled" and his answers were "defensive, unpersuasive or just plain strange". Pointing out that "Prince Andrew claims liaison never happened because he couldn't sweat," the *New York Post* carried the front-page headline: "HIS ROYAL DRYNESS".

Although Andrew was pleased with his performance – even telling the Queen so – those who watched it concluded that he was lying. The interview was judged, by many including the Royal Family, to be a car crash or worse.

"I expected a train wreck," said Charlie Proctor, editor of Royal Central, a website that covers the travails of the British monarchy. "That was a plane crashing into an oil tanker, causing a tsunami, triggering a nuclear explosion-level bad."

The *Sunday Times* reported that Prince Charles "had been divided over the wisdom of the interview". The *Daily Mirror* said Prince Charles had not been given prior notice of his younger brother's interview and told advisers he believed Andrew had made "a huge miscalculation".

Despite the damage to the monarchy, Charles could use it to improve his position in the eyes of the public. He may have admitted committing adultery on TV, but that was nothing compared to the disgrace that had now befallen Andrew. A royal commentator told the *Daily Star* that Charles was stepping up preparations to be king "within the next ten years". Others put his wait at eighteen months, believing that when the Queen reached ninety-five, she would trigger the Regency Act, making him Prince Regent – or King in all but name.

He'd be lucky. At a dinner in Mayfair the year before, Philip joked about the Queen's longevity, explaining that this was to keep Charles off the throne. At ninety-one, he said, she could well live for another ten years, judging by her mother. Charles would have little time to damage the monarchy if he was not king for long. Philip could hardly hide his scorn for his son's achievements and vision. In his eyes, Charles had barely come to terms with the twentieth century, let alone the twenty-first. As a country gentleman hankering for a forgotten world, he would be a danger to the institution of the monarchy. His reign would be about the past rather than the future. The meddling prince might well become a meddling monarch. This could jeopardise the monarchy's very existence.

For the moment, though, Prince Andrew was the real threat to the family. The *Daily Mail* said: "All those years as heir in line to the throne – before Prince Charles had his family – have given Andrew an inflated sense of his own importance."

Peter Hunt, the BBC's former royal correspondent, tweeted: "Will Prince Charles have the courage to do what he should do – and tell Prince Andrew to retire from public life on the basis his judgement has been called into question one too many times? Their mother won't – Andrew is one of her blind spots."

Charles was also miffed because the fallout from the interview would overshadow the week-long tour of New Zealand he was about to embark on with Camilla. It was reported that he advised the Queen to sack Andrew from royal duties to safeguard the long-term future of the monarchy. Buckingham Palace then put out a statement on Andrew's behalf, saying that Andrew was stepping back from public duties for the foreseeable future.

His office in Buckingham Palace was closed down.

"The Queen has been locked in phone calls with Charles, who is on tour in New Zealand, since the crisis broke," wrote royal correspondent Tom Sykes. He also said that the two princes had not been on speaking terms for some time.

Prince William similarly put his oar in, saying that Andrew had "hoodwinked" the Queen by not warning her about the interview.

Nevertheless, the following day, the Queen went riding with Prince Andrew in the grounds of Windsor Castle in a defiant show of support for her beleaguered son.

Returning from the Solomon Islands at the end of his tour of the South Pacific, Charles travelled directly to Sandringham to consult Prince Philip over the scandal. After all, Andrew was hardly the favourite son now. Meanwhile, William was sent to see the Queen at Buckingham Palace, where they too discussed Andrew's fate.

With Philip now retired, Charles took his place next to the Queen at the State Opening of Parliament and would take his mother's place at the forthcoming Commonwealth Heads of Government Meeting. Charles was now seen as "Shadow King" and head of the family. The fate of his errant brother lay in his hands.

CHAPTER TWENTY-SIX

DISGRACE

Virginia Roberts – now using her married name Giuffre – had also recorded an interview for the BBC with the *Panorama* programme to be aired just two weeks later, on 2 December 2019. With days to go, Prince Charles called for a summit at Sandringham. He had consulted his father Prince Philip and his friend Sir Nicholas Soames, the veteran MP and grandson of Sir Winston Churchill, on how best to handle the crisis. Charles, it was said, wanted an "open and honest" discussion with his brother.

"He has told his brother to be completely up front, open and honest with him about his relationship with Epstein and this woman and if there is anything else he thinks could still come out," a source told the *Sunday Mirror*.

But his mind already seemed to be made up. Charles was still planning to strip back the Royal Family to just him, William and Harry, plus their wives and children, when he became king. The Jeffrey Epstein scandal was the perfect opportunity to get rid of his troublesome brother.

Andrew was then summoned to Sandringham for a "crisis lunch" just hours before Virginia Giuffre's interview was broadcast. A royal source told the *Sun*: "It was all very civilised and calm but Charles calmly read him the Riot Act and told him there was no way back for him in the near future." Andrew didn't stick around at Sandringham to watch the *Panorama* interview. While Andrew had been told that he had to give up all royal duties for "the foreseeable future", Charles went back to London to host a NATO reception at Buckingham Palace with his mother.

At Charles's urging, Andrew issued a statement saying: "It has become clear to me over the last few days that the circumstances relating to my former association with Jeffrey Epstein has become a major disruption to my family's work and the valuable work going on in the many organisations and charities that I am proud to support. Therefore, I have asked Her Majesty if I may step back from public duties for the foreseeable future, and she has given her permission.

"I continue to unequivocally regret my ill-judged association with Jeffrey Epstein. His suicide has left many unanswered questions, particularly for his victims, and I deeply sympathise with everyone who has been affected and wants some form of closure. I can only hope that, in time, they will be able to rebuild their lives. Of course, I am willing to help any appropriate law enforcement agency with their investigations, if required."

But he did not offer any assistance to the FBI, and Scotland Yard refused even to look into the matter, though Giuffre had made a complaint to the Metropolitan Police in 2015 and accused him of rape.

In the *Panorama* interview, Giuffre repeated her earlier accusations and urged Andrew to come clean. She pushed back against the idea that a widely circulated photograph that showed Andrew standing with his hand round her waist was doctored.

"The people on the inside are going to keep coming up with these ridiculous excuses like his arm was elongated or the photo was doctored, or he came to New York to break up with Jeffrey Epstein," she said. "I mean I'm calling BS on this, because that's what it is. He knows what happened. I know what happened. And there's only one of us telling the truth."

She insisted that the photograph was real and that she had handed the original to the FBI in 2011. Further forensic examination by Hany Farid, professor of digital forensics and image analysis in UC Berkeley's School of Information, found no signs that the photograph had been doctored.

"I think the world is getting sick of these ridiculous excuses," she said, adding that there was a date on the back of the photo showing when it was printed – just two days after they met, she said.

Michael Thomas, a freelance photographer who copied the original picture before it was handed over, said it was found in a pile of photographs Virginia had given him.

"It wasn't like she pulled the photo of Prince Andrew out – it was just in amongst the rest of them," he said. "These were five-by-seven photos that looked like they had come from Boots, nothing more complicated than that. They were just typical teenage snaps. There's no way that photo is fake."

An affidavit from Tony Figueroa, a man Virginia was dating in 2001, reportedly confirms he saw the picture and that she told him she was forced to have sex with the Prince. The date stamp on the back shows it was developed on 13 March 2001. The stamp also shows that it was processed in the Walgreen's store, just two minutes from Virginia's Florida home. The grain of the film showed that it could not have been altered digitally, according to forensic image expert Bryan Neumeister.

Virginia's account of the evening began with tea at Maxwell's house, where Andrew spoke about his former wife, Fergie, whom Maxwell was bad-mouthing.

"I was just sitting there like I was always told to do," she said. "Be polite and laugh at everything someone says when they're trying to be funny."

She continued with her account of what had happened at Tramp.

"We went to the VIP section. There was no waiting in the lines obviously – you were with a prince. Andrew asked what I wanted to drink then asked me to dance," she said. "He is the most hideous dancer I've ever seen in my life. It was horrible and this guy was sweating all over me, his sweat was like it was raining basically everywhere. I was just like grossed out from it, but I knew I had to keep him happy because that's what Jeffrey and Ghislaine would have expected from me."

When they left the club Maxwell gave her instructions.

"In the car Ghislaine tells me that I have to do for Andrew what I do for Jeffrey and that just made me sick," she said. "I just didn't expect it from royalty. I didn't expect it from someone who people look up to and admire, you know, in the Royal Family."

She grew emotional when she recalled having sex with Andrew upstairs at Maxwell's house in Belgravia.

"There was a bath, and it started there, and then it led into the bedroom," she said. "It didn't last very long, the whole entire procedure. It was disgusting. He wasn't mean or anything but he got up and said 'thanks' and walked out, and I sat there in bed, just horrified and ashamed, and felt dirty. I had to get up and have a shower."

The next day, Virginia recalled: "Ghislaine said, 'You did a really good job,' and pats me on the back and says, 'You made him really happy.'"

It had not made Virginia happy though.

"It was a wicked time in my life. It was a really scary time in my life. I had just been abused by a member of the Royal Family... I wasn't chained to a sink, but these powerful people were my chains," Giuffre said, starting to cry. "I couldn't comprehend how in the highest levels in the government, powerful people were allowing this to happen. Not only allowing it to happen but participating in it."

The interviewer asked if she would like to stop.

"If you don't mind, just for a moment," she said.

When the interview resumed, she acknowledged that a "foggy memory" meant she might get dates or places wrong sometimes, but she stood by the substance of her allegations.

"One thing that I can tell you is you never forget the face of someone who has heaved over you," she said.

Panorama said that it has discovered more evidence supporting Virginia's story. In a 2015 email to Maxwell, Andrew asked for help dealing with Virginia's allegations. He wrote: "Let me know when we can talk. Got some specific questions to ask you about Virginia Roberts." Maxwell replied: "Have some info. Call me when you have a moment."

Another of Epstein's victims named Sarah Ransome supported Virginia's story and the legal deposition, saying Andrew had spent weeks in Epstein's Florida home and got daily massages, was cited. An old girlfriend came forward to say that Andrew was particularly fond of being given a massage by two women at a time. Lawyer David Boies, who was representing the five women who had come forward to say the Prince knew about Epstein's behaviour, said on the documentary: "One of the things that we have tried to do is to interview Prince Andrew and to try to get what his explanation is. He was a frequent visitor."

While Virginia was emotional and straightforward, Andrew had been cold and evasive. *Panorama* painted Giuffre as a victim fully aware of the weight of her accusations. *Newsnight* left many feeling Andrew was devoid of a conscience, self-important and full of a sense of entitlement.

In the media post-mortems of their TV accounts, it was Virginia who was believed, not Andrew. The *New York Post* did not mince its words, saying straightforwardly: "The BBC has come to bury Prince Andrew", having framed the documentary as an exploration of "the prince's friendship with a prolific sex offender".

"Some of Epstein's victims are believed to have been as young as eleven or twelve years old," the *Post* continued. "Sure, Prince Andrew may have had his office at the Palace shut down (hardly a consequence; he doesn't really work) and lost corporate sponsors after his disastrous sit-down with the BBC just two weeks ago, but the Queen has continued to message support for her favourite child. And Andrew, the BBC pointed out Monday night, continues a friendship with Maxwell, long accused of sexually abusing the underage girls she procured for Epstein."

With sponsors fleeing, Andrew was also forced to stand down from 230 patronages he held. He was stripped of his honorary military titles and he agreed not to use his HRH. Charles was still in his inexorable ascent to be king; Andrew was, to all intents and purposes, finished as a royal.

American attorneys representing Epstein's victims called for him to come to the US to make depositions under oath. Others urged the FBI and Scotland Yard to investigate and, possibly, bring charges. All to no avail.

Although Andrew disappeared from sight, the matter was not over. Ghislaine Maxwell was arrested and charged with sex trafficking offences. The US Federal prosecutors sought to interview Andrew as a "person of interest" in the case. When his co-operation was not forthcoming, the US Department of Justice made a request under the US-UK Mutual Legal Assistance Treaty. Under this, Prince Andrew had twenty-one days to submit himself to being interviewed by US federal prosecutors. Otherwise, Scotland Yard were supposed to ask him questions provided by the DoJ. If he refused to co-operate, he should have been subpoenaed by a British court and answer the questions there. None of this has happened, though, and the British government remains in breach of a treaty with our closest ally. Meanwhile, Maxwell was convicted and sentenced to twenty years.

Virginia Giuffre then took a civil suit against Andrew, seeking damages. He did his best to evade having the American court papers served on him, hiding behind the gates of the Royal Lodge or his mother's skirts at Balmoral. It was only when the High Court of England and Wales agreed to act on their behalf that Andrew's legal team accepted them. After several failed attempts to get the case dismissed, Andrew settled for an undisclosed sum, reportedly as much as £12 million. Charles did not oppose his mother funding the payment. While, as part of the settlement, Andrew made no acceptance of liability, handing over such a large sum was seen as a tacit admission of guilt and he was no longer allowed to repeat his claim that he hadn't raped Virginia Giuffre.

By the time his daughter Princess Beatrice married real estate developer Edoardo Mapelli Mozzi in July 2020, Andrew had vanished completely. Even though he walked the Princess down the aisle, he did not appear in any of the official wedding photographs released by Buckingham Palace.

He did briefly resurface at his father's funeral. When he insisted on wearing the uniform of an admiral – apparently having a new one made by his London tailor – the family decided they would all attend in civilian dress. Then he accompanied the Queen to Prince Philip's memorial service in Westminster Abbey, which was seen by the *Guardian* as an attempt by Her Majesty to rehabilitate the "soiled royal". Again, she was seen to be giving special treatment to her favourite son.

But Charles continued to push on his plans for a slimmed-down monarchy, though he managed to get Camilla on to the team when the Queen agreed that she should become queen consort when Charles became king. At least one royal feud was over. Meanwhile, it was widely reported that Charles intended to sideline not only Andrew but also Edward, who had already given up royal duties. What Charles had not anticipated, however, was the departure of another royal he had always seen as an integral part of his modern monarchy: Harry.

He had long been a loose cannon. Spared, like Andrew, the expectation of high office, he could live the life of an over-privileged nepo baby. When he was young, it was all sex, drugs and (not so much) rock 'n' roll. But then, he could arguably be forgiven because of the tragic circumstances of his mother's untimely death when he was just twelve.

Nevertheless, he seemed to have become more respected by joining the Army, serving two tours in Afghanistan and starting the Invictus Games for wounded veterans. Then he fell in love with glamorous American actress, Meghan Markle. When she married into the Royal Family, she was seen as a breath of fresh air, not least because she was a person of colour.

However, the tabloid press eventually turned on her, in many ways for exactly the same reason. MailOnline ran a headline saying Meghan was "(Almost) Straight Outta Compton". Harry pointed out that she had never lived in Compton or anywhere near it. Under this perceived pressure, they stepped back from royal duties at precisely the same time as Andrew was forced to do the same. They withdrew to Canada, then settled in California.

The couple said that they intended to work to become "financially independent". This would not be a struggle. Harry had inherited £10 million from his mother and another £6 million from his great-grandmother, the Queen Mother. What he subsequently inherited from Prince Philip (a penniless immigrant made good) and the Queen (reportedly the richest woman in the world) has not been disclosed. While a working royal, he had also been receiving £2.3 million a year from his father and may have put some aside for a rainy day. The *Daily Telegraph* estimated that he was worth some £30 million. Meghan was hardly a pauper either. For the seven years she worked on *Suits*, she was reportedly paid $50,000 an episode, or $450,000 a year. Nevertheless, Harry complained that he had been cut off without a penny.

They then made lucrative media deals with Netflix and Spotify, and signed up for an interview with Oprah Winfrey that netted somewhere between $7 million and $9 million, according to the *Wall Street Journal*. If the couple's relations with the rest of the Royal Family were not bad enough already, Harry talked of his estrangement from his father and brother. Once close, William and Harry had become increasingly alienated. Subsequently it was revealed that they had had a fight where Harry had been knocked to the floor, his necklace broken and a dog bowl cracked.

Meghan, for her part, told Oprah that an unidentified member of the Royal Family had asked "how dark" their then unborn child would come out. Asked if there were concerns the baby might be "too brown", Meghan said that was a pretty safe assumption. Both she and Harry refused to identify the person who had said it, saying that would be very damaging. Speculation was rife. Could it have been Charles?

Were the Royal Family racist? Harry was asked later. "No," he replied. They suffered from "unconscious bias".

CHAPTER TWENTY-SEVEN
CROWN IMMUNITY

Miraculously, Andrew had escaped prosecution or even investigation over the Epstein affair. Virginia Giuffre had repeatedly approached Scotland Yard to complain that she had been trafficked to the UK at the age of seventeen to have sex with Prince Andrew. The age of consent is sixteen. However, under the 1956 Sexual Offences Act, which applied at the time: "It is an offence for a person to procure a girl under the age of twenty-one to have unlawful sexual intercourse in any part of the world with a third person." The punishment is two years.

Further, Giuffre has alleged rape. However, in 2021, the outgoing Metropolitan Police Commissioner Dame Cressida Dick said that Scotland Yard would not investigate the serious allegations of sexual assault made by Virginia Giuffre, after reviewing the case three times. In the case of Partygate – where there were allegedly social functions in 10 Downing Street against Covid lockdown regulations – Dick spelt out the criteria involved: Did those accused know they were doing wrong? Would they have a reasonable defence in court? And would not investigating bring the law into disrepute? One wonders if the same criteria were applied to Prince Andrew's case. Dick herself once said: "No one is above the law."

Whatever the legal ruling, by then Andrew had already been convicted in the court of public opinion. His reputation remained in the gutter and he rarely dared to show his face in public.

He may have drawn some satisfaction that his older brother has been caught in some wrongdoing, which Cressida Dick then decided that Scotland Yard should look into. In 2021, the media began looking into two of Charles's charities, the Prince of Wales's Charitable Fund and the Prince's Foundation, which had been created in 2018 by a merger of the Prince's Foundation for Building Community and other bodies including the Prince's Regeneration Trust. The *Mail on Sunday* alleged that people were asked to pay £100,000 to have dinner with Charles and stay overnight in Dumfries House. But 25 per cent of the money would end up going to middlemen, according to an email soliciting the donation. The rest of the money would go to the Prince's Foundation.

That email came from Michael Wynne-Parker, a British businessman who has been banned by official watchdogs in the past from giving financial advice and serving as a company director. In the case of the Prince's Trust, he would take 5 per cent while another 20 per cent would go to another fixer. The money should be paid into the account of *Burke's Peerage*, the "Who's Who" of the British aristocracy. Its owner, William Bortrick, was representing Prince Charles.

In August 2021, under pressure from the press, the Prince's Foundation announced that there would be an investigation into money being siphoned off in this way headed by Douglas Connell, the chair of the Prince's Foundation, and Dame Susan Bruce, the chair of its ethics committee. In effect, the Foundation would be marking its own homework.

Separately, the Prince's Foundation returned a donation from Dmitry Leus, a Russian banker whose own foundation lists Wynne-Parker as one of its trustees, after new information surfaced as part of what was said to be the royal charity's due diligence process.

Born in Turkmenistan, Leus was convicted of money laundering in Russia in 2004. Speaking with the protection of parliamentary privilege, Labour MP Liam Byrne claimed Leus had since been recruited by the Russian spy agency, the FSB, which Byrne alleged had secured his release from prison in 2006.

Leus had moved to the UK in 2015. He had since given more than £54,000 to the Conservative Party. The party has not returned the money, despite Byrne's assertion that UK intelligence services believe he was "absolutely dependent" on the FSB.

It was revealed that Leus had been named in a report on kleptocracy in the UK by Chatham House, the respected international affairs institute. But Leus secured the removal of all references to him in the report.

"After seven months of increasing demands, and due to the costs of defending the case – estimated at some £500,000 before trial – Chatham House has been forced to agree to his meritless claim and excise the report of all mentions of Mr Leus," said Labour MP Margaret Hodge, the chair of the All-Party Parliamentary Group on Anti-Corruption and Responsible Tax.

Leus said he believed he was giving a donation of £500,000 to help the Dumfries House project in Ayrshire in 2020 – and received a personal thank you letter from Prince Charles. When the Foundation's ethics committee ruled that Leus was not an appropriate donor, it returned £100,000, saying that was all it had received after the £500,000 had been passed through the middlemen who had brokered the donation. Leus has recovered another £200,000, meaning that £200,000 was still missing.

Leus had even given another £35,000 to help restore the Castle of Mey, the Queen Mother's favourite hideaway, but this had also not been returned.

Latvian businessman Valery Belokon was a donor and trustee of the Prince's Foundation for Building Community from 2010 to 2013. He had a criminal record for money laundering. In January 2023, armed police raided the Baltic International Bank in Riga, which he owned, and closed it down.

Michael Fawcett stepped down as chief executive of the Prince's Fund in November 2021 following reports in the *Sunday Times* and the *Mail on Sunday* that he had fixed a CBE for Saudi businessman Mahfouz Marei Mubarak bin Mahfouz, who donated more than £1.5 million to Prince Charles's charities, contrary to section 1 of the Honours (Prevention of Abuses) Act 1925. According to the newspaper, he had paid "tens of thousands of pounds to fixers with links to the Prince who had told him they could secure the honour".

In leaked correspondence, William Bortrick, who was also one of Mahfouz's advisers, told colleagues that once the Saudi had "Hon OBE… then more money will flow". The OBE, he said, was "promised" to Mr Mahfouz "to get the £1.5m he paid for Dumfries [House] and [The Castle of] Mey".

The interior of the Castle of Mey had been given a £250,000 makeover overseen by Baron Piers von Westenholz, a former Olympic skier and a close friend of Prince Charles, meaning that a stay for a long weekend there now costs £50,000. The money for the makeover had come from a UK businessman in a donation secured by the Prince.

Bortrick added: "MF [Michael Fawcett] needs to keep to his side of the bargain and sort out the Hon OBE immediately – then assist with citizenship."

Charles gave Mahfouz his Honorary CBE at a private ceremony in the Blue Drawing Room at Buckingham Palace in November 2016, though the event was not published in the Court Circular, the official record of royal engagements. He was wearing a black and gold dress uniform, festooned with medals and fancy insignia for the investiture.

Mahfouz was the executive officer of Saudi-based Marei bin Mahfouz Group, founded by his father Sheikh Marei Mubarak Mahfouz bin Mahfouz, who is one of the richest men in Saudi Arabia. He was also the holder of the Lordship and Barony of Abernethy in Scotland.

The Scottish Charity Regulator started an investigation into the Prince's Foundation's funding arrangements, as it was registered in Scotland. Meanwhile, the Prince's office said the foundation would also stop using Fawcett's company, Premier Mode, which had organised events for the charity, charging hundreds of thousands of pounds.

But this was not good enough for royal finance scrutiniser Norman Baker, who told Sky News in September 2021: "It is the Prince of Wales, not Michael Fawcett, who has to answer questions now. His royal fingerprints are all over this. The monarchy has been seriously damaged by the dodgy activities of the boorish Prince Andrew and by the self-obsessed bleatings of Harry and Meghan. The Queen continues to command respect, but she will not go on for ever. This morning, many will be asking themselves how Prince Charles can square such behaviour with the momentous responsibilities he is due to inherit one day."

Baker wrote to Metropolitan Police Commissioner Cressida Dick demanding a police inquiry. Clarence House responded that Charles had "no knowledge of the alleged offer of honours or British citizenship on the basis of donation to his charities and fully supports the investigation now under way".

With Michael Fawcett, former chief executive of the Prince's Foundation, out of the way, Scotland Yard looked into the matter. The trustees' own investigation, handled by auditing firm EY, had already concluded that "there is evidence that communication and co-ordination took place between the CEO at the time and so-called 'fixers' regarding honorary nominations for a donor between 2014 and 2018".

The Charity Commission then launched a statutory inquiry into allegations that donations intended for the Prince's Foundation went instead to the Mahfouz Foundation, and leaked correspondence suggested that Fawcett had told Mahfouz that royal charities would be "happy and willing" to support his application for citizenship and help further upgrade the CBE to a knighthood.

Then the *Mail on Sunday* reported that Charles met Bruno Wang, who described himself as a Chinese philanthropist and donated £500,000 to the Prince's Foundation. The newspaper claimed that Wang was wanted in Taiwan for alleged money laundering and being a fugitive from justice, allegations he strongly denied.

In February 2022, the Metropolitan Police put the unit that had been investigating Partygate on to the Prince's Foundation. On 31 October 2022, the Metropolitan Police passed their evidence to the Crown Prosecution Service for deliberation.

Other investigations were also under way. In June 2022, *The Times* reported that between 2011 and 2015, Charles accepted €3 million in cash from his old friend the Emir of Qatar, Hamad bin Jassim bin Jaber Al Thani. The money was in €500 notes, handed over in person in three tranches – in a suitcase, holdall and carrier bags from Fortnum & Mason, grocers to the Royal Family. Charles's off-the-record meetings with Al Thani did not appear in the Court Circular. The royal bank Coutts collected the cash and the payments were deposited into the accounts of the Prince of Wales's Charitable Fund.

While there is no evidence that the payments were illegal, Norman Baker pitched in again.

"A million euros in cash stuffed into bags, or shoved into a holdall or a suitcase, and handed over behind closed doors is what you might expect from a South American drug baron, not the heir to the British throne," he said. "This is grubby, scuzzy behaviour, which reinforces the view many are reaching, that Charles is not fit to be king."

The sheikh had faced controversy in recent years, including claims that, while he was in office, Qatar financed the al-Nusra Front, the Syrian branch of al-Qaeda. Al Thani was also accused of licensing the alleged torture of a British subject who reported being subjected to solitary confinement and psychological abuse. Sheikh Hamad's lawyers said the claims were "distortion, exaggeration and wholesale fabrication".

The Charity Commission announced they would review the situation. The following month, they announced that they would not be launching an investigation into the donations, as the information submitted had provided "sufficient assurance" that due diligence had taken place.

"We have assessed the information provided by the charity and have determined there is no further regulatory role for the commission," a spokesperson for the Charity Commission said. However, it was announced that Charles would not be accepting plastic bags full of cash in future.

The Charity Commission had barely washed their hands of that one when *The Times* reported that the Prince of Wales's Charitable Fund received a donation of £1 million from Bakr bin Laden and Shafiq bin Laden, half-brothers of terrorist leader Osama bin Laden, at a private meeting in Clarence House in October 2013, two years after Osama bin Laden had been killed by US special forces in Pakistan. Charles and Bakr bin Laden had known each other since

2000 and dined together at the Oxford Centre for Islamic Studies, where Charles was a patron, two weeks after the 9/11 attacks in 2001. When they met in June 2001, Charles reportedly asked: "What's your brother up to these days?"

The Charity Commission described the decision to accept donations as a "matter for trustees".

"Based on current information, this historic donation does not appear to be unlawful. There is therefore no role for the commission," a spokesman said.

However, in 2022, the Office of the Scottish Charity Regulator was investigating transactions by a property company called Havisham Properties which bought homes on an Ayrshire estate from a subsidiary of the Prince's Foundation. The company was owned by Lord Brownlow, a Tory peer ennobled by Charles who became a trustee of the Prince's Foundation in 2013.

Prince Charles laid on a black-tie dinner for Lord Brownlow and awarded his company a £1.2 million construction contract after accepting millions of pounds in donations from him, shrugging aside advice from senior aides that there may be a "myriad of conflicts of interest". Brownlow spent £1.7 million bailing out Charles's failing Scottish eco-village, Knockroon. He bought eleven properties and converted them into buy-to-lets and a café.

Only thirty-one of the proposed 770 homes in Knockroon had been sold. Charles had seen the construction and sale of faux-Georgian homes there as an ideal way of repaying the debt on Dumfries House. The development was also supposed to bring jobs and homes to a former mining community and exhibit his values of traditional and sustainable architecture.

By 2015, Hope Homes, the developer, had withdrawn from the project and Professor Alan Dunlop, a leading Scottish architect, described the Prince's vision as an "imported pastiche" and a "curious mix" of relatively expensive homes dropped into a rural setting that should never have been built. Charles rarely visited what had become a ghost town, despite regularly spending weekends entertaining donors and relaxing at his estate nearby.

In 2018, after Brownlow completed his purchase of the unwanted properties and quit as a trustee, the Prince made him a Commander of the Victorian Order at a ceremony in Buckingham Palace. The project's value was written down from £15 million to £700,000 in 2022. Once again, Charles had whatever one would call the opposite of the Midas touch.

Nevertheless, the various investigations into cash for honours and other financial peccadillos will go nowhere. As King, Charles is immune from prosecution.

CHAPTER TWENTY-EIGHT
THE FINAL RECKONING

Charles became king when the Queen died on 8 September 2022 at Balmoral. She had served as monarch for seventy years and, in all that time, had barely put a foot wrong. The only criticism that can be levelled at her is that she was not a good mother. Her death threw the feuding brothers – Charles and Andrew, and William and Harry – into the arena again.

Prince Charles and Princess Anne were already in Scotland as the Queen's last moments approached. He was at Dumfries House, while Camilla was staying at Birkhall. They raced to Balmoral. Charles and Anne were there in time to be beside their mother's bedside when she died.

Prince Andrew was with Prince William, Prince Edward and Sophie, Countess of Wessex when they flew from Northolt to Aberdeen, arriving around two hours after the death of the Queen. Harry, who was in London for a charity award ceremony, followed. Catherine, Duchess of Cambridge and Meghan, Duchess of Sussex stayed behind in Windsor.

Prince Andrew seized centre stage in Scotland two days later, leading senior royals as they gathered for a small private service at Crathie Kirk, before walking across the River Dee to inspect floral tributes laid outside the wrought iron gates of Balmoral. Princess Anne was there with her husband, Commander Timothy Laurence. Also taking a back seat were Prince Edward and Sophie. Consoling his clearly emotional daughters, Eugenie and Beatrice, the Duke thanked members of the public for their support through his family's grief.

However, he soon felt Charles's iron hand on his shoulder. He was not allowed to wear a uniform when following his mother's coffin in the procession up the Royal Mile to St Giles' Cathedral in Edinburgh. Marching beside him, his siblings – Charles, Anne and Edward – were in full military attire. This was not lost on a young man in the crowd who shouted at him: "Andrew, you're a sick old man."

He wore a morning suit, this time with medals, on the procession following his mother's coffin from Buckingham Palace to Westminster Hall where she lay in state. He was allowed to wear the uniform of an honorary vice admiral for the Vigil of the Princes where they stood as an honour guard around the coffin. The others wore guards' uniforms, but Andrew had been stripped of his ceremonial role of colonel of the Grenadier Guards by his mother. Along with Harry, he was back in a civilian morning suit for the Queen's funeral, further cementing their demotion.

As Andrew had been inspecting the flowers at Balmoral on 10 September, Camilla was making her first appearance as queen consort at the Accession Council where Charles was formally proclaimed king. As he went to sign the historic Proclamation, Charles frantically motioned to an aide to move a pen box from his desk which was far too small to accommodate the huge document.

Three days later he grew frustrated again, this time with a leaky pen he was using to sign the visitors' book at Hillsborough Castle.

"Oh God, I hate this!" Charles said, brandishing the pen and handing it to Camilla.

"Oh look, it's going everywhere," Camilla said as her husband wiped the ink from his fingers.

"I can't bear this bloody thing... every stinking time," Charles said as he walked away.

He also got the date wrong, before checking with an aide who informed him that it was 13 September not 12 September.

These incidents must have given Andrew a brief moment of mirth. He could handle a helicopter in action. Surely he'd make a better job of wielding writing implements.

As king, Charles seems to have won the War of the Windsors for the moment. Fergie has inherited the Queen's corgis and Andrew has been reduced to the rank of Royal High Dog Walker. But the slugfest continues, with Netflix's *The Crown* reimagining Charles's troubled relationship with Diana and Prince Harry revealing some of his father's problematic parenting and his fears that Camilla would become the archetypal "wicked stepmother" in his autobiography *Spare*. Charles had been king for less than a month when protesters starting throwing eggs at him and Camilla.

For Andrew, there came a ray of sunshine when Virginia Giuffre dropped her civil case against Harvard law professor Alan Dershowitz, saying that she could not be sure he was one of the men who abused her while she was being trafficked by Epstein. Suddenly Andrew's friends said that he thought his reputation could be resurrected and he could resume royal duties, though Charles had already made it clear that he couldn't after the Sandringham summit.

This did not stop Lady Victoria Hervey rallying round on every media outlet available to her, saying that the photograph of Andrew with his arm round the waist of Virginia Giuffre was a fake (it isn't) and that Ghislaine Maxwell was a "victim" of Epstein and "scape-goat". As to the girls who accused Ghislaine of sex trafficking: "a lot of these girls are liars". The jury in a Federal court in Manhattan in December 2021 disagreed. Maxwell was convicted of five sex offences and sentenced to twenty years.

Fergie took to the airwaves too, even though she had not been invited to the coronation. Andrew was a "thoroughly good man", she insisted, who was trying to rebuild his life.

Despite Andrew's optimism, he was a no-show at the Cenotaph on Remembrance Sunday 2022, even in spite of it being the fortieth anniversary of the Falklands War, where he had served. But Andrew picked up the cudgel and flew privately to Bahrain, seemingly trying to carve a role as an envoy between the West and the oil-producing Middle East states. That seems to have come to nothing too.

Worse was to come. Moves were afoot to evict him from the pala-tial Royal Lodge and downsize him to the five-bedroomed Frogmore Cottage, then being forcibly vacated by Harry and Meghan. It was also announced he wouldn't be receiving any money from his moth-er's estate. Everything has been left to Charles as assets passed directly from monarch to monarch do not attract inheritance tax.

Andrew no longer receives the £249,000 that "working royals" get to carry out their duties, so he could not afford the upkeep on Royal Lodge, which he pays the peppercorn rent of £250 a week on, even if he was not forced to leave. Nor would he have the money to launch a promised legal battle to overturn the settlement he made with Virginia Giuffre in a hopeful attempt to restore his good name.

Financially, Andrew is now dependent on handouts from his brother and the generosity of his ex-wife, now a successful children's author with a £5 million Mayfair mansion. But, excepting Fergie, he is totally in Charles's hands.

There then arose the question of what the Duke of York was going to wear to Charles's coronation, as he had been forbidden to wear the regalia of the Order of the Garter, which he would ordinarily have been entitled to. The Garter robes would have been inappropriate, as supposedly the Order was founded to demonstrate respect for women. According to legend, during a court ball the garter slipped from the leg of the Countess of Salisbury while she was dancing. When the courtiers sniggered, the King picked it up and handed it back to her, exclaiming: "*Honi soit qui mal y pense!*" – "Shame on him who thinks ill of it!" That became the Order's motto.

While expressing "the depth of his personal sorrow" over the suffering caused by slavery and allowing academics access to the royal archives to investigate the involvement of the monarchy in the slave trade, King Charles wore on his head the very symbol of slave trading – St Edwards Crown, as worn by his mother and provided in 1661 by Sir Robert Vyner, one of the founding directors of the Royal African Company, the biggest slave-trading operation on the Atlantic. The slaves were branded with the letters "DoY", for its governor, the Duke of York, who succeeded his brother Charles II in 1685 to become James II. Subsequently William III occupied the post Governor of Royal African Company after being given shares by Edward Colston, the slave trader whose statue was toppled in Bristol in 2020. Indeed, every monarch from Elizabeth I to Queen Victoria has profited from the slave trade, and both Kensington Palace and Clarence House were built at least partially on the proceeds.

However, out of postcolonial sensitivity, it was decided that Queen Camilla would not wear the crown used at the coronation of Queen Mary in 1911 and Queen Elizabeth the Queen Mother in 1937 as it carries the Koh-i-Noor diamond. This had been taken from the ten-year-old Duleep Singh, the last Maharaja of the Sikh

Empire in 1849 under the Treaty of Lahore. India, Pakistan, Iran and Afghanistan have asked for its return.

But a crown's a crown. Even if Andrew remarried Fergie, neither of them would ever get one.

That aside, the feud between Andrew and Charles, it seems, will never be over. But, as this book has tried to demonstrate, the two brothers are more alike than they know – petulant, churlish, self-regarding, self-important, self-serving, self-aggrandising, grasping, greedy, amoral and corrupt. Addicted to pomp and uniforms. They acquire wealth, privately and publicly, as if no amount of money is ever enough. If they weren't living the high life as royals, protected by their royal status, they would surely have suffered much worse fates for their misbehaviour.

As I also hope this book proves, they are everything their mother was not. Where she commanded respect, they get sycophancy. They can't understand why she was loved and they're not. It's the story of Cain and Abel all over again. Andrew is dead, reputationally at least, while Charles will always carry the mark of Cain.

SOURCES AND
FURTHER READING

In the research for this book, the author used a variety of sources, including the publications listed below; articles from *The Times*, The *New York Times*, the *Daily Express*, the *Daily Mail*, The *Sun*, the *Daily Mail*, the *Mail on Sunday*, Global NewsBank, The Times Digital Archive and the electronic archives in the British Library and ProQuest. All facts and quotations included are in the public domain.

Andrew: The Playboy Prince, Andrew Morton, Severn House, 1983

Camilla: From Outcast to Queen Consort, Angela Levin, Simon & Schuster UK, 2022

Charles, Anthony Holden, Corgi, 1999

Charles: Victim or Villain, Penny Junor, HarperCollins, 1998

Diana: Her True Story, Andrew Morton, Michael O'Mara, 1992

Elizabeth: An Intimate Portrait, Gyles Brandreth, Michael Joseph, 2022

Fall of the House of Windsor, Nigel Blundell and Susan Blackhall, Blake, 1992

Fergie: Her Secret Life, Allan Starkie, Michael O'Mara, 1996

The King: Life of Charles III, Christopher Anderson, John Blake, 2023

Majesty: Elizabeth II and the House of Windsor, Robert Lacey, Hutchinson, 1977

The Myth of British Monarchy, Edgar Wilson, Journeyman, 1989

Palace Papers, Tina Brown, Penguin, 2022

Prince Andrew: Boy, Man and Prince, Graham and Heather Fisher, WH Allen, 1982

Prince Andrew: The War Hero from Buckingham Palace, Jessica Jayne, Platinum Publishing, 2012

Philip: The Final Portrait, Gyles Brandreth, Coronet, 2021

Prince Charles: The Passions and Paradoxes of an Improbable Life, Sally Bedell Smith, Penguin, 2017

The Prince of Wales, Jonathan Dimbleby, Warner, 1995

Queen of Our Times: The Life of Elizabeth II, Robert Hardman, Macmillan 2022

Revenge: Meghan, Harry and the war between the Windsors, Tom Bower, Blink Publishing, 2022

Rebel King: The Making of a Monarch, Tom Bower, William Collins, 2018

Remember Diana: The Way We Were, Paul Burrell, HarperCollins, 2007

A Royal Duty, Paul Burrell, Penguin, 2004

Scoops: The BBC's Most Shocking Interviews from Prince Andrew to Steven Seagal, Sam McAlister, Oneworld Publications, 2022

Shadows of a Princess, Patrick Jephson, HarperCollins, 2000

The Tarnished Crown: Princess Diana and the House of Windsor, Anthony Holden, Random House, 1993

Young Prince Philip: His Turbulent Early Life, Philip Eade, HarperPress, 2011

RELATED TITLES ALSO FROM THIS AUTHOR

Call Me Diana: The Princess of Wales on Herself, Nigel Cawthorne, Gibson Square Books, 2017

Ghislaine Maxwell: Jeffery Epstein and America's Most Notorious Socialite, Nigel Cawthorne, Gibson Square Books, 2022

Kings and Queens of England, Nigel Cawthorne, Arcturus Publishing, 2010

Prince Andrew: Epstein, Maxwell and the Palace, Nigel Cawthorne, Gibson Square Books, 2021

Prince Harry: His Mother's Son, Nigel Cawthorne, Sharpe Books, 2021

Prince Philip: I Know I am Rude But It's Fun, Nigel Cawthorne, Gibson Square Books, 2020

Sex Lives of the Kings and Queens of England, Nigel Cawthorne, Welbeck Publishing, 2012

Virginia Giuffre: The Extraordinary Life Story of the 'Playtoy' who Pursued and Ended the Crimes of Millionaires Ghislaine Maxwell and Jeffery Epstein, Nigel Cawthorne, Gibson Square Books, 2022

Windsor Spares: The Prince Harry and Prince Andrew Soap Opera, Nigel Cawthorne, Gibson Square Books, 2023